IMAGES
of America

SAN JUAN ISLAND

I0806320

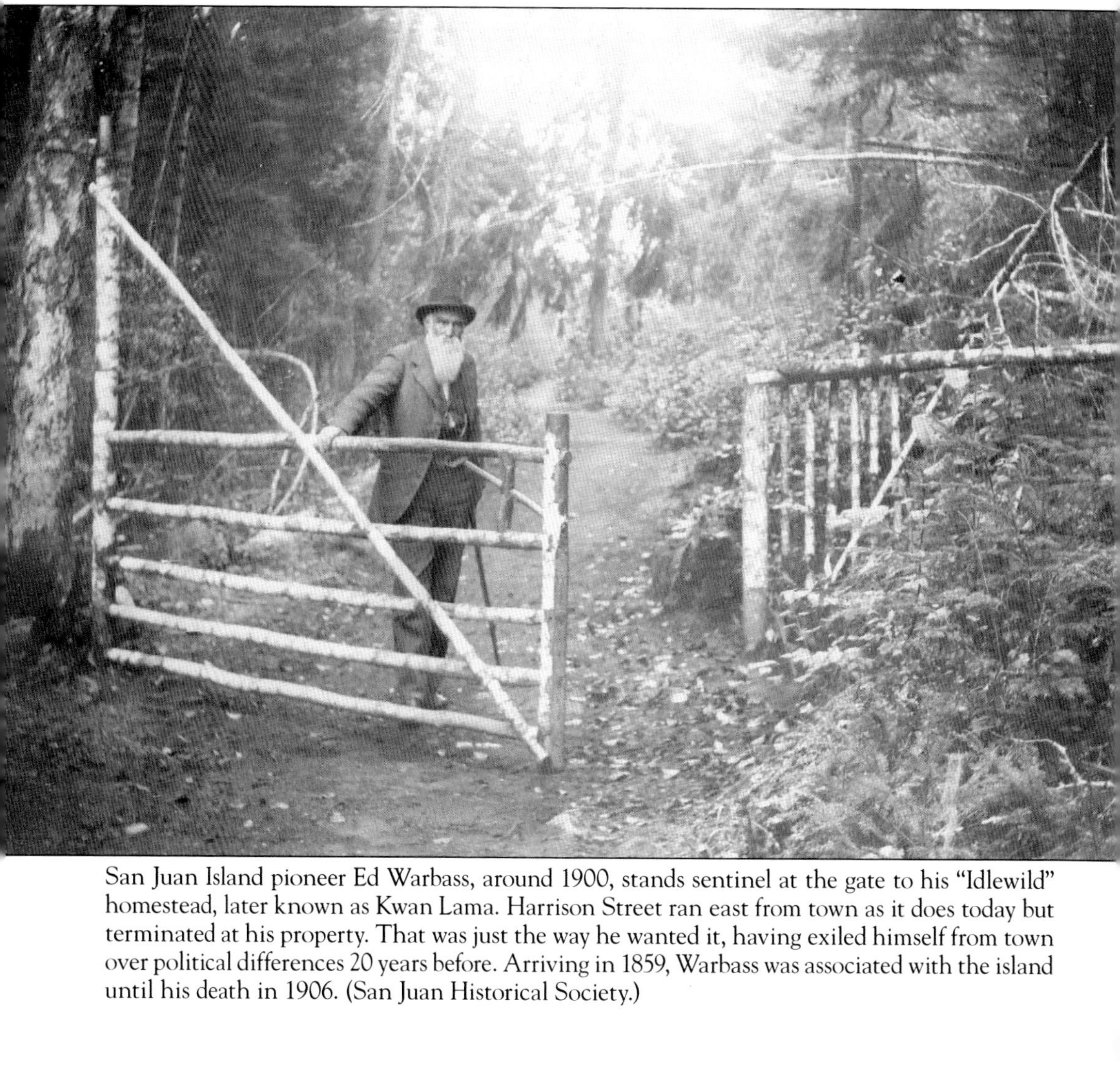

San Juan Island pioneer Ed Warbass, around 1900, stands sentinel at the gate to his "Idlewild" homestead, later known as Kwan Lama. Harrison Street ran east from town as it does today but terminated at his property. That was just the way he wanted it, having exiled himself from town over political differences 20 years before. Arriving in 1859, Warbass was associated with the island until his death in 1906. (San Juan Historical Society.)

On the Cover: The former "Home Prairie" of the Hudson's Bay Company, today's American Camp, fell under the plow and became a vast grain field under the ownership of San Juan town storekeeper Israel Katz and successors. Here in the 1890s, a horse-drawn binder cuts the grain—probably rye, which was well-suited to the dry, glacial till—and bundles it with string while two hands (Rudolph Rosler at right) gather it into shocks in preparation for threshing. The house on Mount Finlayson's lower slope is the George and Eliza Jakle homestead. The old county road is at left. (San Juan Historical Society.)

IMAGES
of America

SAN JUAN ISLAND

Mike and Julia Vouri and the
San Juan Historical Society

ARCADIA
PUBLISHING

Copyright © 2010 by Mike and Julia Vouri and the San Juan Historical Society
ISBN 978-0-7385-8147-7

Published by Arcadia Publishing
Charleston, South Carolina

Printed in the United States of America

Library of Congress Control Number: 2010927902

For all general information, please contact Arcadia Publishing:
Telephone 843-853-2070
Fax 843-853-0044
E-mail sales@arcadiapublishing.com
For customer service and orders:
Toll-Free 1-888-313-2665

Visit us on the Internet at www.arcadiapublishing.com

For the first ones and all of their children

Contents

Acknowledgments		6
Introduction		7
1.	A Brand New Start	9
2.	Bringing in the Harvest	29
3.	The Salmon Bank	49
4.	A Vanished Commerce	61
5.	Hearth and Home	77
6.	The Schoolhouses	93
7.	In the Spirit of Things	97
8.	Community Connections	105

ACKNOWLEDGMENTS

It was a pleasure spending time with descendants of the pioneers, who loaned photographs and/or helped us identify and interpret them. Special thanks to Mary Jean Cahail and Kevin Loftus for moving this project along; to E. A. "Ted" Middleton and Rob Roy McGregor, whose donations once again made an island history book possible; and to Jim Cahail and Al Sundstrom for hours of patient explanation and amazing stories. Thanks also to Kitty Roberts, Mary Jane Anderson, Diane Timm, Peggy Sue McRae, Shaun Hubbard, Joe Bettridge, Richard Walker, Kelly Cahill, John Wade, Ed Johnson, Marlene Crosby, Guard Sundstrom, Bob Guard, Mildred Sandwith, Lynette Guard, Nola Boyce Nash, Ed Rouleau, Carla Higginson, Jean Rogers, Boyd Pratt, and Al Nash. Hugs to Denise Vouri for research support and to Dakota for a lifetime of love.

SOURCE ABBREVIATIONS

Beinecke Rare Book and Manuscript Library, Yale University (BRBML)
Library of Congress (LOC)
San Juan Island National Historical Park (SAJH)
Washington State Archives (WSA)
Guard Sundstrom (GS)
Al Sundstrom (AS)
Mary Jane Anderson (MJA)
Kitty Roberts (KR)
Shaun Hubbard (SH)
Marlene Crosby (MC)
Carla Higginson (CH)
Peggy Sue McRae (PM)

The San Juan Historical Society owns all images not otherwise credited. For information on purchasing prints of these images, please call the San Juan Historical Society at (360) 378-3949, e-mail museum_admin@sjmuseum.org, or write P.O. Box 441, Friday Harbor, WA 98250.

Introduction

If you know where to look, the past is almost always at hand on San Juan Island. From the tracks of the continental glacier, to the fields of camas that bloom each spring, to the weathered barns of the pioneer homestead, the story is seamless in the telling and timeless in scope.

It wasn't easy to pioneer here. Even though food was abundant and means of shelter readily at hand, it still required hard work, a little luck, and, more often than not, the assistance of others, which was readily given. This is one of the central themes of island history, which will hopefully be evident in these pages.

In many respects, the island itself gave rise to these attributes. The ancestors of today's Northern Straits Coast Salish people began to appear in the wake of the continental ice sheet that started to recede 11,000 years ago. Archaeological evidence suggests that the island supported hunting and gathering between 6,000 and 8,000 years ago. The marine culture encountered by the first Europeans to the area developed about 2,500 years ago, and traces of its once thriving villages remain in the shell middens found along the shoreline.

European diseases reduced this population to a scattering of villages long before 1791, when the *Isla y Archipelago de San Juan* was first named by Francisco Eliza, a Spanish explorer charged with retrenching the Spanish presence in the Pacific Northwest. Eliza's cartographers introduced the San Juans as a single mass blocking what became known as the Strait of Georgia. But they did not provide any hint of the island's attributes, which in 70 years would nearly trigger a war between Great Britain and the United States.

That was left to the Royal Navy's Lt. William Broughton, 29, who in May 1792 charted the San Juans aboard the HMS *Chatham* under orders of Capt. George Vancouver. His sailing master, James Johnstone, left this description: "The land is delightful, being in many places clear and the soil so rich that the grass in several parts grew to man height."

Fifty years later, in October 1853, James Alden of the U.S. Coast Survey enthused about the maritime resources. "Salmon abound in great quantities at certain seasons of the year, when the water in every direction seems to be filled with them . . . The Hudson's Bay Company has a fishing establishment at San Juan . . . where I am informed they have put up this season 600 barrels of salmon."

Not one month later, Vancouver Island governor James Douglas wrote London, "These islands are exceedingly valuable, not only on account of their relative position to Vancouver Island, but also from the fact that their shores and inlets abound with salmon and other fish which form a productive export and an inexhaustible form of great wealth."

By "relative position," Douglas was alluding to the fact that the San Juans had been in dispute since the signing of the Treaty of Oregon between the United States and Great Britain in June 1846, which divided the Oregon Country along the 49th Parallel. The treaty, however, did not specify on which side of the archipelago the boundary would pass—the Haro or Rosario straits. Hoping an act of possession would solidify the British claim, Douglas established Belle

Vue Sheep Farm on the island's southern extremity in December 1953 through the Hudson's Bay Company (HBC).

International tensions climaxed in June 1859 when an American "squatter" (so-called by the Hudson's Bay Company) shot a Company pig, spurring threats of arrest by the British and the landing of nearly 500 U.S. Army soldiers to protect him. A comic opera standoff ensued over the next several months until the nations agreed to a joint military occupation of the island by the American soldiers and the British Royal Marines. This mostly stable military presence not only maintained the peace, but also provided basic infrastructure in the form of a Military Road that transected the island, which invited settlement by citizens of both nations.

The fact that the islands were in dispute did not dissuade these pioneers from staking claims among the frigid waters, dark forests, rocky bights, and wind-swept prairies. From 1860 to 1870, the civilian population on San Juan jumped from 73 to 457, hardly spectacular by later standards but significant for a 54-square-mile island on the pale of settlement.

These people were stouthearted and gritty. To get to the island, some sailed around the Horn from England, Germany, and Denmark. At least one of San Juan's pioneer women—Fannie Deardon Lawson—came aboard a British bride ship, while another crossed the Great Plains from Tennessee by covered wagon. Often the final leg of the journey to San Juan Island was by canoe or rowboat.

Some of these first Euro-Americans snapped up the best grazing and croplands in valleys enriched by runoff and creeks from the island's rocky uplands and the glacial till savannahs giving on to the Strait of Juan de Fuca. Those of an industrial bent noted the lime excavation undertaken by the Royal Marines at Roche Harbor and commenced operations of their own at several points along the shore, most notably at what is known today as Lime Kiln State Park. Others took the cue from Governor Douglas and cast their lots each summer in the abundant salmon fishery.

Financiers and storekeepers from Victoria, Port Townsend, and eventually Friday Harbor were eager to underwrite these and other ventures, especially farming. Belle Vue Sheep Farm had already demonstrated that farming could be a profitable, albeit back-breaking, enterprise. Preparing the land for cultivation involved cutting down trees, removing stumps, clearing brush, and schlepping rocks—thousands of rocks.

People were, by necessity, self-sufficient. They raised turkeys, chickens, cattle, sheep, and pigs and put up food from their orchards and vegetable gardens. They fished, dug clams, and hunted rabbits, birds, and deer. Just as the Native Americans banded together for common benefit in seasonal fishing villages, so too did San Juan's early settlers.

Survival depended upon community, and they learned to rely on one another for everything from raising barns to pooling farm equipment. Families embraced orphaned children or homeless adults. Neighbors and businesses relied on the barter system. And when hard times hit, they got by. "If anyone was short of food, everyone shared," recalled Beryl Boyce Wade of the Depression years. "It was just like one big, happy family." Sometimes they *were* family, as early settlers often intermarried, creating a network of cousins for whom the past is an essential part of the present.

The island continues to echo those early times. Look for Peter Lawson's hand-hewn barn on Eagle Point, pear trees planted by Isaac Sandwith on his West Valley Road farm, rocks piled high by the Roslers and Firths at American Camp while clearing building sites, and swaths of daffodils along Roche Harbor Road, which bloomed every spring on Winnie Sundstrom's farm.

But the past is perhaps most visible in the character of descendants of the pioneers who shaped the community. Their spirit endures in the way islanders rally to those in need, gather for the funerals of its elders, and preserve for generations to come the same fertile valleys and wild shorelines that attracted their forefathers.

One

A Brand New Start

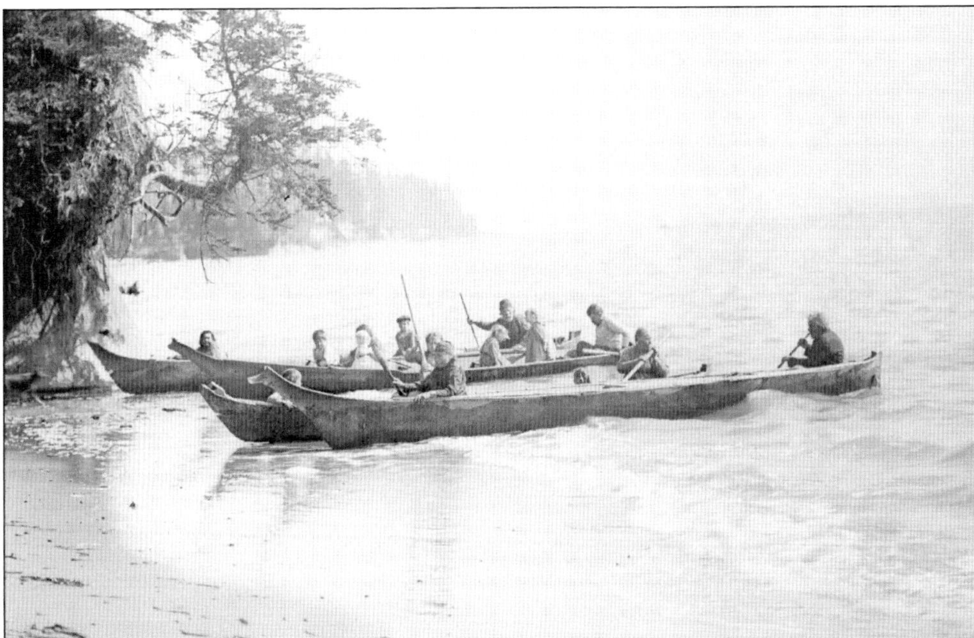

Four West Coast–style canoes pull up on the beach with European passengers aboard, around 1900, somewhere in the Northern Straits region. In the early days of Euro-American settlement, a degree of comity—in some cases codependency—existed between whites and Native Americans. Groups from as far as southeast Alaska would arrive to camp, fish, dig clams, and smoke their catch for the winter months. The whites watched them fish and took note of their techniques. Often fish would be exchanged for farm produce, including, on several occasions, legs of lamb. Pioneer women skilled in healing, such as Lucinda Boyce, ministered to whites and Native Americans, who brought her fish and clams in gratitude. On one occasion, when Peter Lawson's daughter Annie broke her leg while milking a cow, Lawson hired two Native American men to paddle her to Victoria for treatment. San Juan Historical Museum founder Etta Egeland, who donated this image to the museum, also remembered crossing Haro Strait by Native American canoe to the community that in the 1850s and 1860s was commonly known as "The Fort."

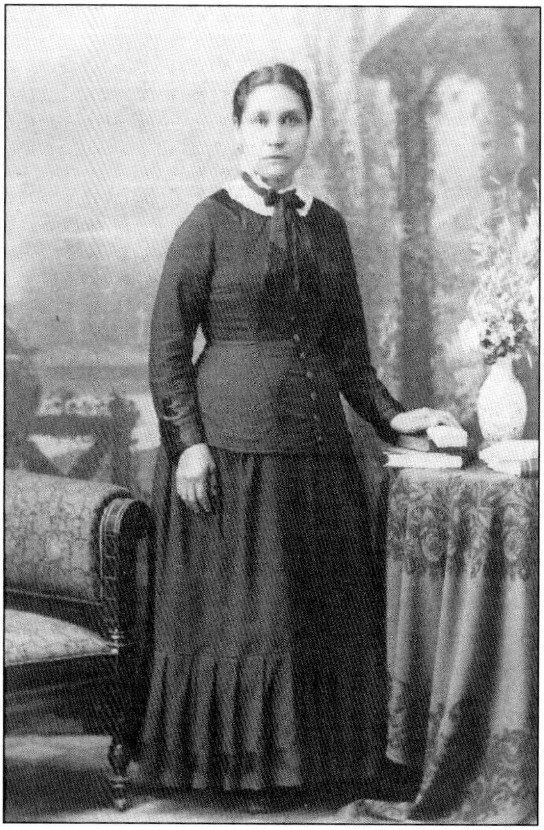

In 1861, Tsimshian (*Ts'msyan*) Anna Pike Rosler arrived from Alaska with her family to fish the Salmon Bank. She married Christopher Rosler, a recently discharged German immigrant soldier from American Camp. As shown at left, Anna adopted European ways and dress, epitomizing many Native American women whose descendants became known as the "San Juan Tribe of Indians" and "Mitchell Bay Band." (CH.)

Founded in 1843, the Hudson's Bay Company's (HBC) Fort Victoria was headquarters of a vast trading, mining, and agricultural empire in the Pacific Northwest. Vancouver Island governor James Douglas later insisted that HBC servants already claimed San Juan Island in 1845 by placing a plaque atop Mount Finlayson. The claim was specious because it was not voiced until after the Oregon Treaty of 1846, which did not resolve possession of the islands. (LOC.)

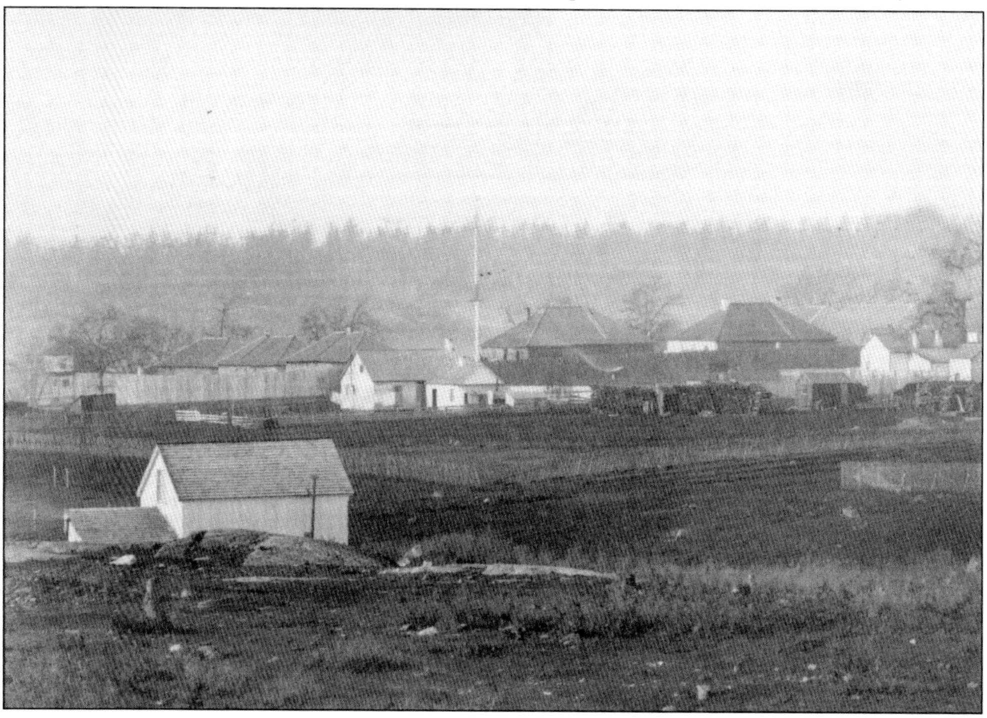

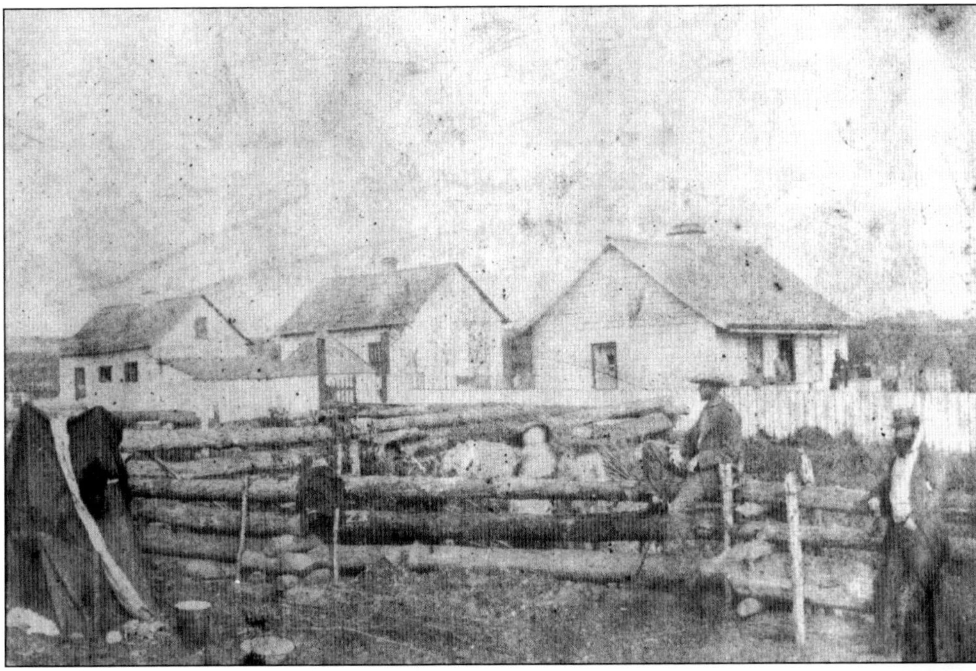

The Hudson's Bay Company established a salmon salting station on the island in 1851 to purchase fish from Native Americans. Two years later, Belle Vue Sheep Farm (above) was established to discourage Americans from moving to the island. By 1859, however, it had become a profitable operation, establishing farming patterns on San Juan that continue to this day. (BRBML.)

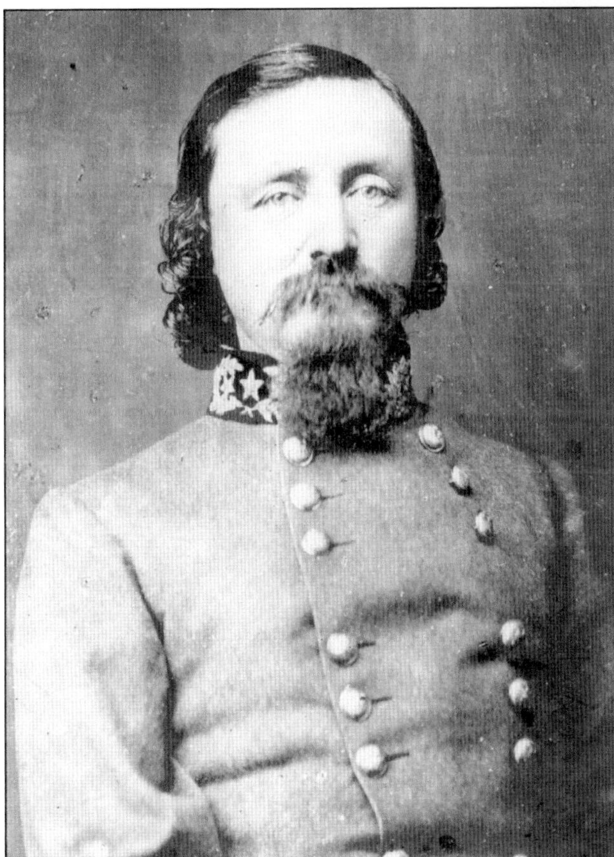

U.S. Army captain George E. Pickett landed on San Juan Island in July 1859 believing he was defending U.S. territory—and an American who shot an HBC pig—from Great Britain. He somehow missed the fact that the archipelago had been in dispute since 1846. He married a Northwest Coast woman who bore him a son before she died but left the boy when he returned to Virginia in 1861. (LOC.)

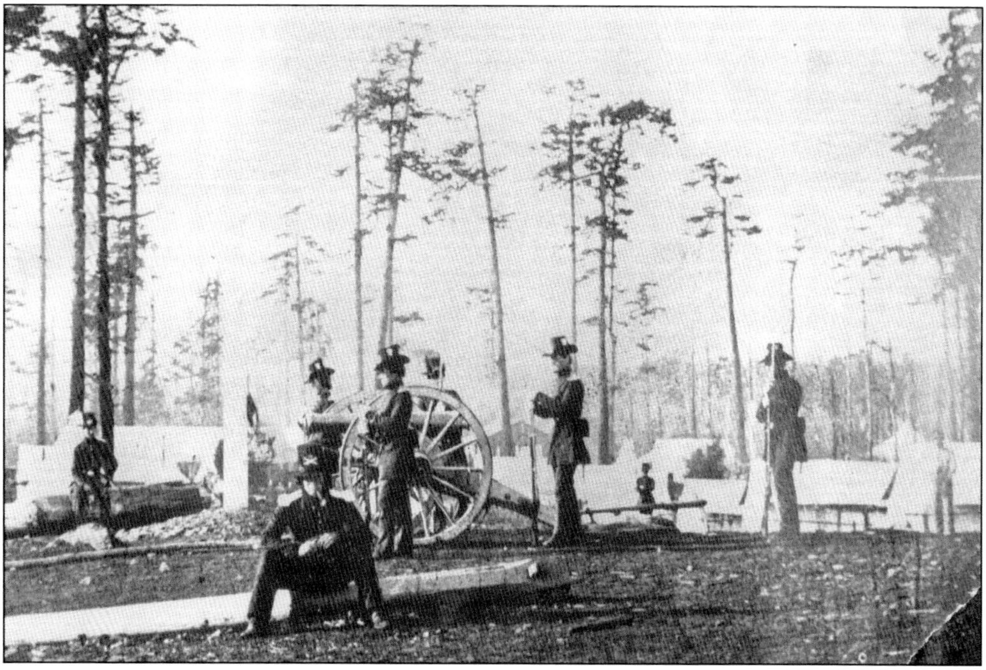

Nearly 500 U.S. soldiers, including the 3rd U.S. Artillery, occupied San Juan in July and August of 1859, when American Brig. Gen. William S. Harney decided all 18 U.S. squatters needed protection. A standoff ensued between the Americans and the Royal Navy that ended only when U.S. Army commander Lt. Gen. Winfield Scott traveled from Washington to make peace. (SAJH.)

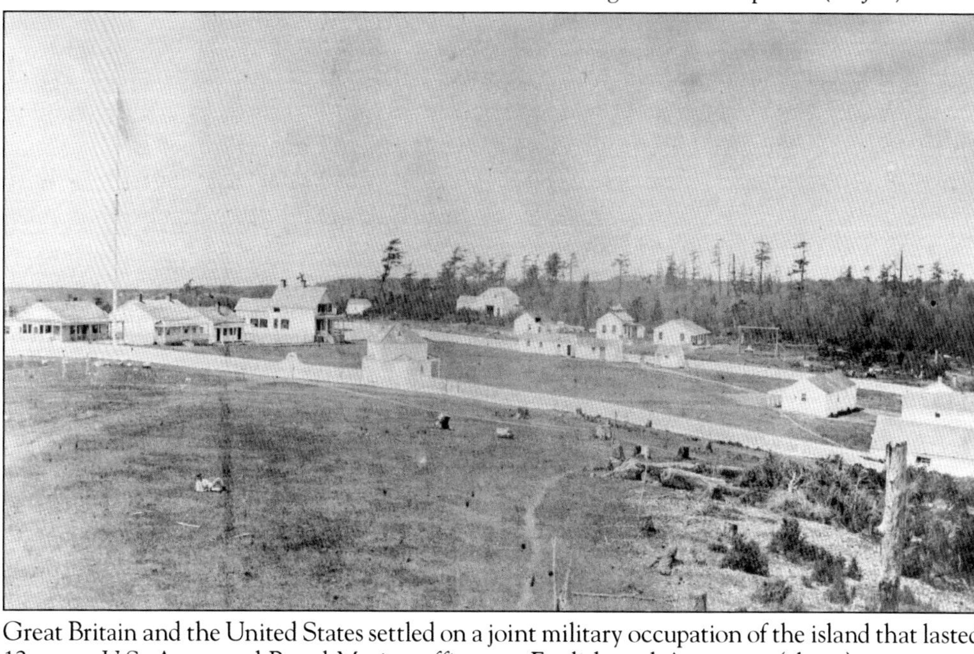

Great Britain and the United States settled on a joint military occupation of the island that lasted 12 years. U.S. Army and Royal Marine officers at English and American (above) camps were mostly congenial except to settlers of both nationalities who caused friction. They were evicted. After the joint occupation, many of these buildings were moved to farms, Argyle village, and Friday Harbor, where they still stand. (SAJH.)

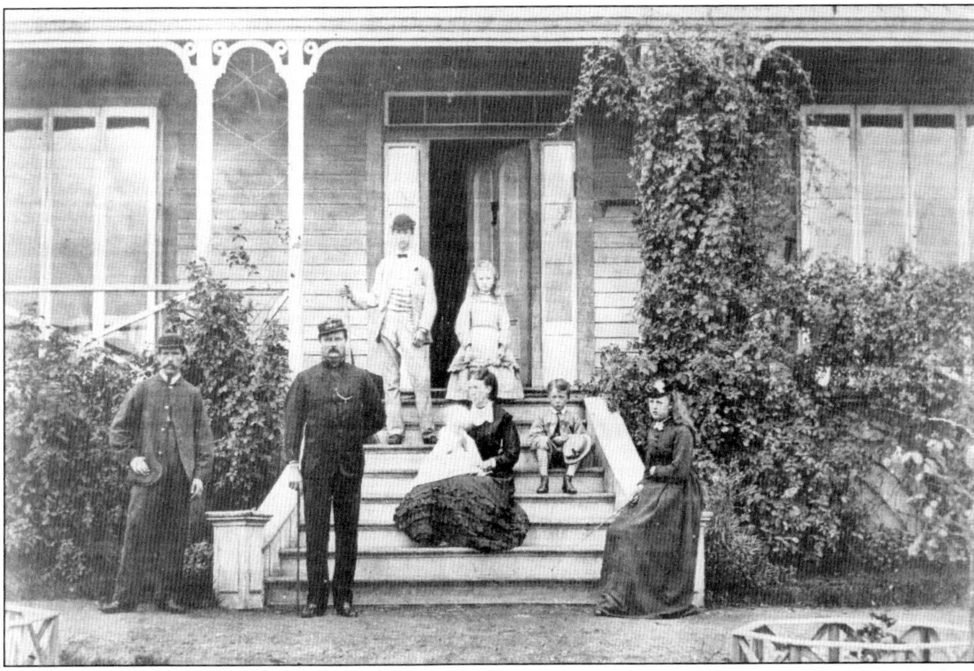

Capt. William A. Delacombe, shown with his family at their English Camp home (second from left), was the second of two Royal Marine commanders during the joint military occupation. He ensured the peace by evicting a British subject squatting on an absentee American's homestead claim. His inherent fairness compelled British and American settlers alike to petition for him to stay a little longer when the boundary was settled. (SAJH.)

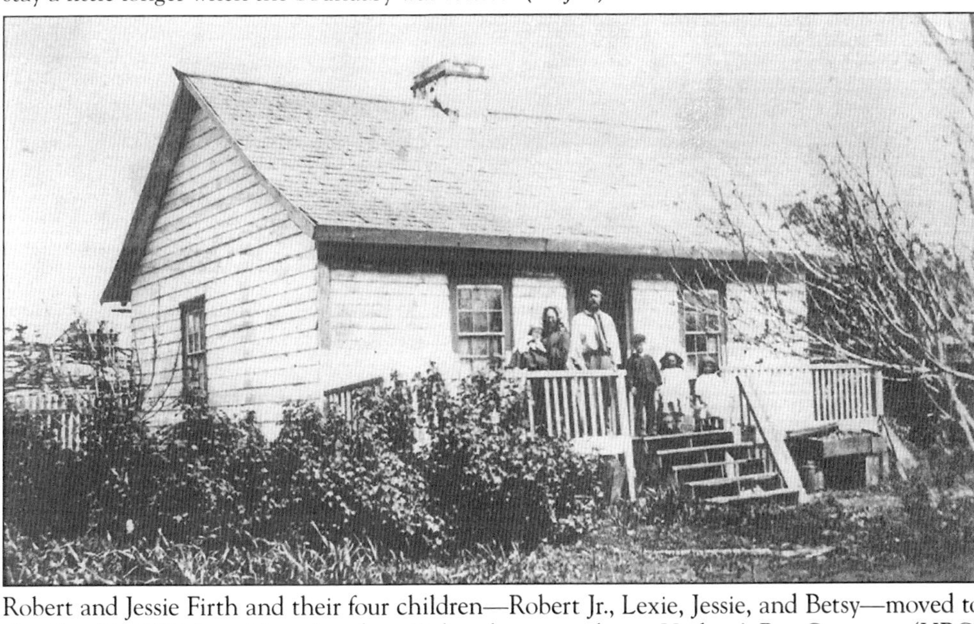

Robert and Jessie Firth and their four children—Robert Jr., Lexie, Jessie, and Betsy—moved to the island in 1862 from Victoria, where Robert began work as a Hudson's Bay Company (HBC) servant in 1851. He went home to his native Scotland to marry Jessie in 1857, then replaced Charles Griffin as Belle Vue Sheep Farm manager in 1862. He worked the farm under lease to HBC until 1873. (SAJH.)

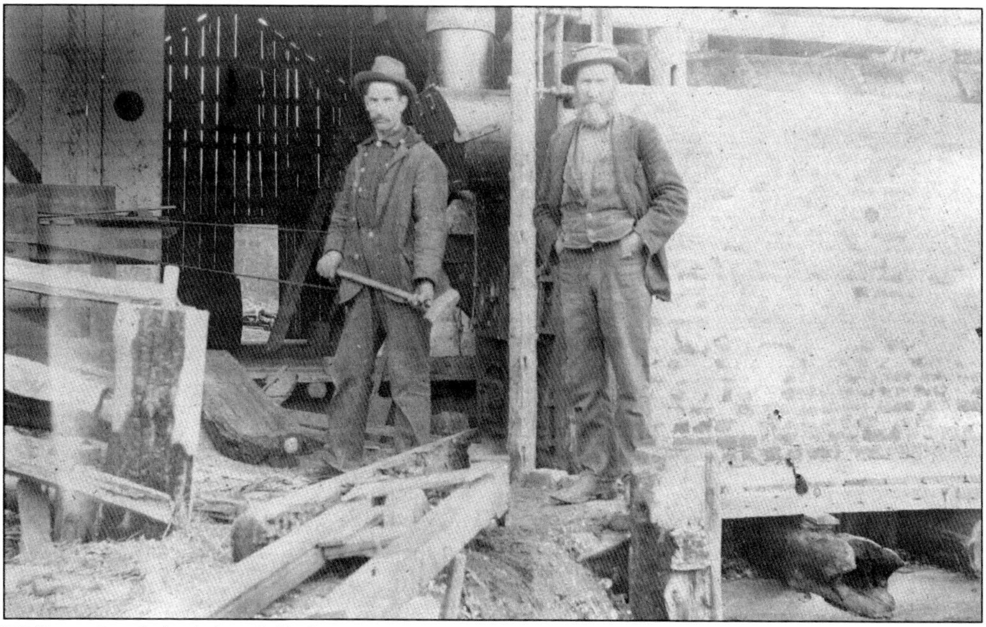

William Crook (right), a skilled carpenter, immigrated to Ontario, Canada, in 1856 from Yorkshire, England, where he met and married Scotland native Mary Forrest. The couple started west by ox cart in 1867, with William building houses along the way and Mary giving birth to Mary and James (left). They arrived at the site of the former Royal Marine Camp on San Juan Island in November 1875.

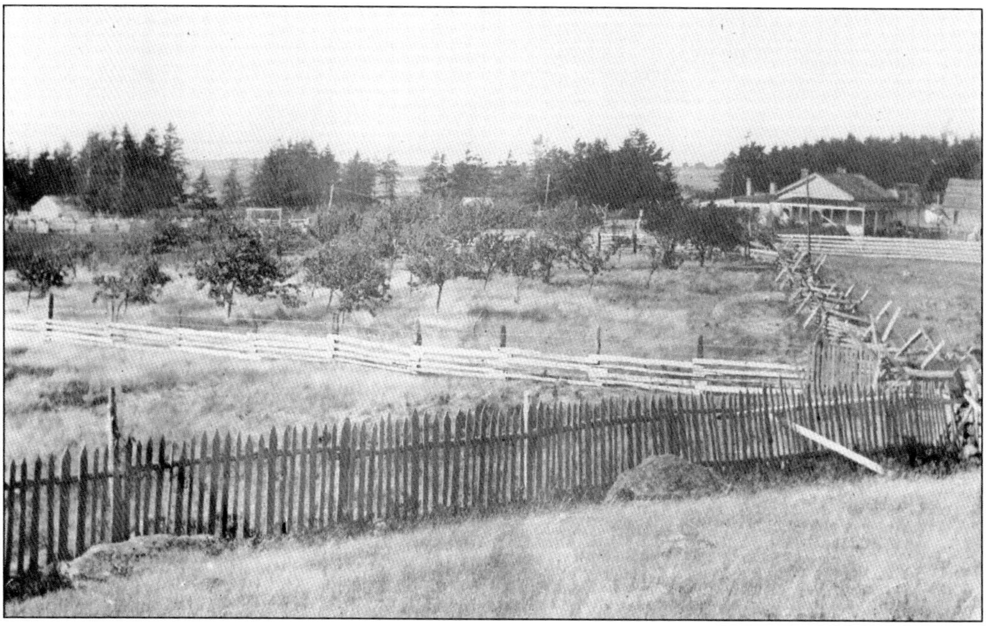

After the boundary dispute was settled, Robert Firth remained at Belle Vue Sheep Farm, becoming a U.S. citizen in 1878. By 1884, he held title to 226 acres, including the old U.S. Army camp (above). Jessie bore six more children on San Juan Island. After the army left, the Firths moved into the officers quarters (still standing) where "one could see lights from Victoria, a good 12 miles away," according to Lila Hannah Firth.

In 1859, native Louisianan Robert Frazer, with his brother William, came to San Juan just in time to witness the Pig War crisis and snap up the claim of pig murderer Lyman Cutlar, just north of the army camp. Frazer married Mary Jane Fleming and expanded his farm to 360 acres, which included a fruit orchard. Through it all, he made time to be San Juan County's first treasurer. (MJA.)

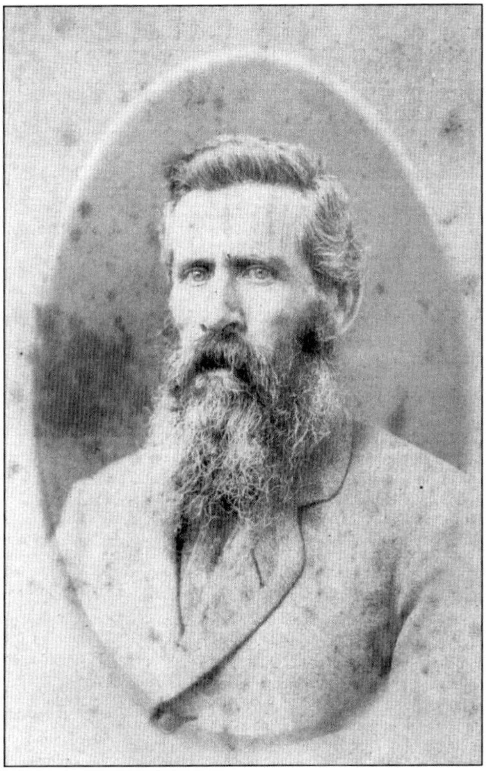

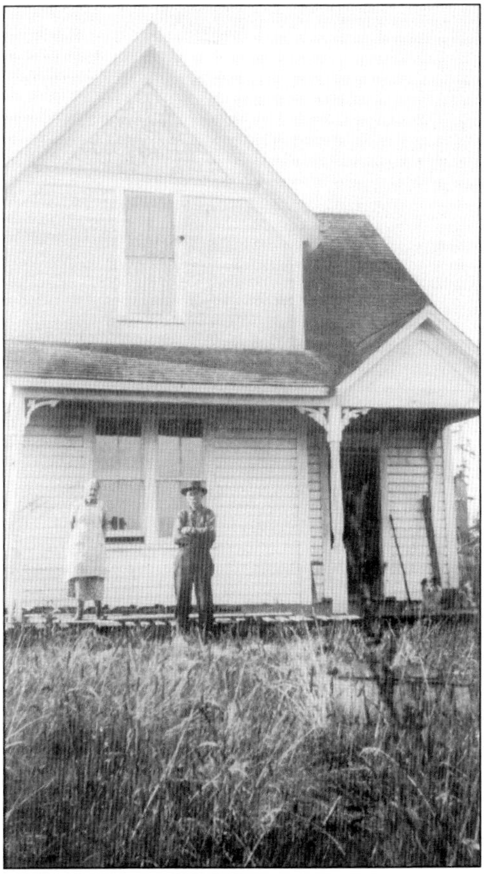

Mary Jane Fleming Frazer and son Norman greet visitors at the family home (still standing) on Cattle Point Road. She landed on the San Juan Town dock in 1863 with her parents, Thomas and Mary Jane. She once ordered an aging Norman to visit neighbor Lizzie Lawson, getting on and single, and propose marriage. He dutifully obeyed, but according to family lore, Lizzie responded, "Why would I do that?" (MJA.)

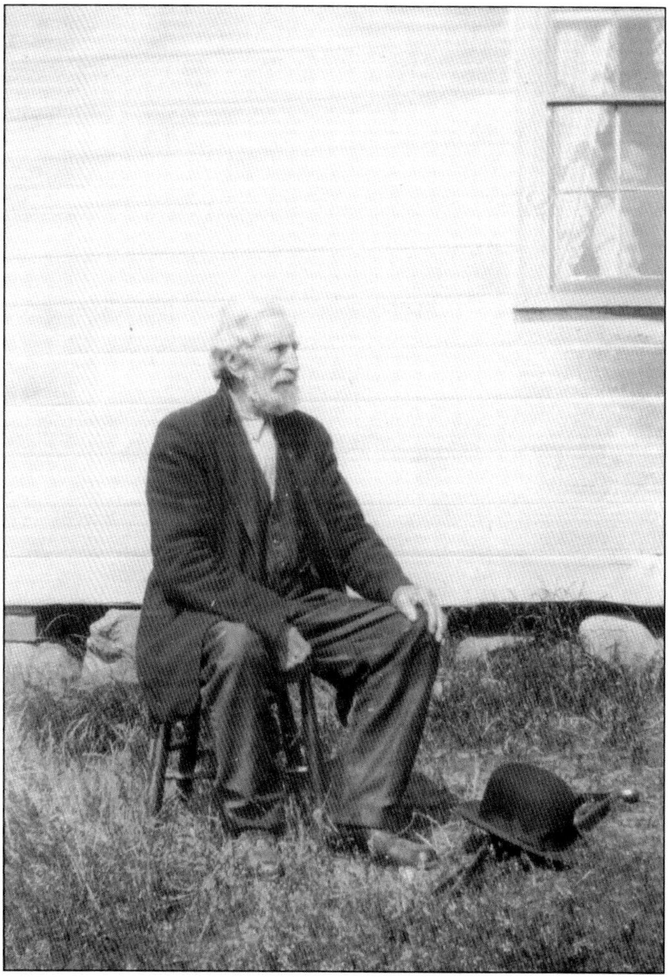

Peter Lawson left his native Denmark at 14, signed on to a square-rigged ship, and spent the next 14 years at sea before landing at Port Townsend in 1855. After hauling mining supplies up the Fraser River, he arrived on San Juan in 1859. He squatted on and later claimed 160 acres, including two "forties" at Eagle Point, built a log cabin, then married Fannie Deardon from Manchester, England.

When Peter Lawson announced he was going to build this barn in 1874 (image from around 1900), he was told the structure would never withstand the winter winds that howl up the Strait of Juan de Fuca. Undaunted, Lawson started work, and a barn raising was organized by his neighbors. The barn still stands, and the broad axe used to hew the beams is on view at the San Juan Historical Museum.

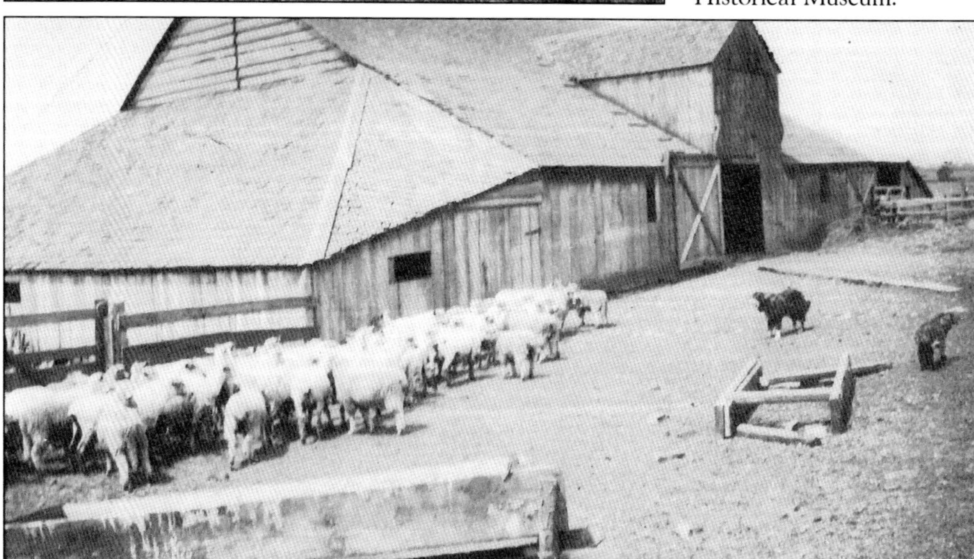

San Juan County's first sheriff, Stephen Boyce, started life as an incorrigible, running away from his New York home at 13 to dig gold in California. He met and married Tennessean Lucinda Stewart in San Francisco but did not shed gold fever until 1860, when the couple settled on San Juan. Boyce was a trusted public servant, respected by all. The Native Americans called him "Hyas Tyee," or "great and powerful man."

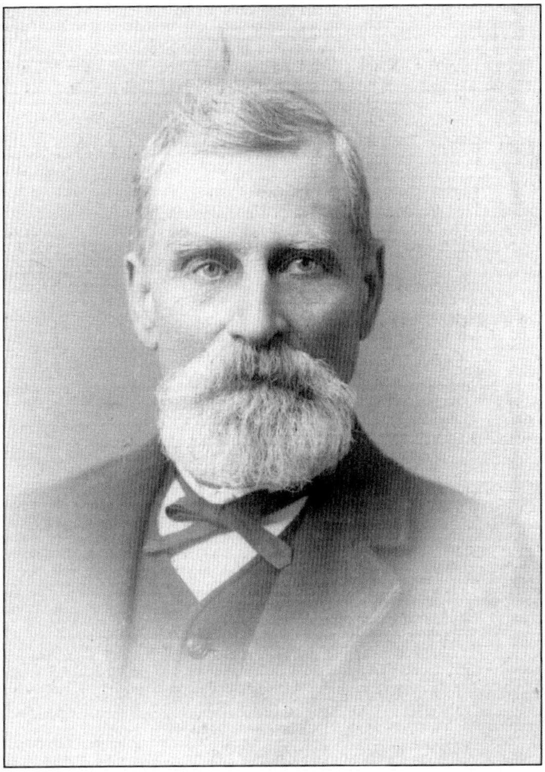

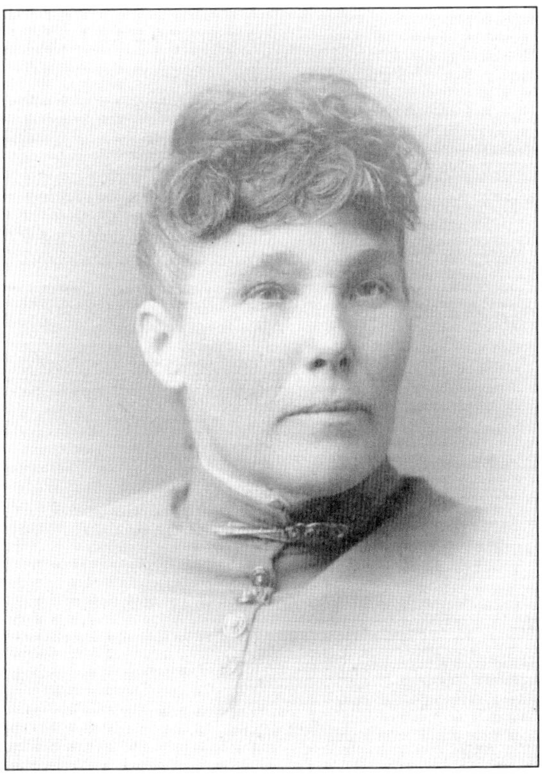

The first Euro-American woman to live permanently on San Juan Island, Lucinda Stewart Boyce, was also the island's first paramedic. Toughened by crossing the Great Plains in a covered wagon at age 12, she was a compassionate nurse and midwife, delivering more than 500 babies—while bearing 11 of her own—and venturing out in any weather and to other islands to care for the sick and injured.

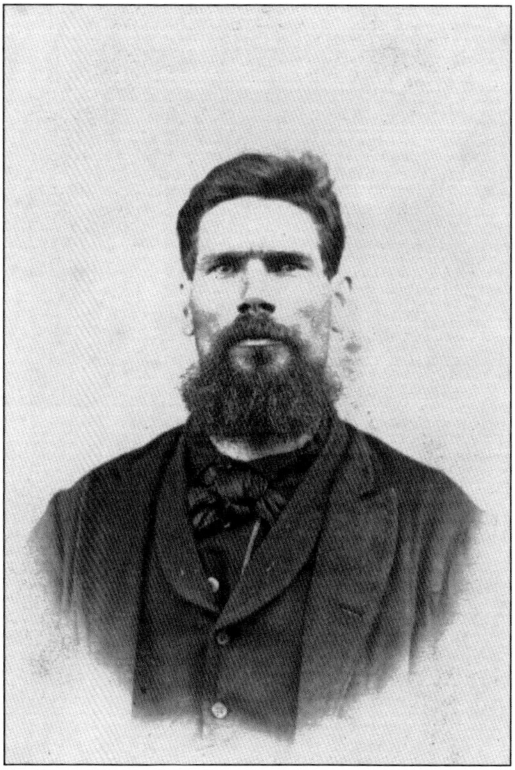

Harry and Selena Dwyer were victims in the island's first sensational murder case, now known as the "Kanaka Joe Murders." A native of Nova Scotia, Dwyer had owned a successful shipping business between San Juan and Victoria until the boundary settlement and resultant duties drove up costs. Dwyer sold his business and, in 1872, moved with his young wife Selena to a farm he had purchased on the island, located off today's Bailer Hill Road. A year later, he was plowing his field when Joe Nuanna shot him in the back of the head. Nuanna then made his way to the house and shot a pregnant Selena. Though only eight years old, Lila Hannah Firth never forgot the sight of Harry's and Selena's dead bodies, nor "the baby clothes scattered about where it seemed she had been sewing."

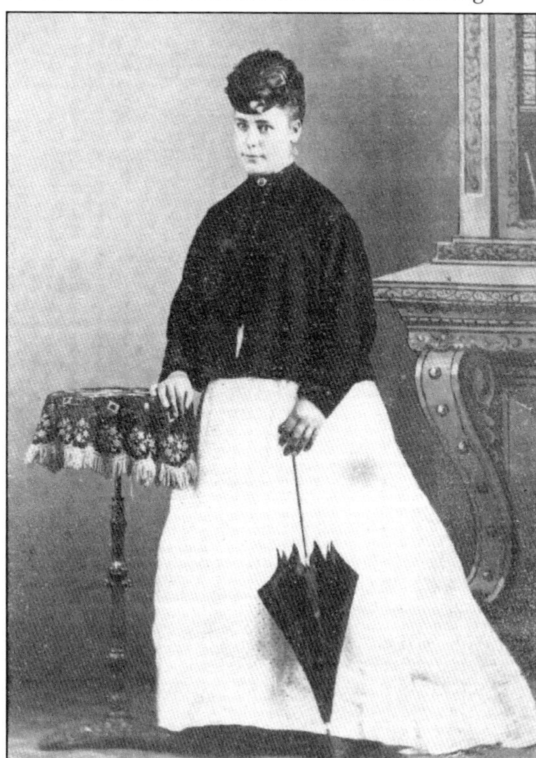

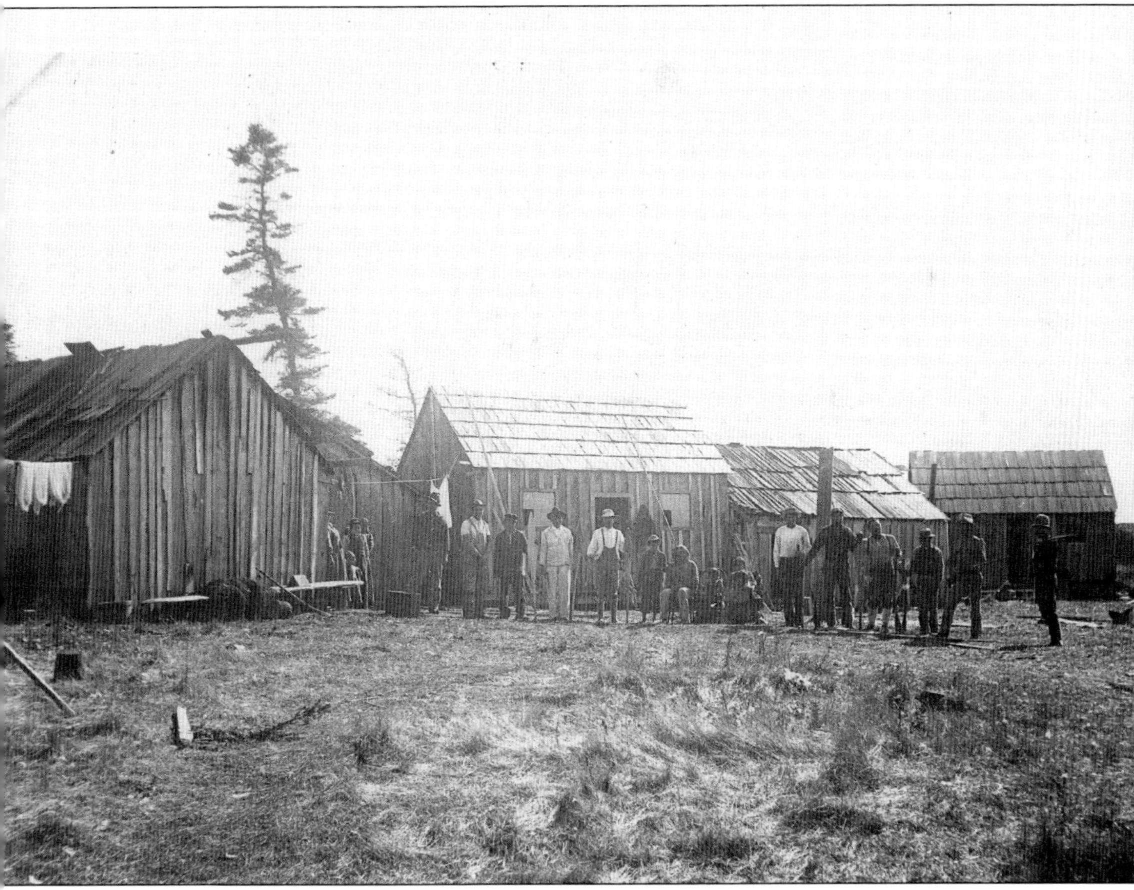

Law enforcement officers from Whatcom County and Vancouver Island pose at the Hawaiian village on Kanaka Bay, home of the then-suspected killer Joe Nuanna, better known as "Kanaka Joe." The village had been home to the Hawaiian herdsmen under the employ of the Hudson's Bay Company, and was by 1873 occupied by hangers-on who fished seasonally and worked on nearby farms. Following an extensive manhunt on the island, Nuanna was arrested in Victoria. After confessing to the killings of San Juan Islanders Harry and Selena Dwyer, and William Fuller, he was extradited to Port Townsend, where he was tried and convicted. More than 200 gathered to witness the hanging. Sheriff Stephen Boyce sprung the trap, but the knot failed and Nuanna thrashed as he slowly strangled. Boyce swung onto the rope above the trap and attempted to tighten the noose with his boots, but it still took 20 minutes for Nuanna to expire. On the way to the scaffold, he had pleaded with Boyce to "die quick." Boyce never forgot and later spared another killer from a similar fate.

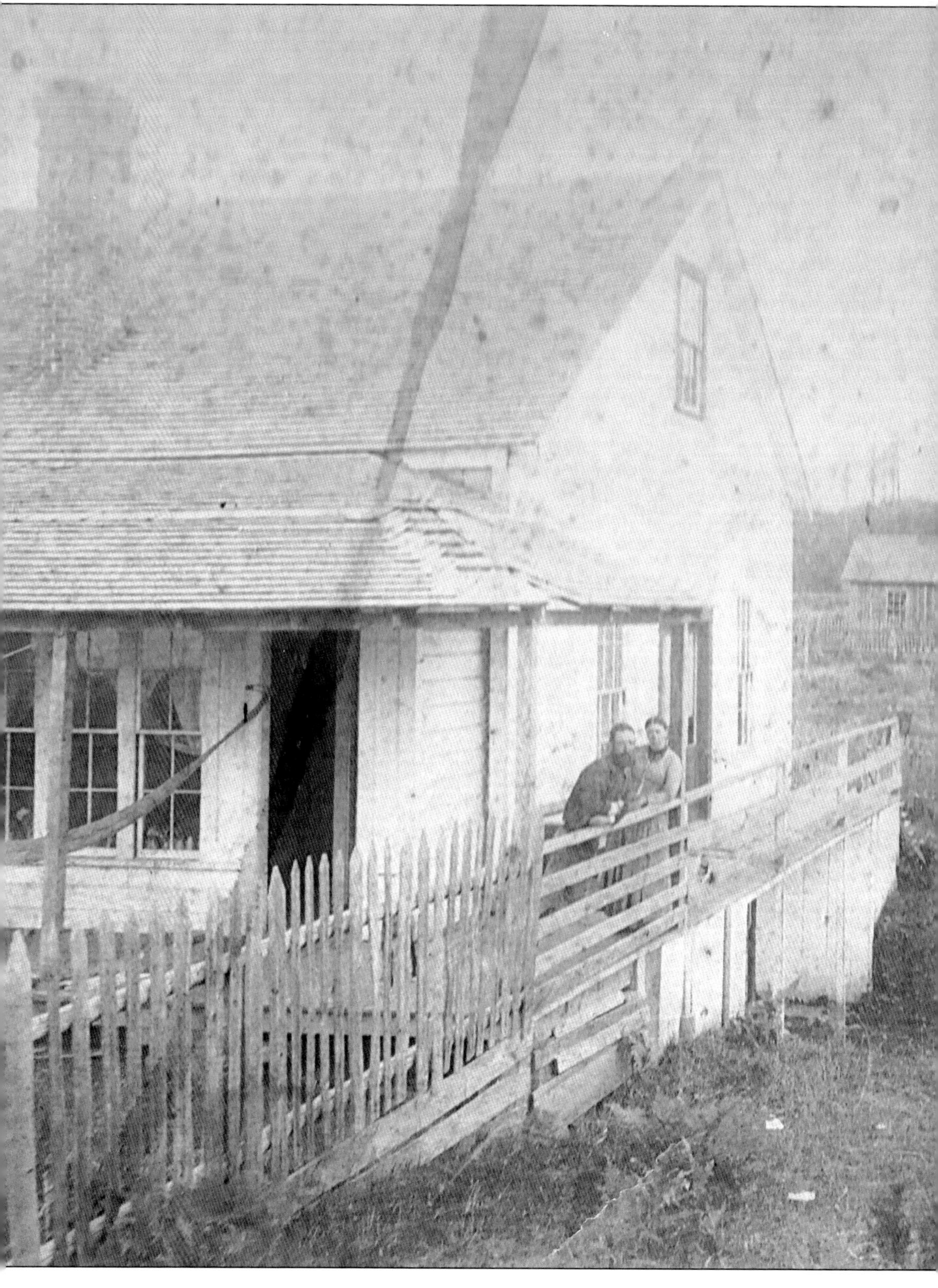

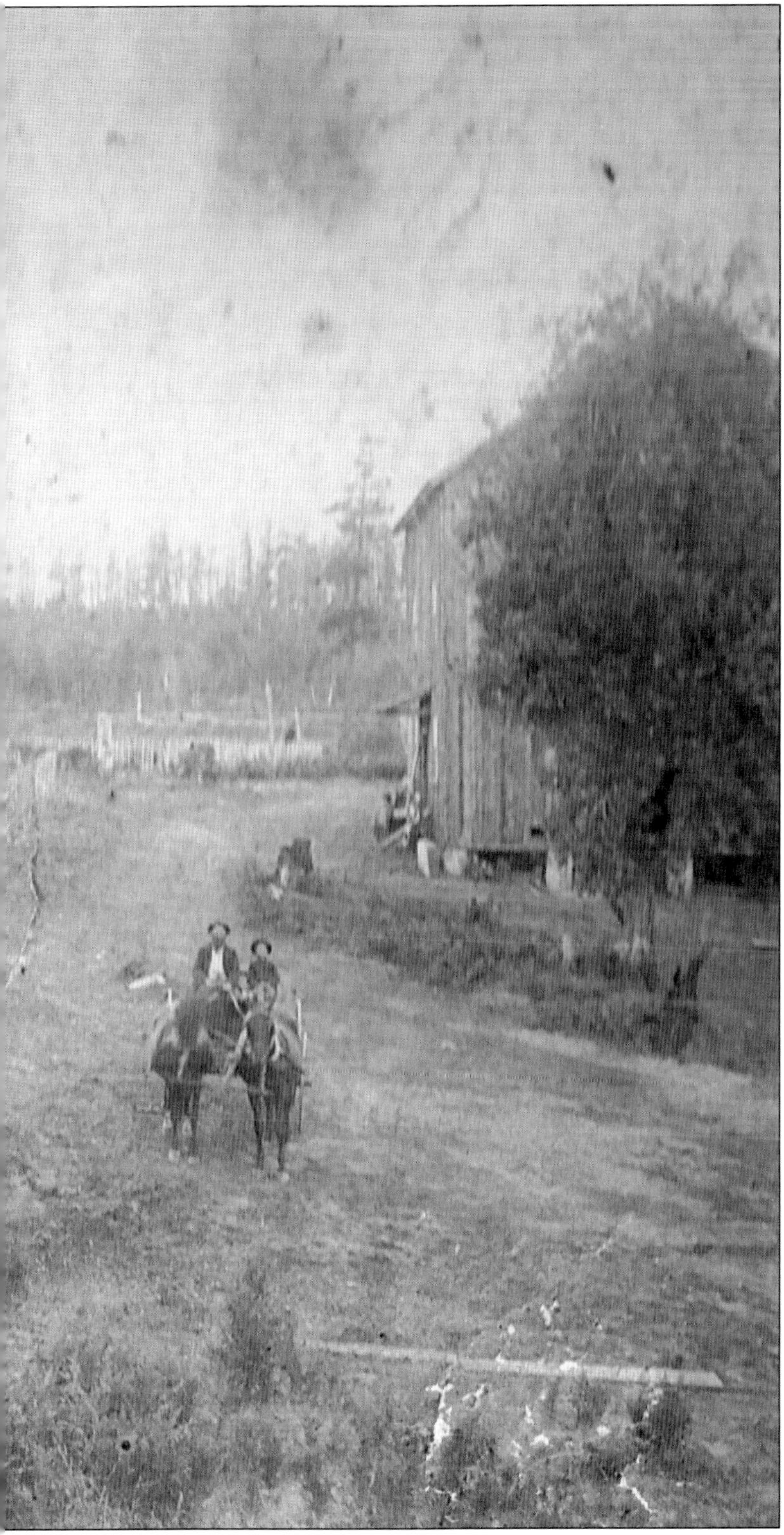

Andrew and Jenny Anderson watch from the porch of their home in Argyle, which was founded in 1873 and boasted a gristmill (at right), store, and post office through the 1890s. The house (still standing) was moved from American Camp. Two young partners from the mainland, Elijah H. "Ham" Nash and Herbert L. Coffin, ran the store from 1893 to 1894, during which Coffin kept a detailed diary. On February 6, 1893, he reported the following: "[It] was a quiet, uneventful day aside from the fact that the mail steamer was going so fast that she stopped by running into the dock, knocking off the main corner fender pile. The captain would be a good man to run an express train when he didn't have to stop to put off the mail." A shallow harbor doomed the village to neighborhood status.

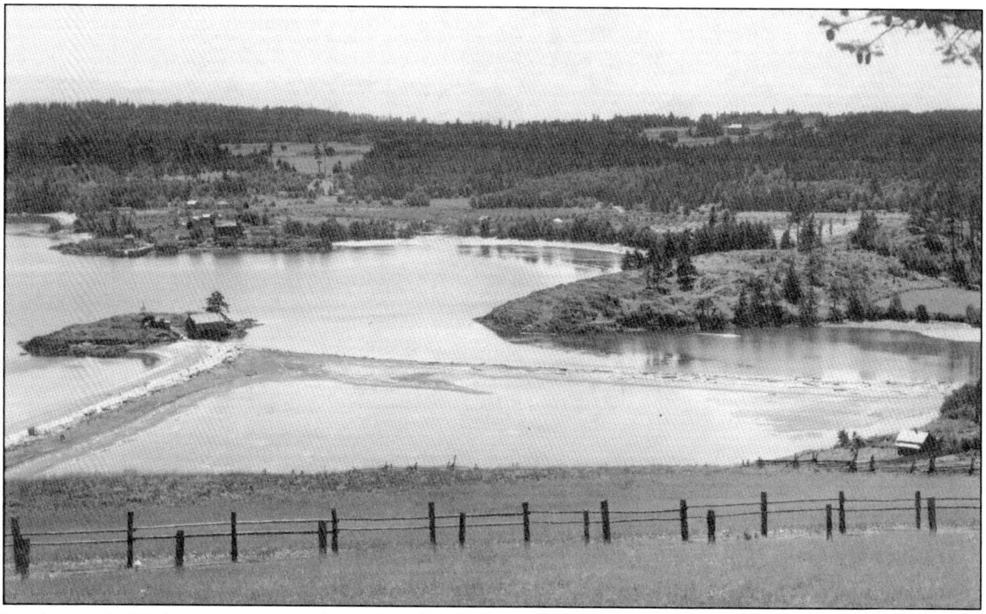

In this early 20th century view from Bald Hill, Jones Lagoon is in the near foreground, separated by a spit from the inlet where many island children learned to swim (see page 110). An old smokehouse sits on the rocky knob that would one day accommodate John Jackson's cannery. The Argyle gristmill and store are on the far shore, and the post office is left of the store.

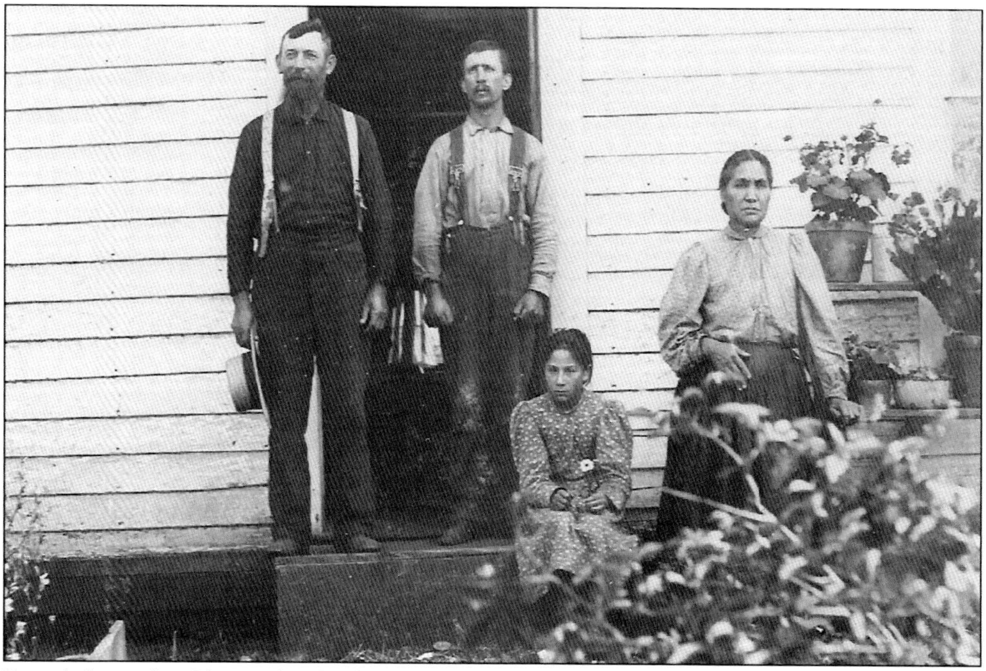

From left to right, Christopher Rosler; an unidentified man; Rosler's youngest daughter, Laurena; and wife Anna enjoy their home near American Camp around 1895. Rosler left his native Germany at 14, dug for gold, went bust, and joined the army. When his enlistment was up, he drew his pay; bought a farm, cattle, and sheep; and married Anna. She loved flowers and planted hundreds of bulbs and a tiny elm sapling that still survives.

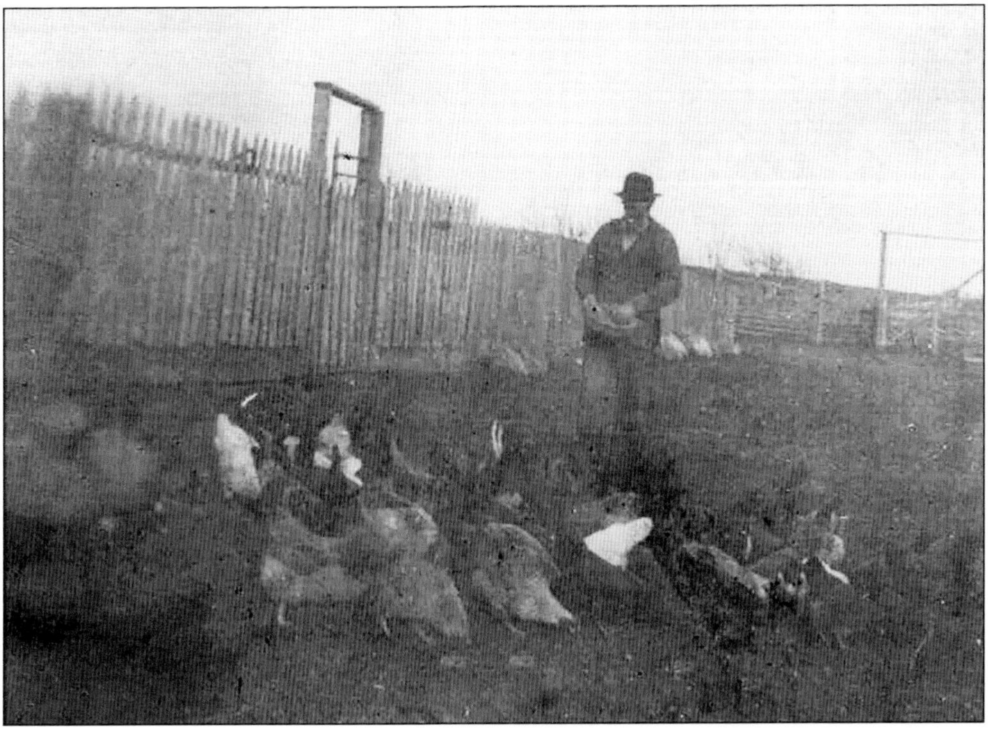

Robert Firth feeds his chickens in the yard of his home at the former U.S. Army post at American Camp. As one of his granddaughters wrote, "Grandfather was a wonderful man and loved children . . . He had a pet crow who followed him all over the farm . . . and when he spied grandfather coming up the lane would caw and fly down and ride on his shoulder and sometimes on his hat."

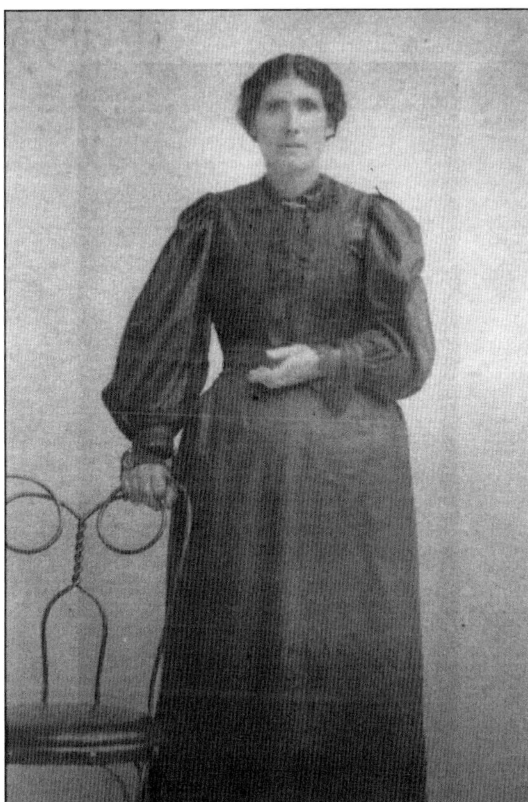

Eliza Furlong Jakle came to San Juan Island in the 1860s with her first husband, James Bryant, an American Camp soldier with whom she had a son, Frank. Pregnant with her second child, Eliza miscarried running for help when James drowned in the lagoon. She then married another soldier, George Jakle (for whom the lagoon is named), and they had five children who married into a number of island families.

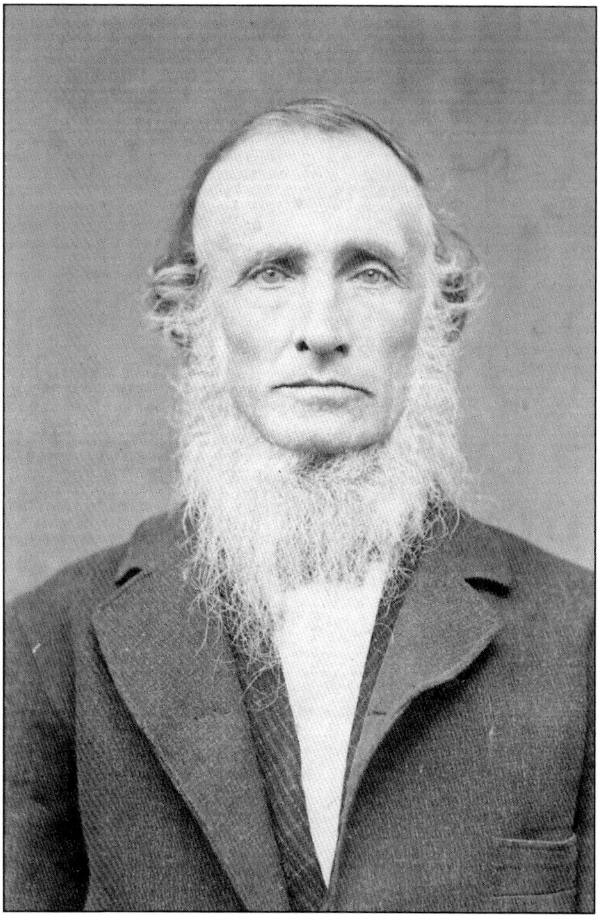

Thomas Fleming, another Scotsman, and his family came to San Juan Island in 1863 following stops in Australia and California. He staked a squatter's claim in San Juan Valley between San Juan Valley and Bailer Hill roads. The family's daily life on the island is revealed thanks to the diary he kept until his death in 1907, which contained pithy entries such as this one: "Feb. 27—Roof Blowed off my barn."

The Patrick Gorman family came to San Juan Island in 1862–1863, also staking a claim in San Juan Valley. Upon Patrick's death, the farm passed to his sons Peter and Joseph. Their sister, Mary Gorman Madden, is second from left in the second row below husband Daniel Madden. Her baby is Josie Madden, who would one day marry John Sundstrom (see page 80). Mary died of tuberculosis six months after this photograph was taken.

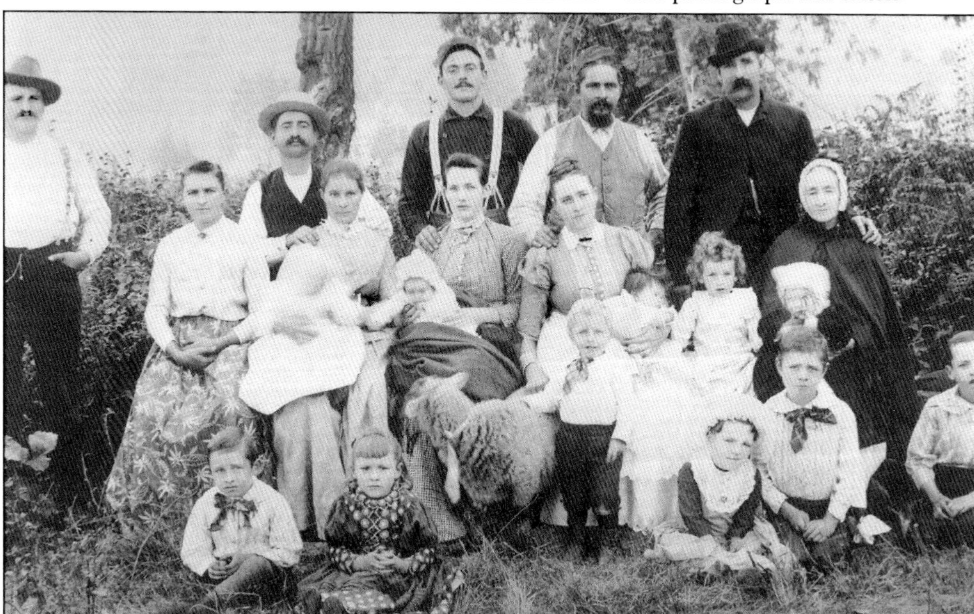

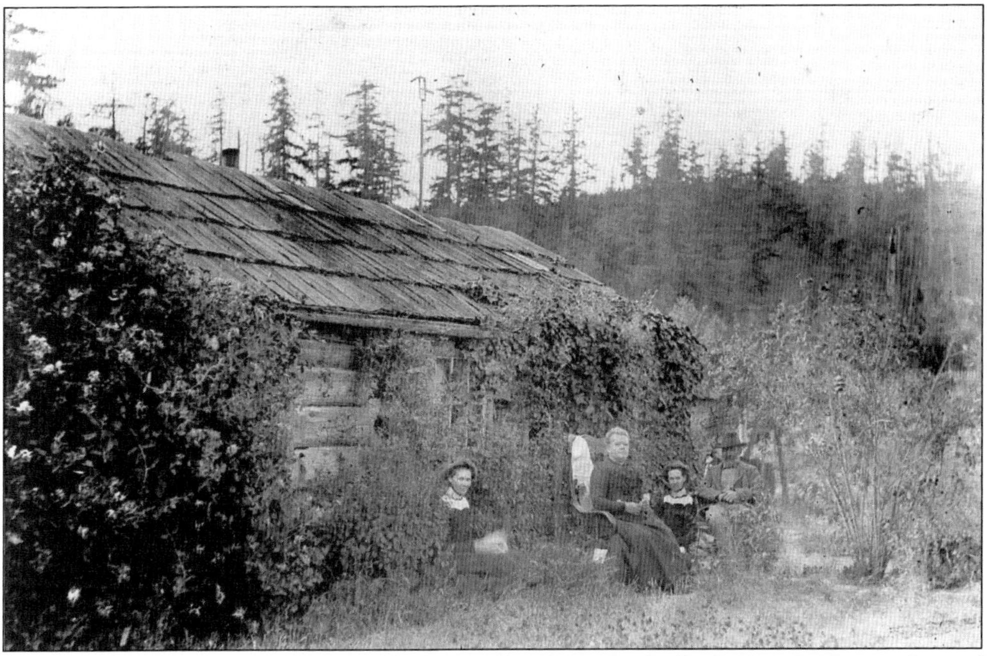

Paul and Elizabeth Guard pose with their granddaughters Emily (far left) and Alice in front of their old cabin, located on their homestead in Beaverton Valley. Guard immigrated to the United States from England in 1867 to join a utopian community in Kansas. He arrived on San Juan in 1888 and—working with his son Frank, who owned the adjoining 80 acres—began the enormous task of cultivating the valley's marshes. (SH.)

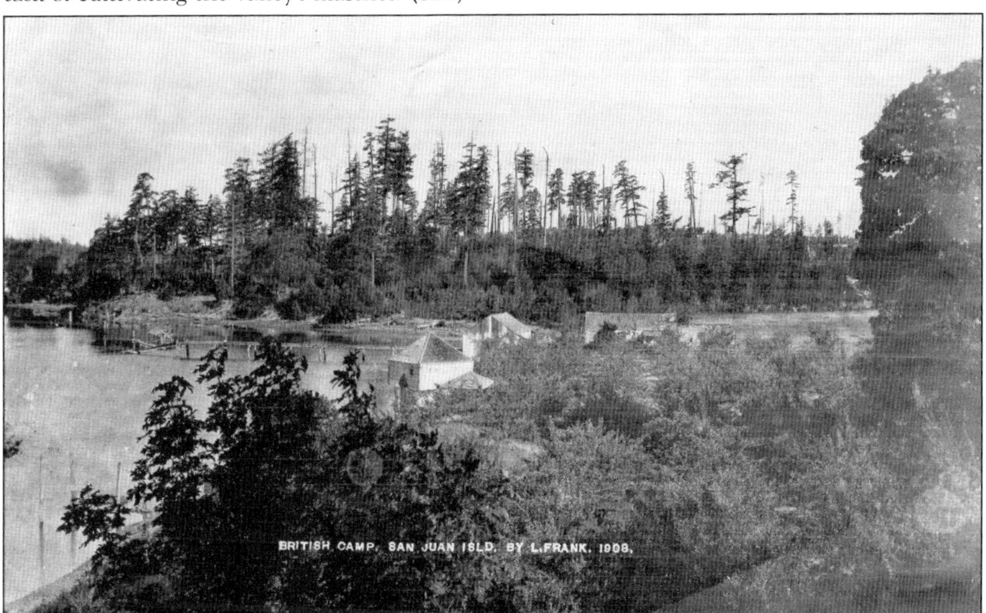

William Crook filed his claim for the English Camp lands in January at the U.S. District Lands Office in Olympia. Family opinions differed as to which structure they first inhabited. Jim Crook said it was the existing barracks building, but his sister Rhoda maintained it was the "Lieutenant's House," where she was born in 1880.

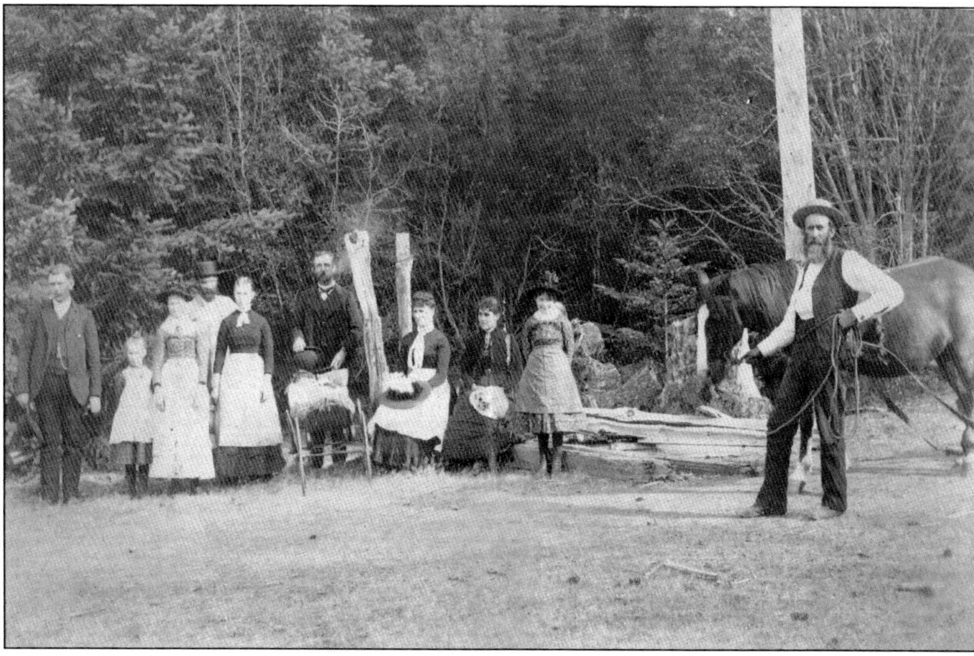

Island families and friends enjoy the orchard planted on the Isaac Sandwith homestead adjoining English Camp around 1885. A native of Cumberland, England, Sandwith arrived on San Juan in 1867 and accumulated 840 acres. From left to right are Gus Anderson, Rhoda Crook, Hannah Sandwith, Charles Hawkins, Mary Crook, Captain Yeager, infant Sarah Sandwith (in carriage), mother Sarah Sandwith, Kate Boyce, Jane Sandwith, and Cy Stowe with horse.

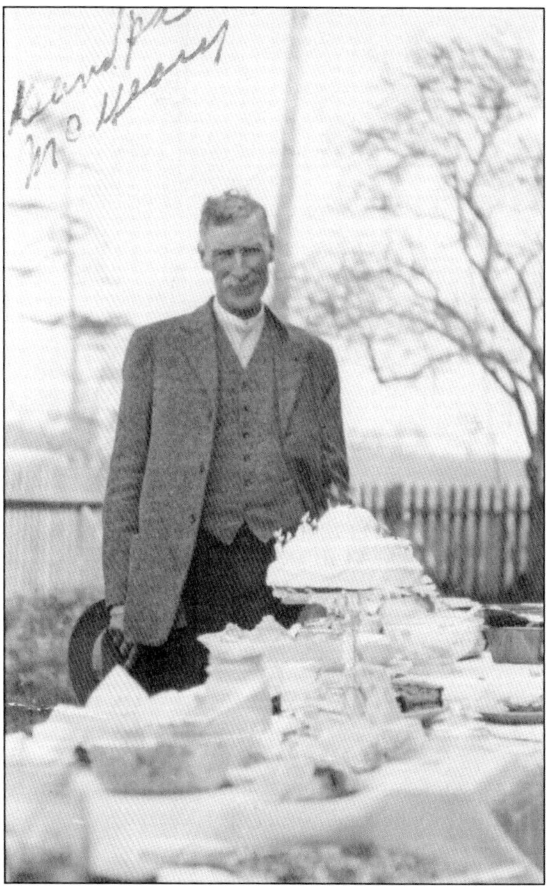

When George Pickett landed on San Juan in July 1859, so did the camp laundress, Catherine McGeary, and her two children, Mary, four, and Edward "Ed", four months. A lifelong islander, Ed was ever accommodating, said Al Sundstrom. "No matter what party you were in, or who you were running against—could have been his best friend—if you were standing for office, Ed would say, 'I'll vote for you!'"

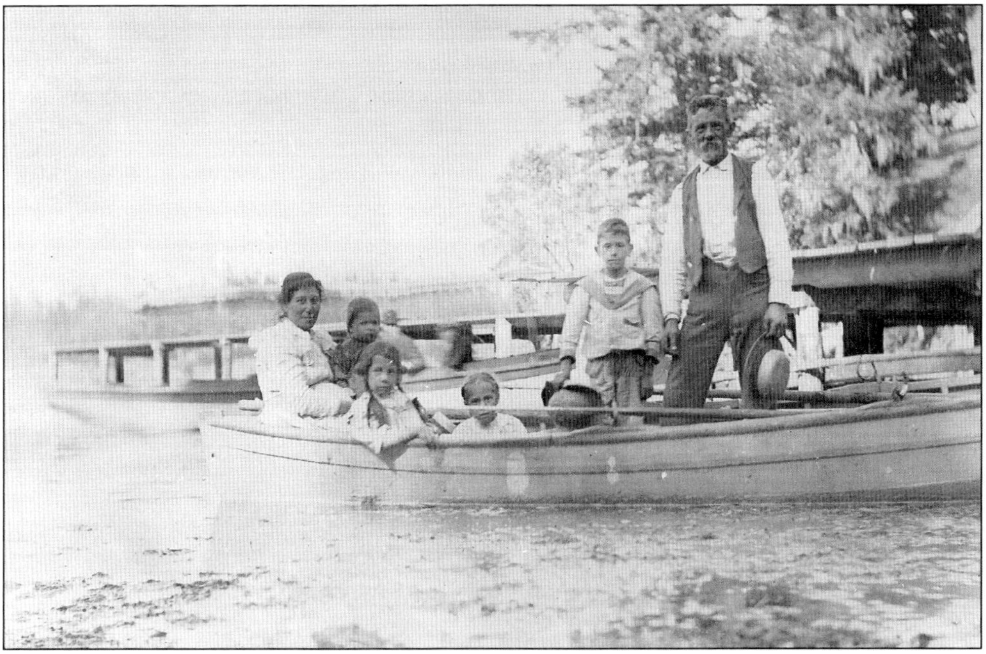

Kate Rosler Mordhorst; her husband, Barnhart; and their children (from left to right), Adeline, Louisa, Ollie, and Casper, prepare for a return trip to their home on Stuart Island. Kate was the third child of Christopher and Anna Pike Rosler. Rowboats and canoes remained the common mode of inter-island transportation well into the 20th century, so a stay at the in-laws was regulated by the weather and tides.

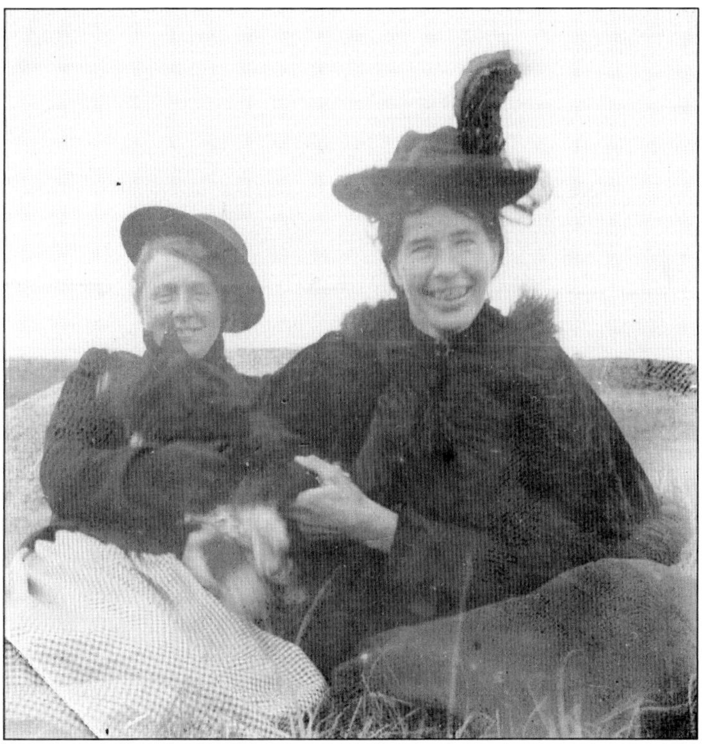

Mary Jane "Mamie" Firth (left) and Lizzie Lawson enjoy a lighthearted moment with a squirmy dog around 1899. They are probably at the redoubt, situated on the hillock above the old U.S. Army camp, that later became the Firth family farm. Mamie would, in a few years, marry Joe LaChappelle, and together they would run the farm until 1923. Lizzie, meanwhile, would never marry anyone—especially Norman Frazer (see page 15).

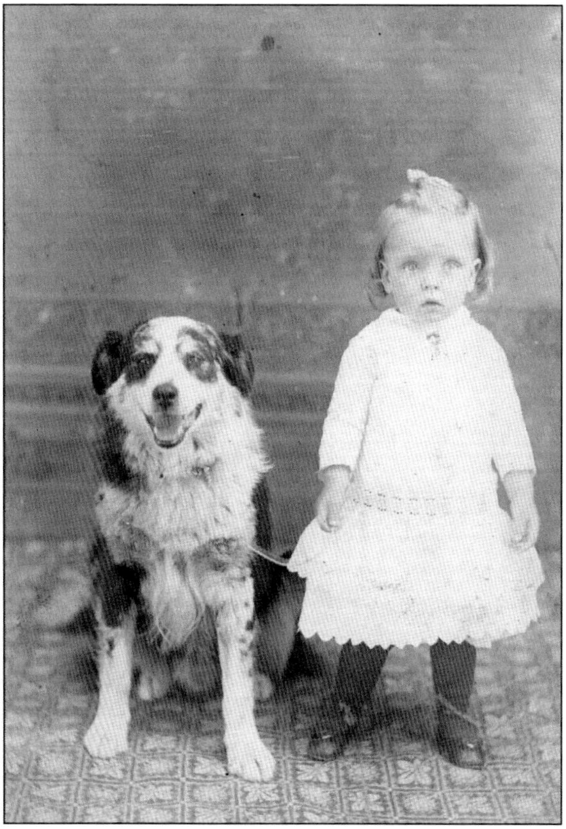

This slightly apprehensive child clutching the tether of her father's favorite sheepdog is Jessie Firth (see also page 87), born in 1863. Some have proclaimed her "the first white child born on San Juan Island." However, the 1870 census indicates that Lucinda Boyce gave birth to Alice in 1861 and Emma in 1862, though perhaps in Victoria where the family lived for a time. A good bet is that Lucinda delivered Jessie.

Englishwoman Fannie Deardon Lawson (seated in front with her son-in-law William Munroe) traveled around the horn to Victoria aboard a "bride ship" with 500 other women. She met her husband, Peter, at the Boyce home, and they married in 1865. With her in this c. 1898–1899 portrait are, from left to right, Alfred Lawson; Emma Lawson Munroe; Joseph and George Lawson; Mary McDowell; and Fannie, Peter, and Lizzie Lawson.

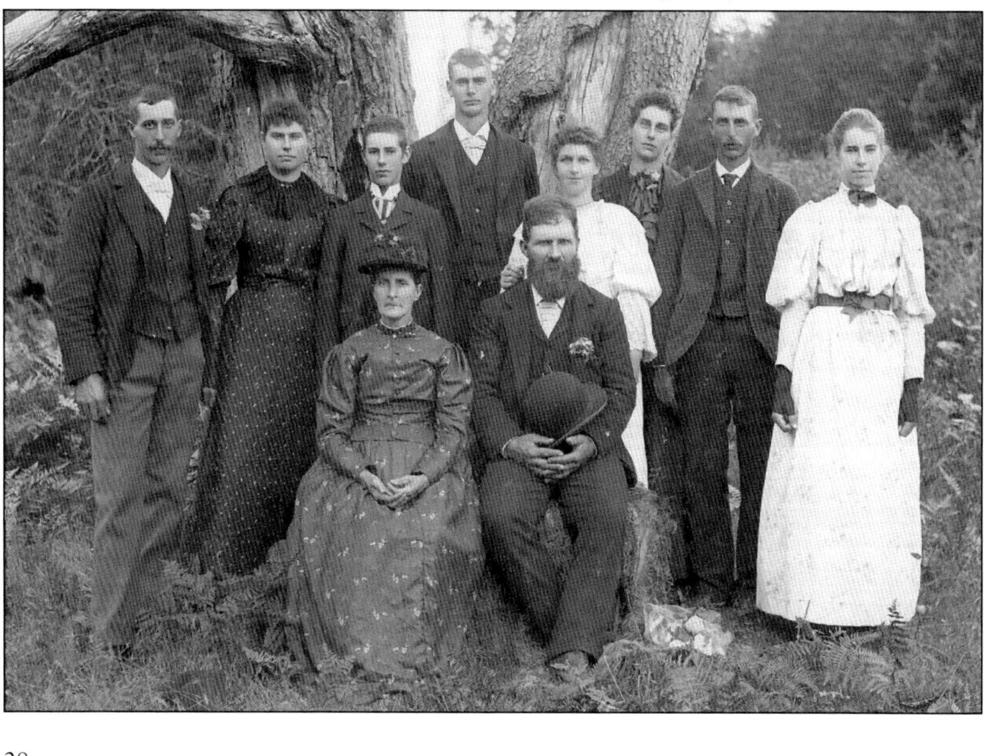

Two

Bringing in the Harvest

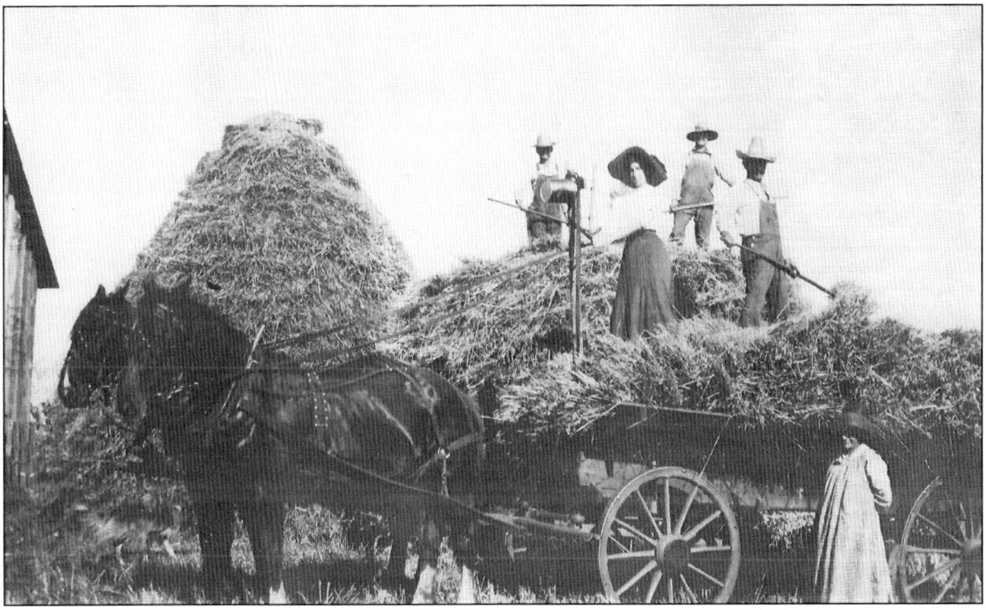

With help from friends and neighbors (Adeline Thrones watches from below), Lizzie Lawson transfers grain from wagon to stack in preparation for threshing on her father, Peter Lawson's, Eagle Point farm. San Juan was literally ripe for the plow when Euro-Americans arrived. First came the establishment of Belle Vue Sheep Farm in 1853, followed by scattered subsistence farms such as Lyman Cutlar's potato patch. It was at the onset of the latter that Dr. Caleb Kennerly, naturalist for the Northwest Boundary Survey, extolled the island's agricultural potential proclaiming San Juan "second to none" when it came to farmland. He noted the "extensive prairies" for plants and grasslands where flocks could graze "throughout the year." That promise was fulfilled in ensuing decades as San Juan shipped agricultural produce throughout the state and across the country. But following World War I, large corporations absorbed small farms and mechanized on a massive scale in California's Central Valley, driving down prices and making it difficult for small farmers, especially those on San Juan, who had to contend with the cost of transportation and fuel.

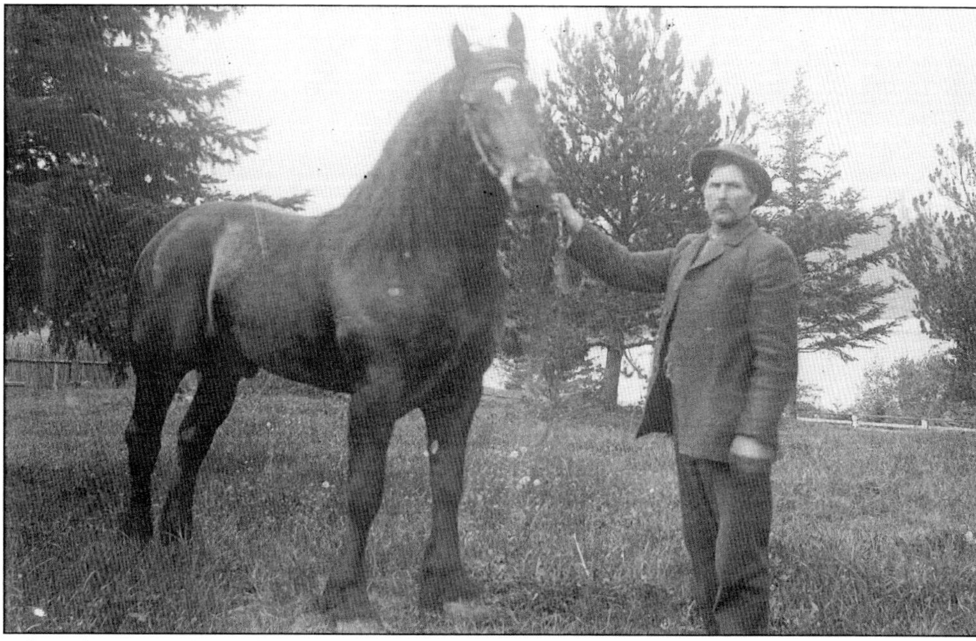

Bill Buchanan made headlines in the *Friday Harbor Journal* when he imported a massive Percheron stallion directly from France for stud. Bred in the Middle Ages to be warhorses, they were ideal for pulling stagecoaches, plows, or stone boats (sleds used to haul glacial rocks from farm fields). Islanders often rode their workhorses. According to Al Sundstrom, it was "a little like riding a wheelbarrow, with your legs sticking straight out."

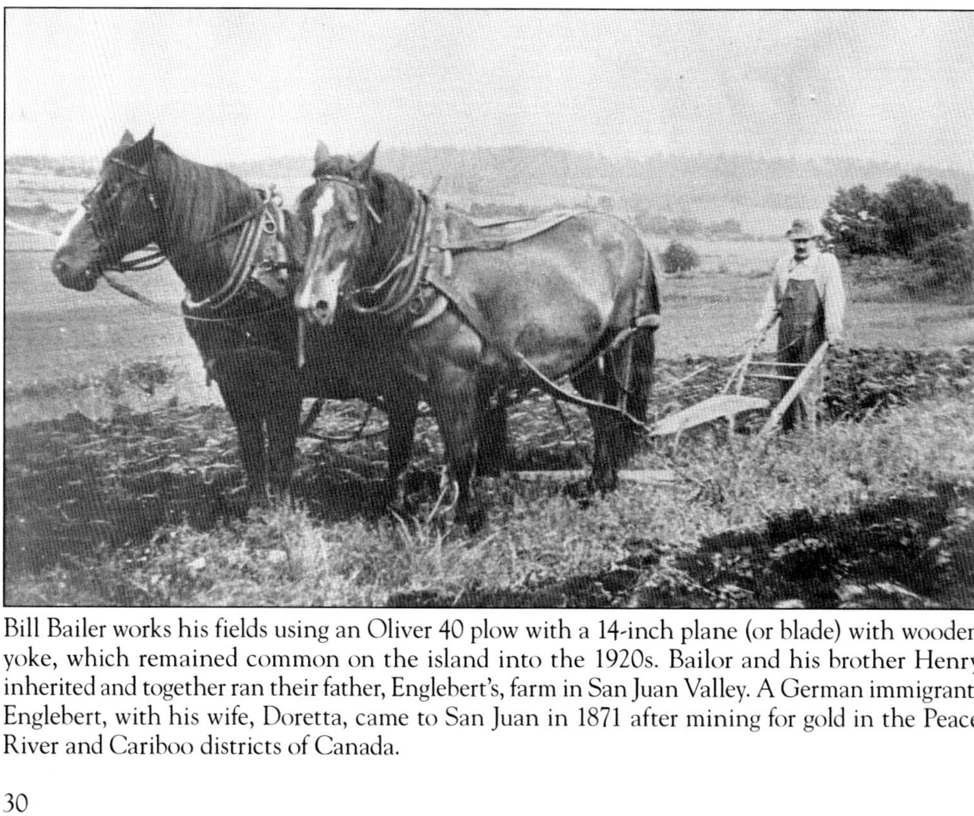

Bill Bailer works his fields using an Oliver 40 plow with a 14-inch plane (or blade) with wooden yoke, which remained common on the island into the 1920s. Bailor and his brother Henry inherited and together ran their father, Englebert's, farm in San Juan Valley. A German immigrant, Englebert, with his wife, Doretta, came to San Juan in 1871 after mining for gold in the Peace River and Cariboo districts of Canada.

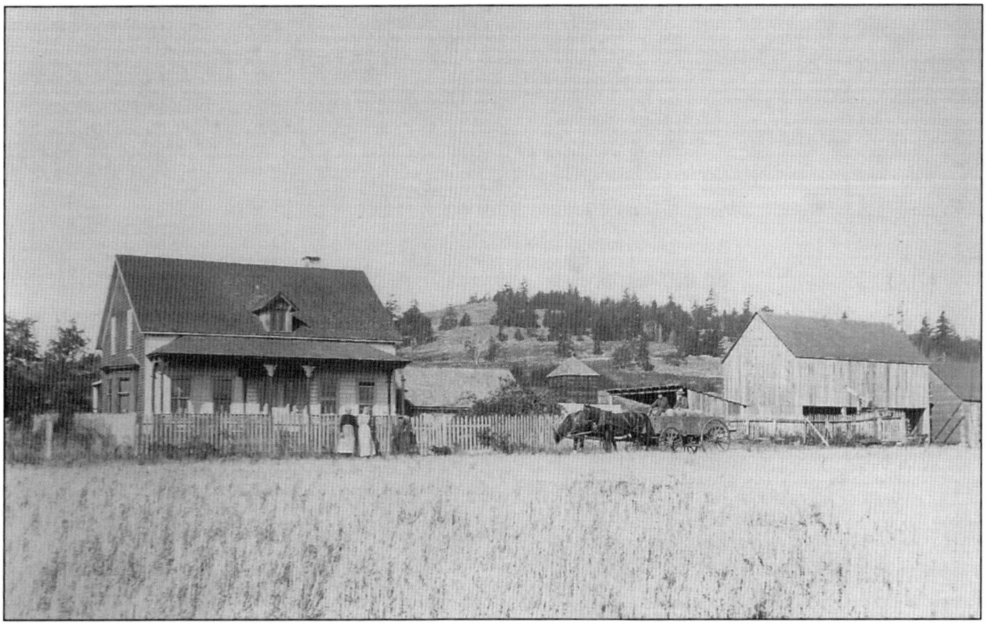

Engelbert Bailer once hosted 70 people for a dance at his San Juan Valley homestead. As Bert Coffin wrote in his journal, "Although I have heard many say that they didn't believe in dancing on Sunday I noticed that they, or rather we, kept it up pretty lively until 4 o' clock in the morning and then didn't stop from any sting of conscience but because we were tired and couldn't dance anymore."

Belle (McKenzie) Erickson is clearly amused as her husband, Eric, demonstrates how to cut weeds with a long-handled scythe. Both hands were required to move its curved, sharpened blade parallel to the ground. A 1901 *Friday Harbor Journal* article reported that the Ericksons farmed 20 acres of wheat and some hay and had 50 sheep and "a number of cattle." Eric was remembered by islanders for never being without a hat.

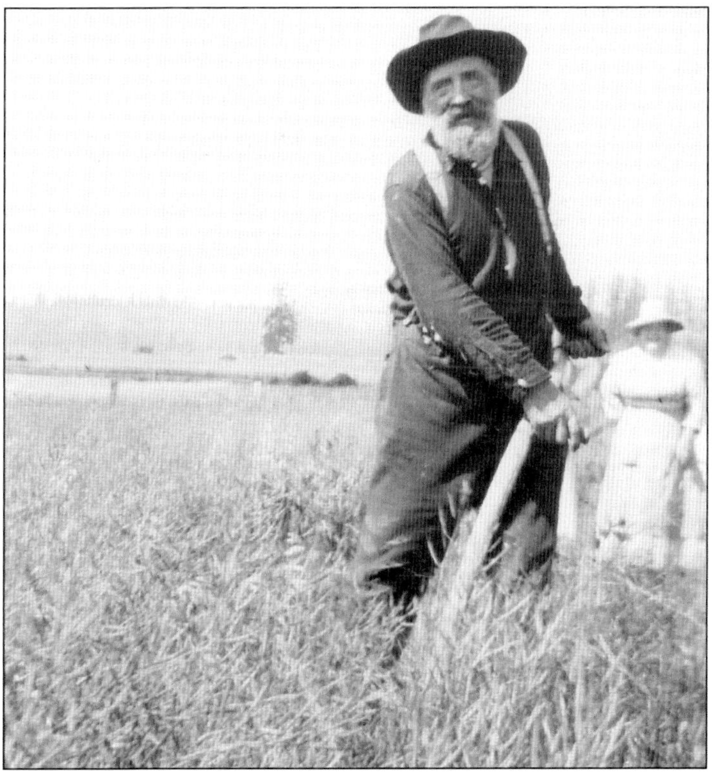

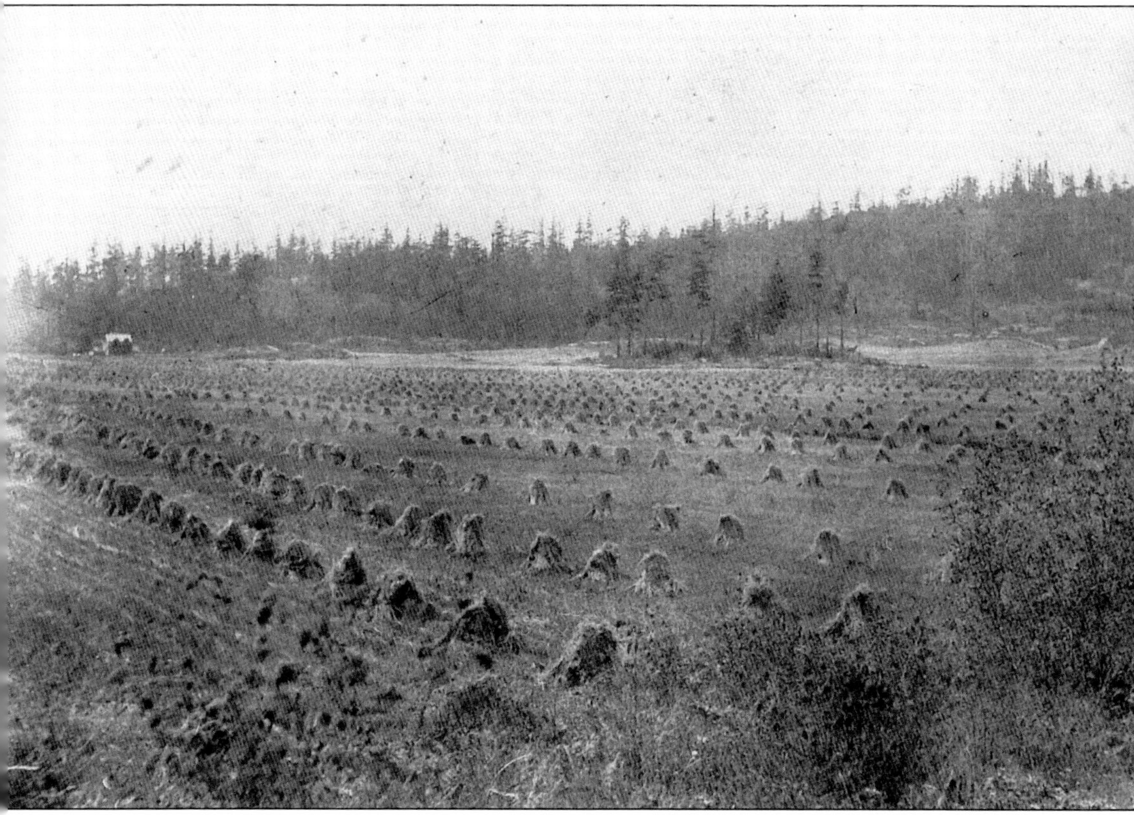

The Paul and Frank Guard homesteads were located in Beaverton Valley, a stretch of marsh giving onto grassy uplands that today runs from the Foxhall Development to the Number Two Schoolhouse Road. Concern over standing water in the field compelled farmers in 1913 to form a "Ditch Association," which met as needed in ensuing decades in a cooperative effort to excavate and maintain a drainage ditch in the valley. When drained, the valley was a farmer's dream. "You could grow anything in there because it was 90 percent humus and only required 100 pounds of fertilizer per acre," recalled Al Sundstrom. "It was good for fattening lambs—if you could keep the dogs away from them—because the grass grew so high." The committee disbanded and the work ceased in 1952. In the early 1940s, the county built a shortcut across the valley, linking Halverson and Beaverton Valley roads. But with each passing year, the puddles expanded and the road sank beyond redemption. The county also attempted drainage but finally gave up and closed the "Sunken Road." (SH.)

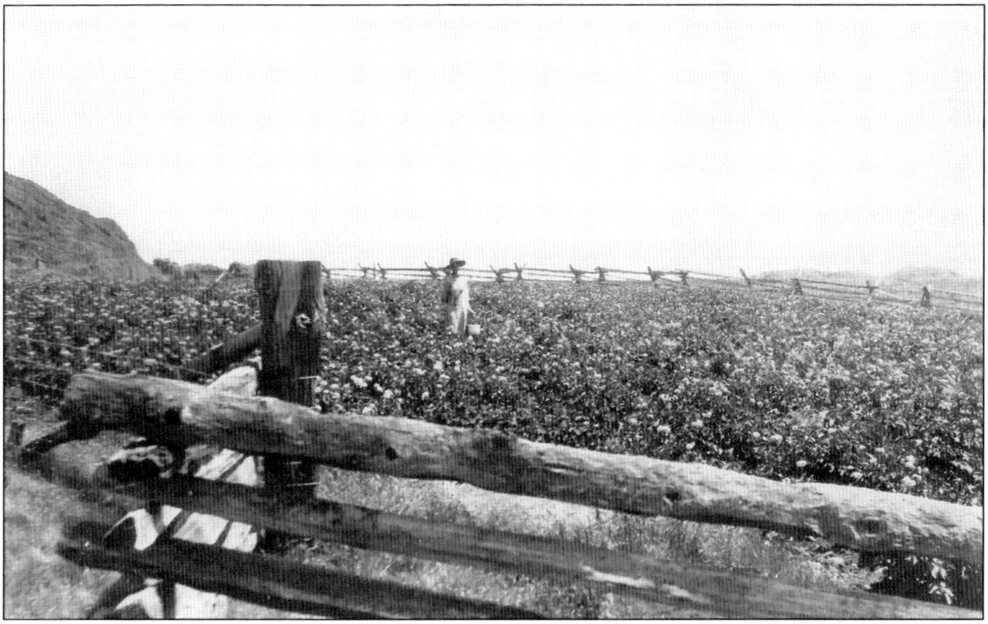

Lizzie Lawson proudly surveys her potato patch on the 40 acres her father deeded to her at Eagle Point. The youngest daughter of Peter and Fannie Lawson, Lizzie was born on the homestead in 1879 and worked the farm until she was nearly 60 years old. She sold out then and bought a modest cottage at the edge of Friday Harbor, where she spent the rest of her life.

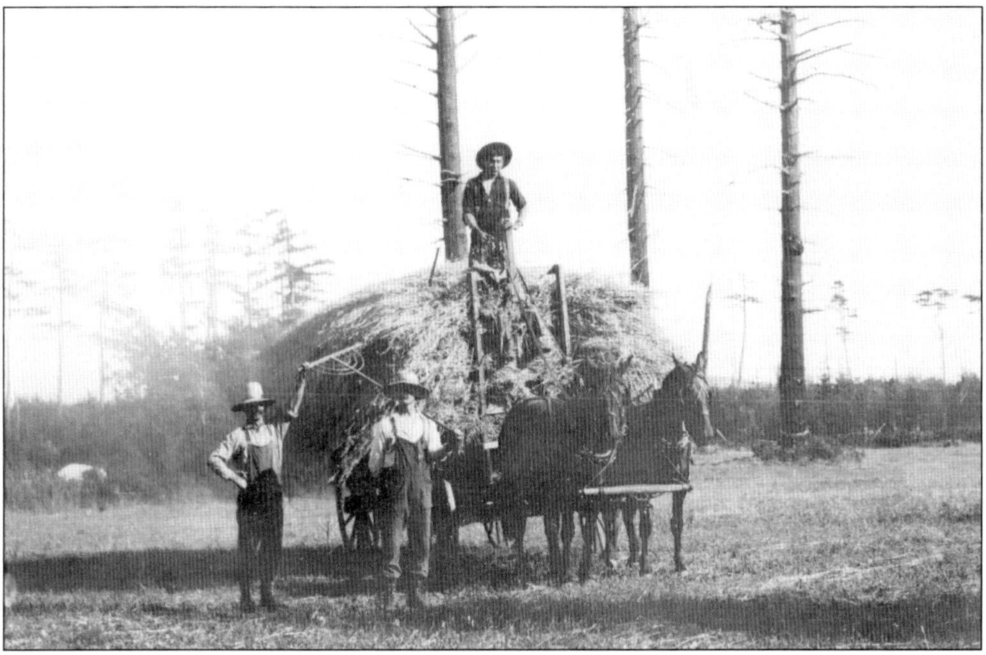

Bill Rosler holds the reins on a wagon of grain, the residue of which had been swept up by the old-fashioned rake carried over the shoulder of one of the men on the ground, who may be Bill's close friend and neighbor George Lawson. They are probably hauling the grain to the threshing machines for separating. Born in 1878, Bill was the youngest son of Christopher and Anna Pike Rosler.

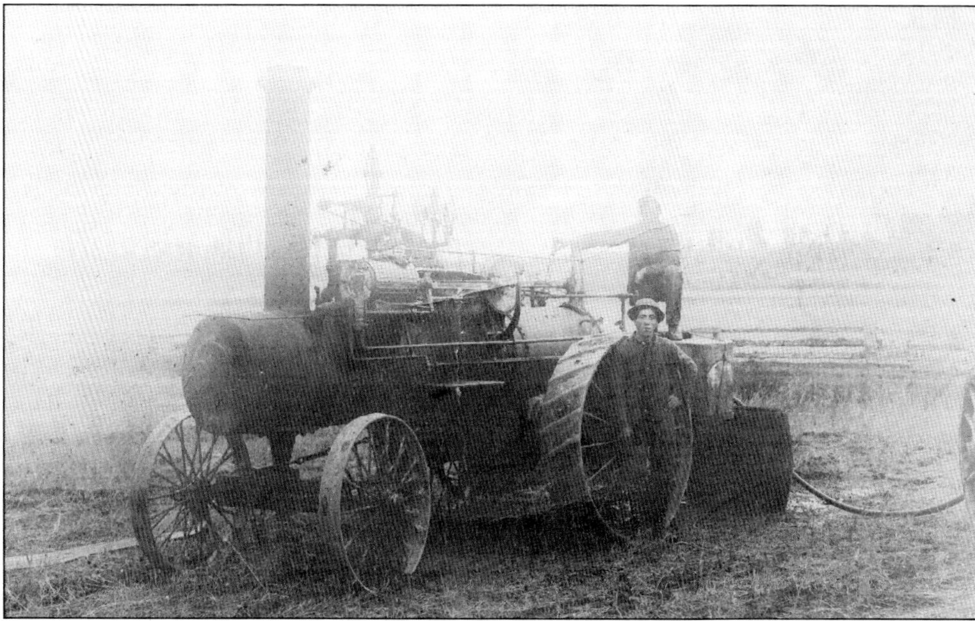

Bill Buchanan, at the throttle of a traction engine, moved comfortably between the equine (page 30) and mechanical worlds. Steam-powered "road locomotives" entered the U.S. market in 1850 and remained in use on the island until 1936, even after gasoline tractors were introduced. They were ponderous and difficult to steer and would sink in the mud if farmers parked them in the same spot two years running.

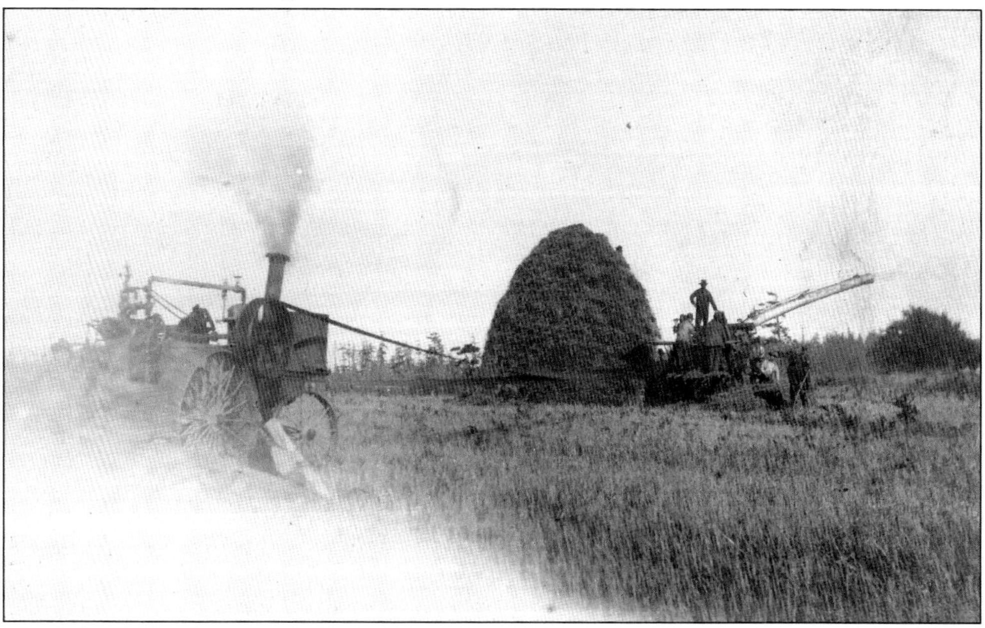

The sight and sound of traction engines rumbling up country lanes with threshing machines in tow was a much-anticipated annual event, but the engines usually remained stationary while powering other equipment. Here on the Lawson farm, an engine belching smoke drives the grain separator via the leather belt from engine to separator. The length of the belt ensured that it would not slip off the giant pulleys on both machines.

Neighbors Adeline Thrones (left), Lizzie Lawson, and Bill Rosler fork grain into the separator as they did during the harvest each August. The traction engines and threshers were purchased cooperatively and shared among neighbors, as was the labor of bringing in the harvest. The agricultural combine rolled all these tasks into one machine. Al Sundstrom brought the first to the island in 1945.

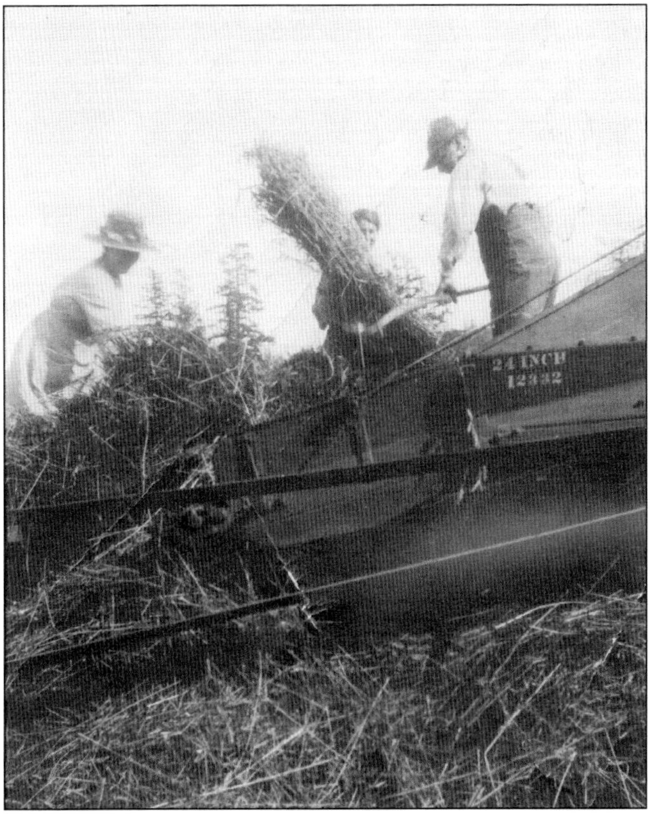

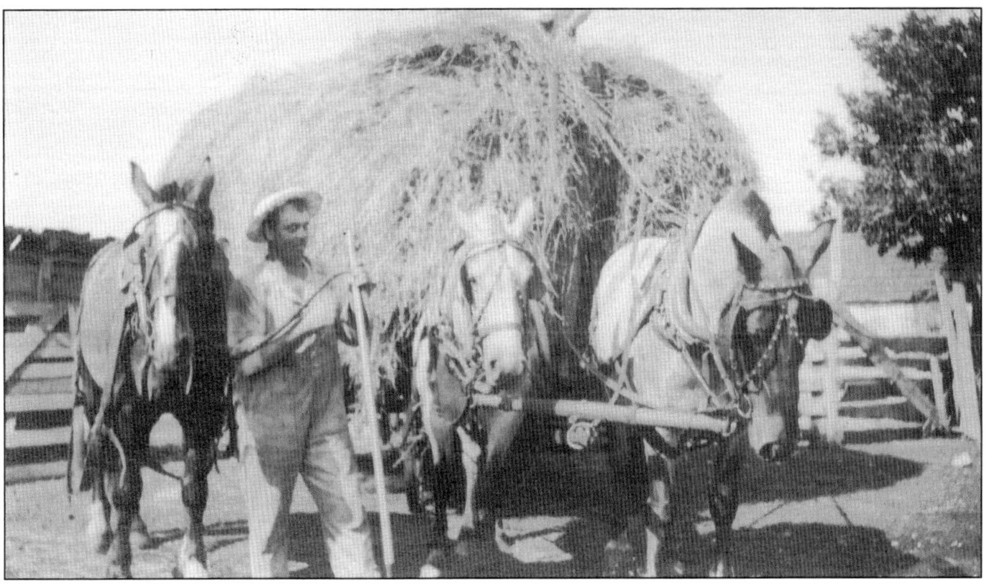

Charles "Charlie" Landahl lingers by his hay wagon around 1912 on the Rosler homestead just north of American Camp. Like his neighbor Stephen Boyce, Charlie ran away from home at age 12, leaving behind his native Hamburg, Germany. He sailed around the world several times and at 18 landed on San Juan Island. The third horse was probably hitched to a hayfork that elevated the hay to the barn loft.

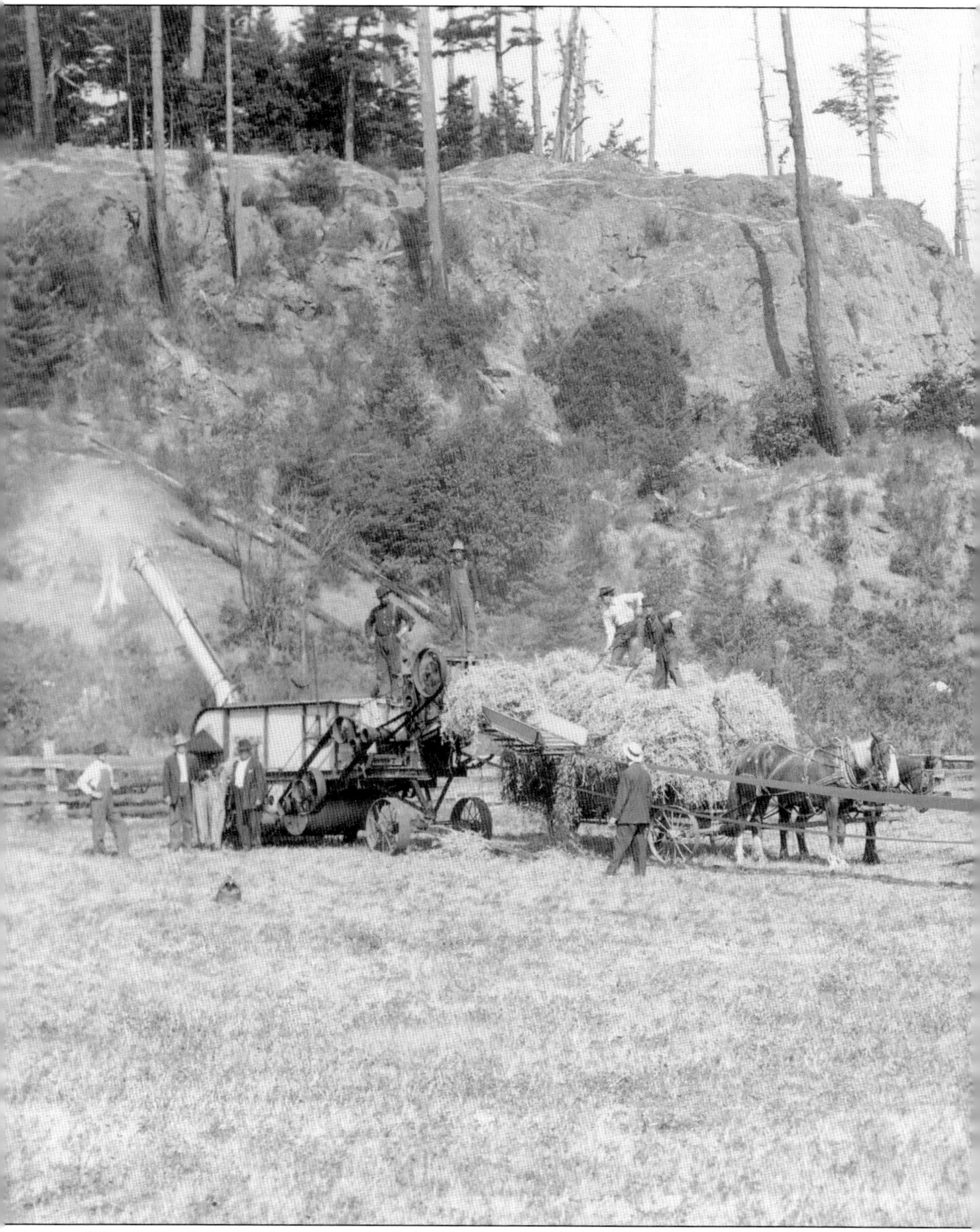

The James King family and hired hands thresh grain below King Mountain, today more commonly known as the "water tank hill," at the head of Spring Street in Friday Harbor around 1900–1910. The man standing atop the separator at far left was the "separator tender," who ensured that the machine did not hang up during operations. It was built by J. J. Case Company, which produced

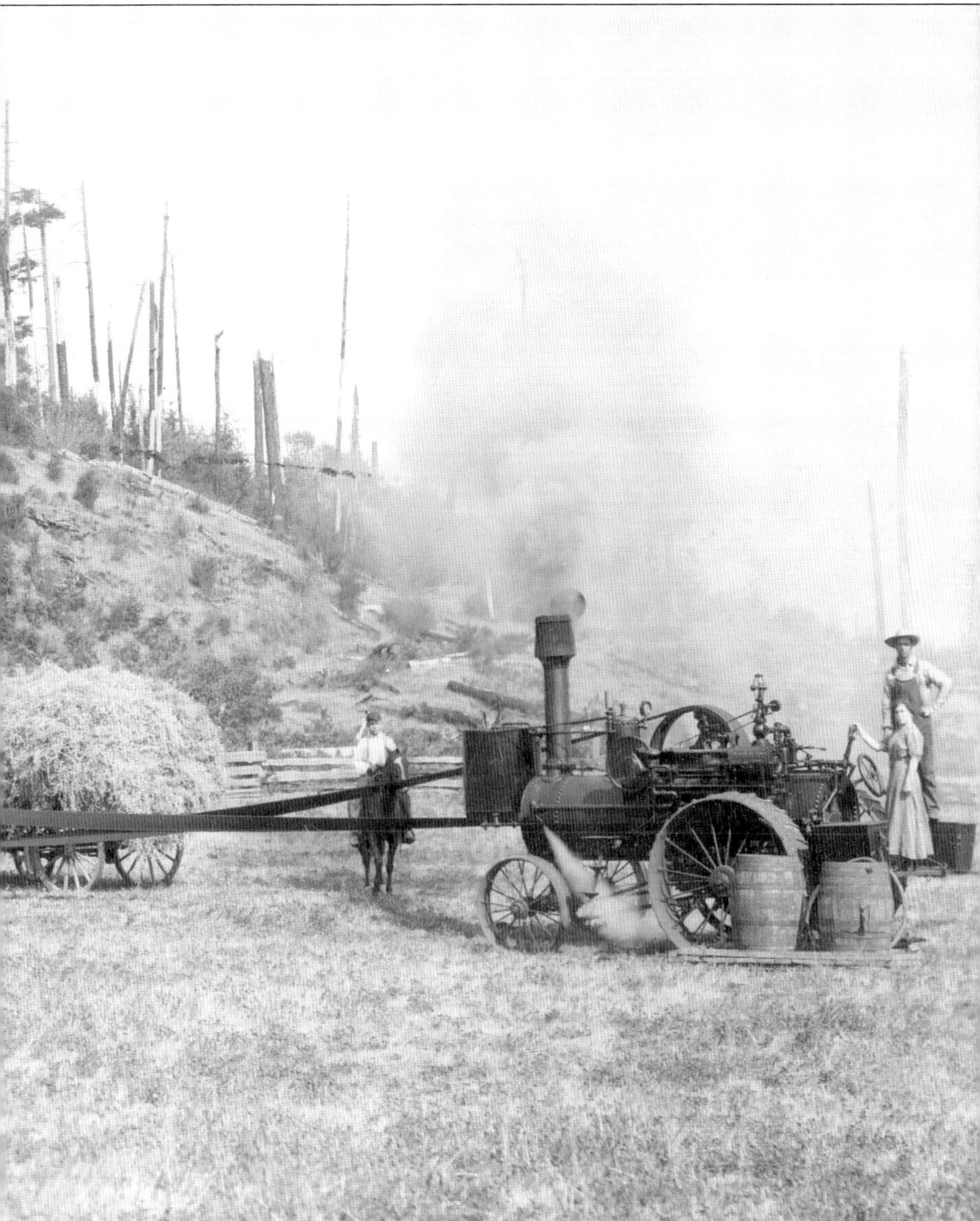

threshers through 1953. The grain bundles are shoved into the feeder, cleaned, and separated; the straw blows out the long stack; and the grain flows into the sacks below, which are then sewn shut. A huge crop usually meant the water barrels by the engine's rear wheel had to be refilled. Note the woman at far right, perhaps Adeline King, with her hand on the throttle.

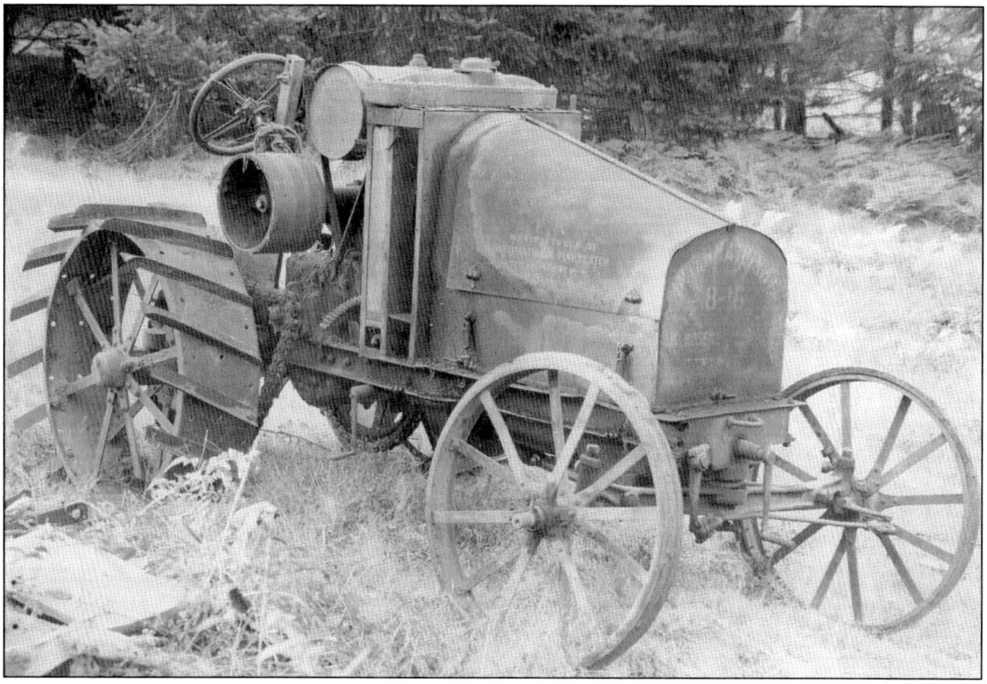

Jim Crook's gasoline-powered International Harvester tractor performed multiple tasks on his English Camp farm, including driving Rube Goldberg devices such as a "power rake" and Crook's famous wool-carding machine. Note the fat pulley just below the gas tank. The extended cleats extending from the rear wheels kept the treads free of mud while the front steel wheels were grooved to prevent slippage.

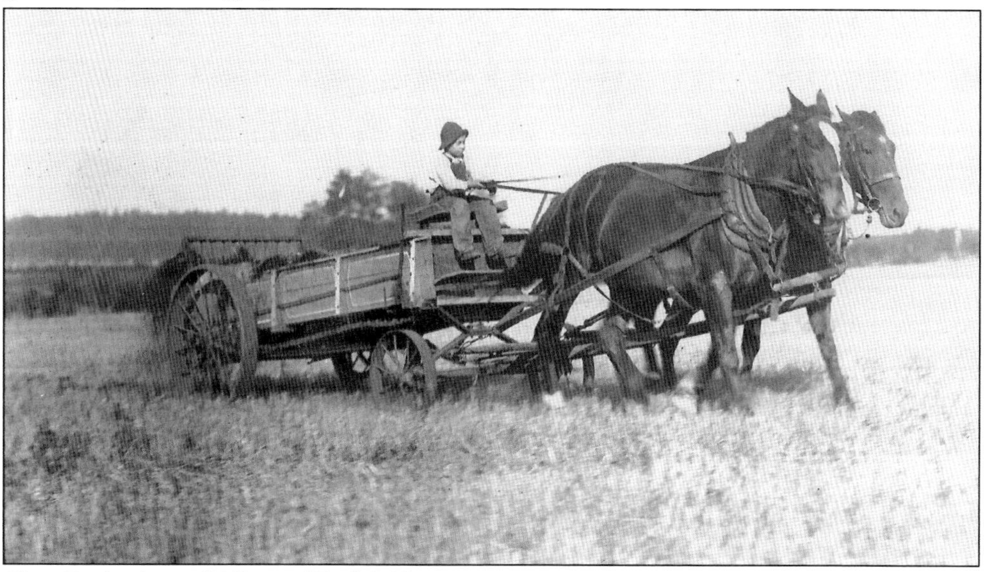

Chris Rosler (son of Tillie and Rudolph), 10, navigates a manure spreader on his father's fields in preparation for plowing. A lever engaged a chain that twirled the spikes at the end of the wagon bed, breaking up and scattering the manure. No implement was embraced as wholeheartedly as the spreader. Before then, someone had to ride in the wagon bed with a shovel and break it up by hand.

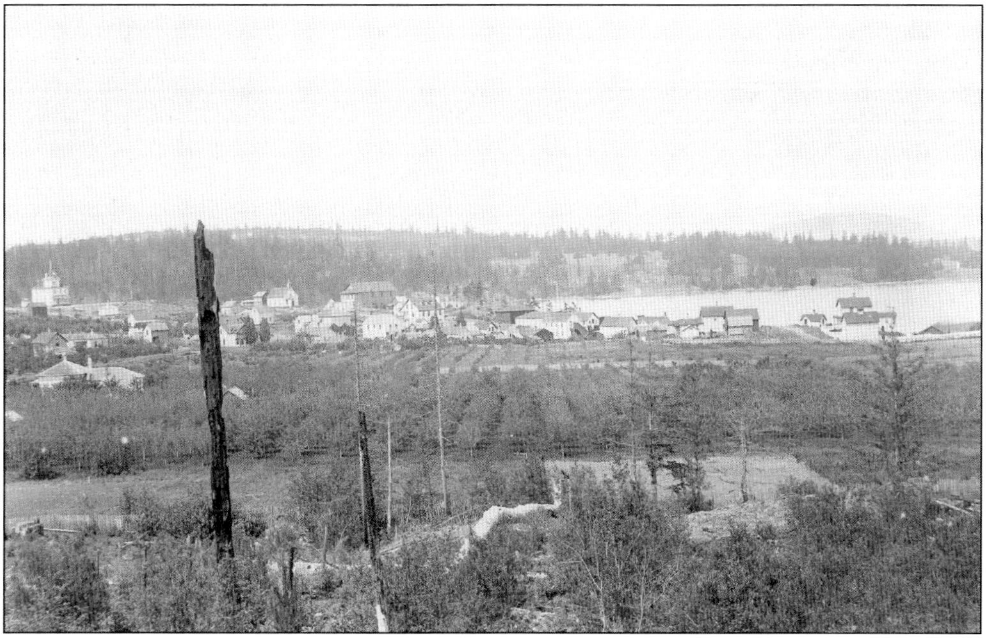

Granville B. Driggs's plum trees line the edge of town in this 1890s view of Friday Harbor. Driggs established the fruit orchard, as did many on the island, as a cash crop in the days before irrigation made central Washington flower. His house, at far left, was one of the first built on the Argyle Wagon Road. A few scraggly trees survive on the lot behind the Surina Business Center.

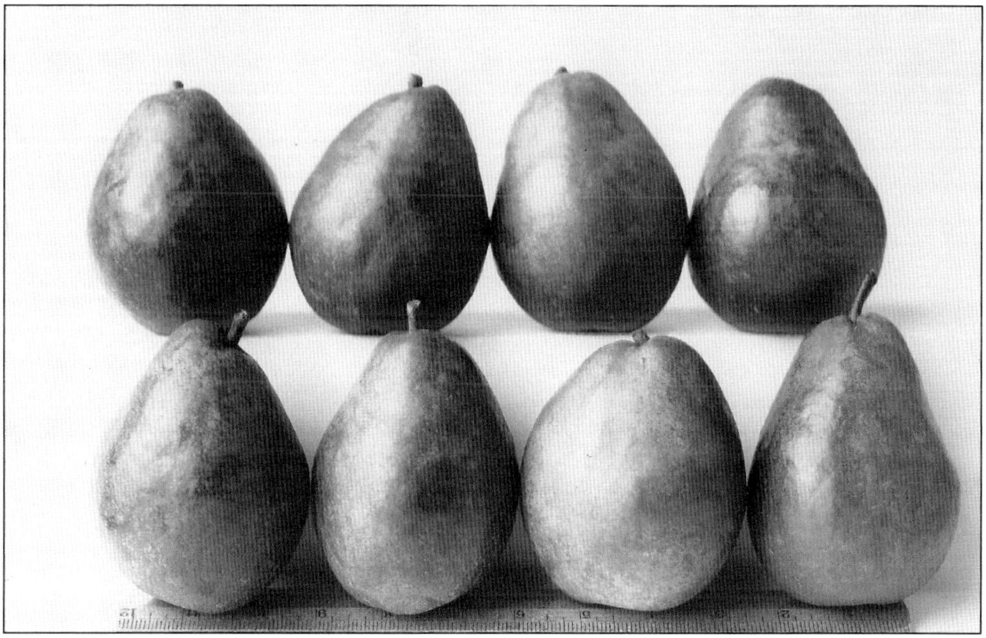

This catchy promotion boasted "Four Pears to a Foot" during the island's foray into the fresh fruit market. Apples, pears, peaches, strawberries, and apricots were grown throughout the island, including most of the backyards in town. In 1907 alone, 72,000 boxes of apples, at 80¢ each, were shipped to points south, such as the Pike Place Market in Seattle. Pears ranked second with 12,000 boxes at $1.25 each.

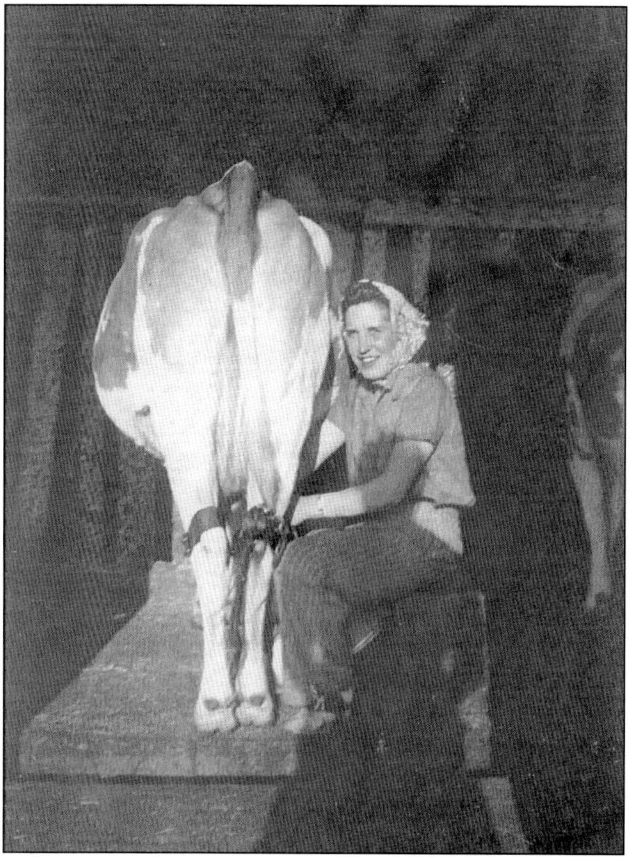

Clyde and Ruth Guard Sundstrom were born to the island life, both in 1920. Ruth milked cows, chocked hay, and disked fields. Clyde was a dairyman and logger, built island roads, and delivered mail by horse and tractor. They married in 1943 when Clyde was on leave from the navy and bought the Valley View farm from Ruth's parents. While working, they would tuck their six children under a tree or on the tractor seat. For 14 years, they hosted "farm stays" for city folks, surrendering their bedroom for the cellar. "We had bunks in the milk house, the garage, and the Birdie house." They loved to dance (dancing shoes lasted Clyde just a week, said one son) and loved their children. Clyde repaired a lot of bed frames over the years—bent and broken in the days before trampolines. (Both, GS.)

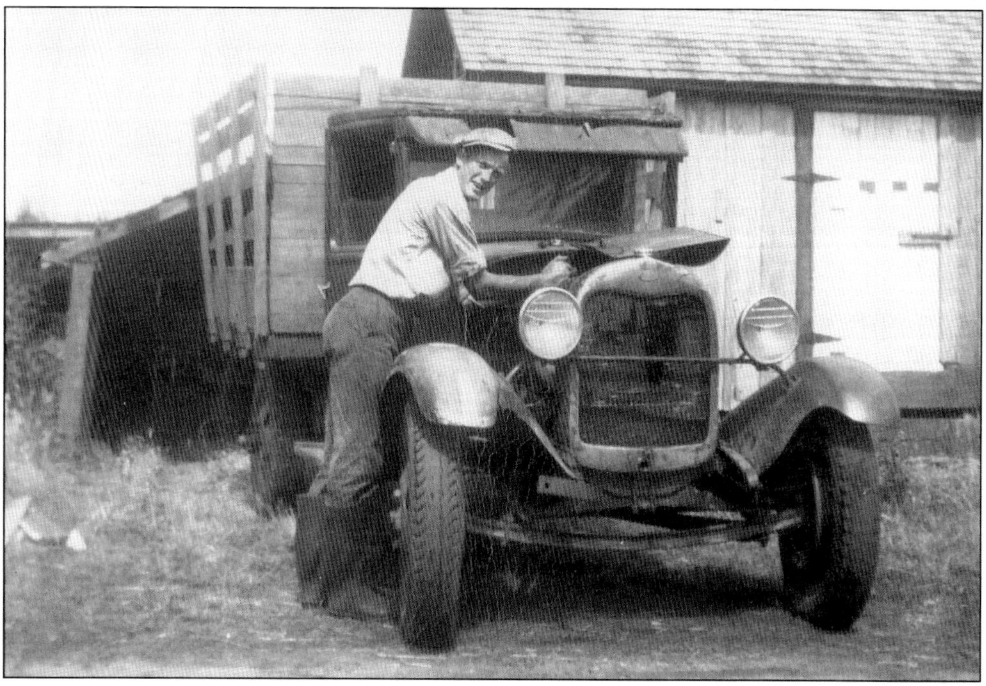

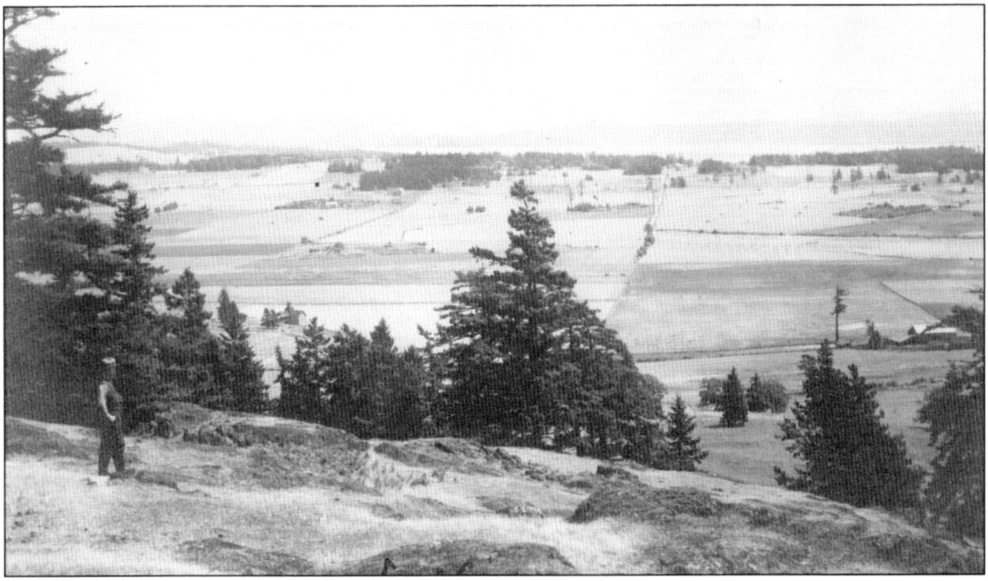

Big-time agriculture imposed on San Juan Valley in 1922 when grower John M. "Pea" Henry bought up farms and turned the valley into a vast pea field. He built a cannery on the dock in Friday Harbor and marketed "Saltair Peas." In 1936, aphids and weevils attacked the plants, decimating the industry by 1940, although there was a brief revival in the 1960s. Note the hop barn lower left.

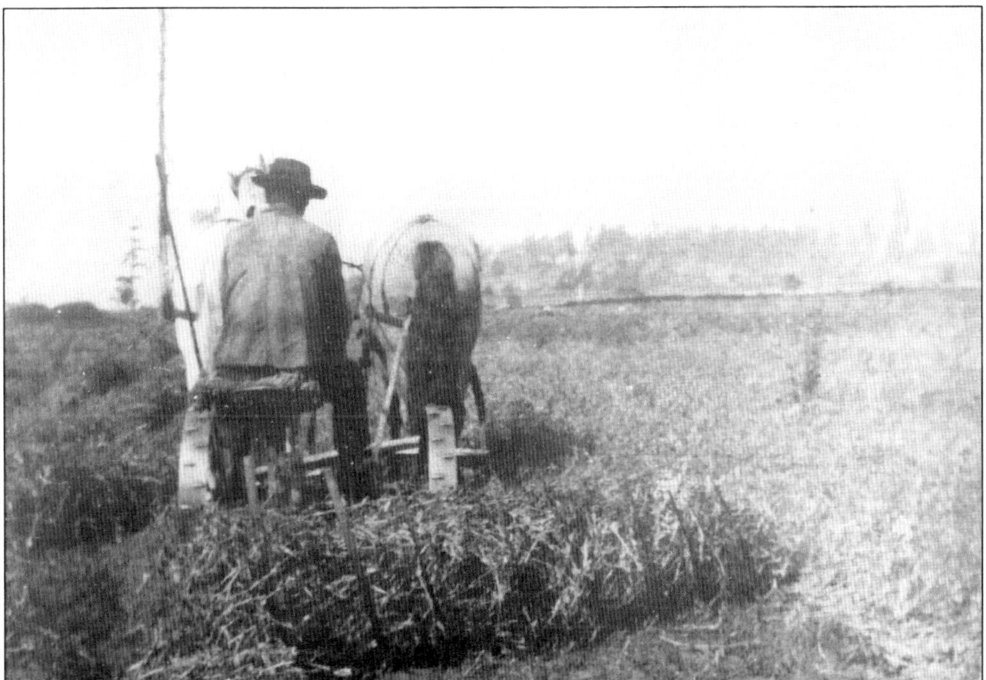

A farmer uses a "buncher" to bunch or windrow the pea harvest at the Lawson farm near Eagle Point. Another worker would usually follow the machine with a pitchfork that would be inserted between the buncher tines, allowing the vines to build and form into rows such as the one at left. The rows would then be raked, placed on a carrier, and taken to a pea viner.

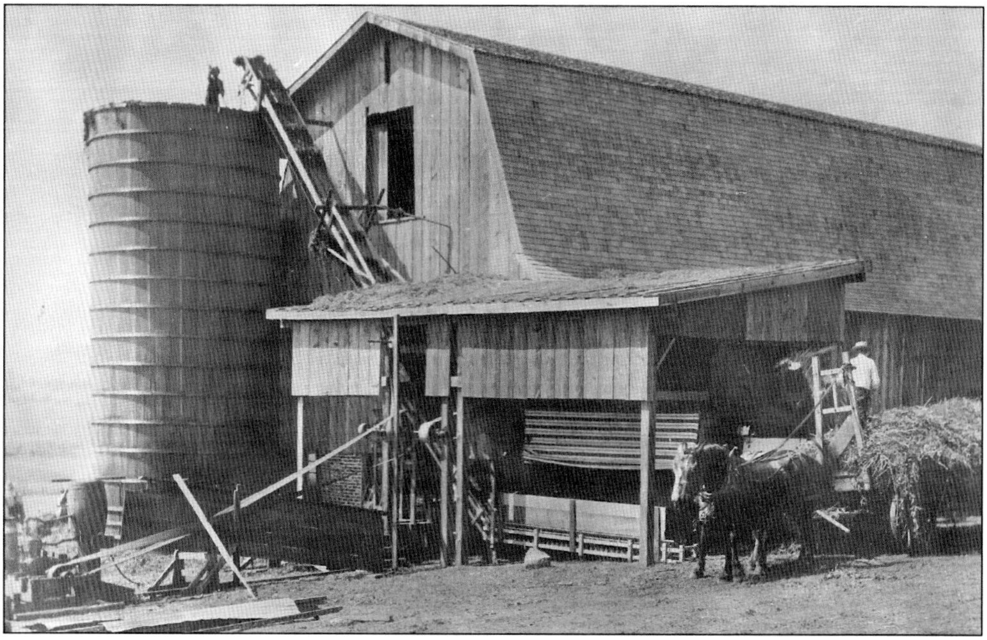

Tommy Davis's new silo created a stir in 1924 and again when it collapsed eight years later. "It was just too big around and fell in on itself," Al Sundstrom said. The farm, now owned by the Hudson family, is located on Douglas Road. Here the workers are feeding the vines on the wagon into the viner, which shells and cleans the peas and conveys the vines to the silo.

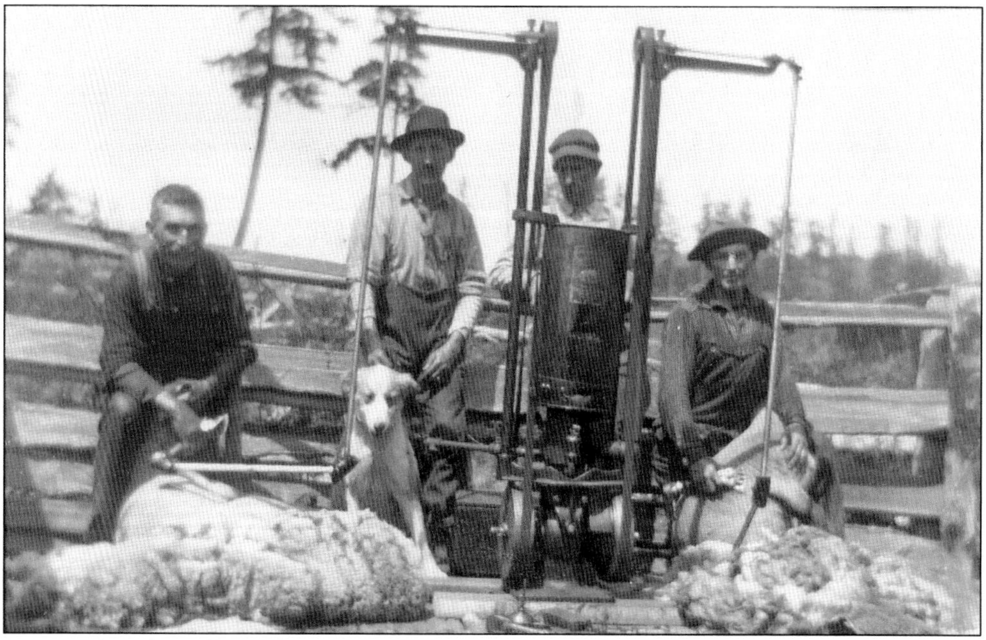

Jim Crook and neighbors shear sheep with the wonder of the age—a gasoline-powered shearing machine. Note the belt drive on each side connecting to a transfer gear. The machine operated on the same principle as today's electric shears. The sheep were tethered to the vertical bars while the gasoline engine drove the belt drives on each side, which, through reduction gears, powered the shears.

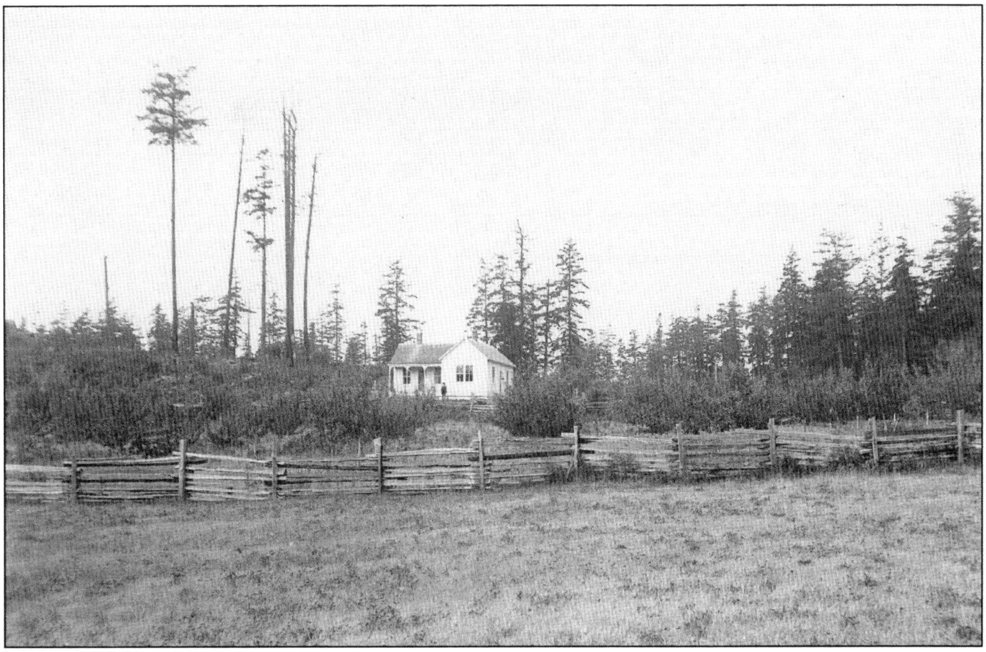

Alfred Lawson struck out on his own from his father Peter's Eagle Point farm and claimed rolling pasture at the foot of Cady and Sugarloaf mountains. He steadily expanded this holding into more than 420 acres on which, in 1900, he raised 2.5 tons of oats per acre and grazed 300 head of sheep. Farm children became intimately aware of the annual cycles at an early age. Here Margaret and William Lawson watch freshly sheared sheep milling about the pens on their farm around 1905. Raising sheep has been a constant on the island since the Hudson's Bay Company imported the first 1,369 head in 1853 and expanded that flock to more than 4,500 by the Pig War crisis in 1859 (see page 11).

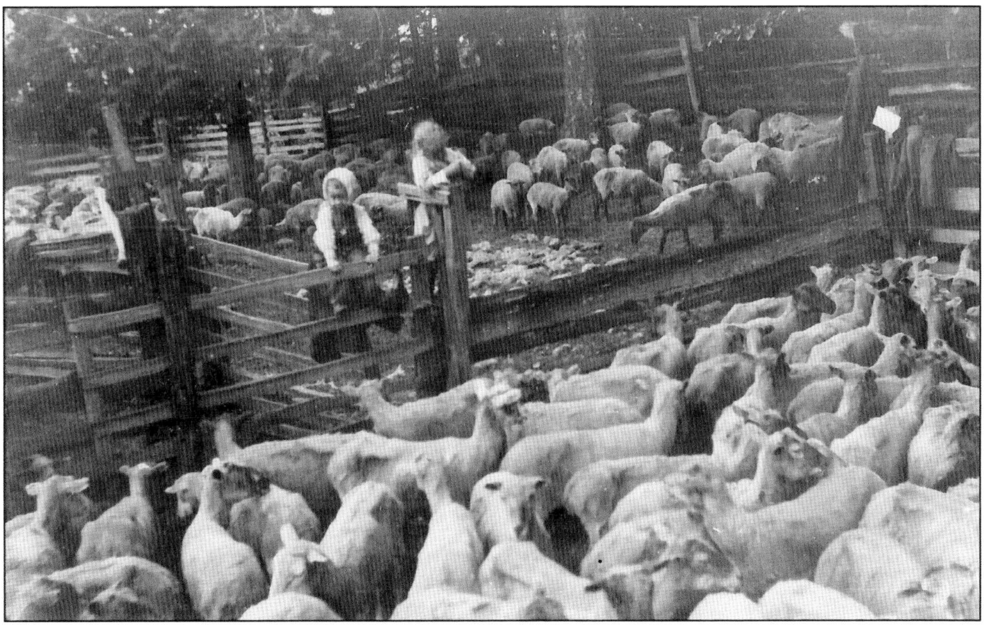

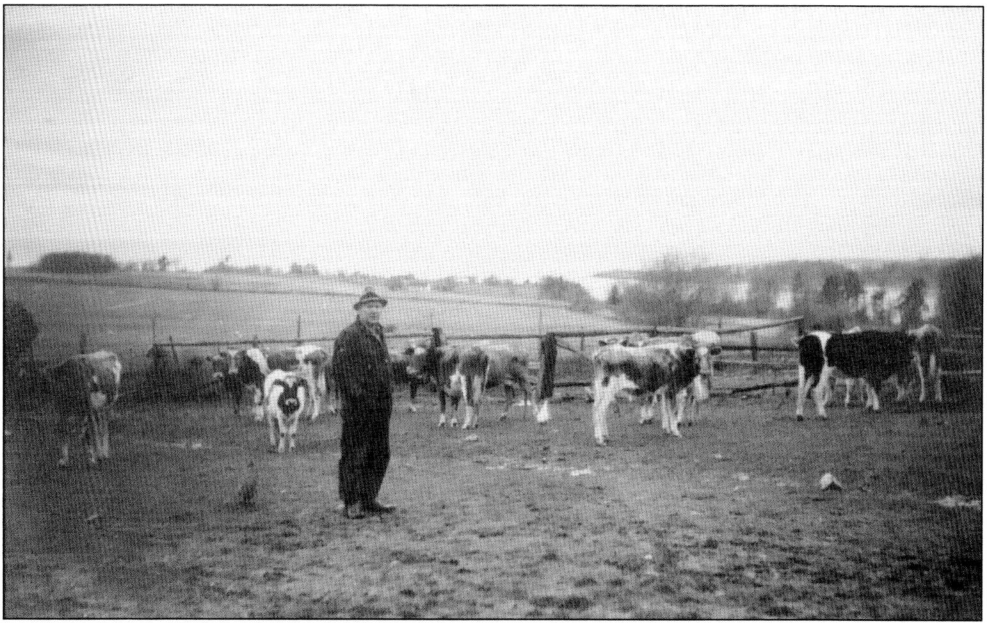

Julius Johnson, the eldest child of Andrew Johnson and Isabella Firth, surveys his stock on his farm, which had a sweeping view of False Bay. He farmed by day and cut cordwood at Cowell's Lime Kiln by night, where he met and married Edna Dougherty. Story has it that Edna's grandfather, Thomas Wotton, jumped ship in Victoria on his journey from England and rowed across the straits on a log.

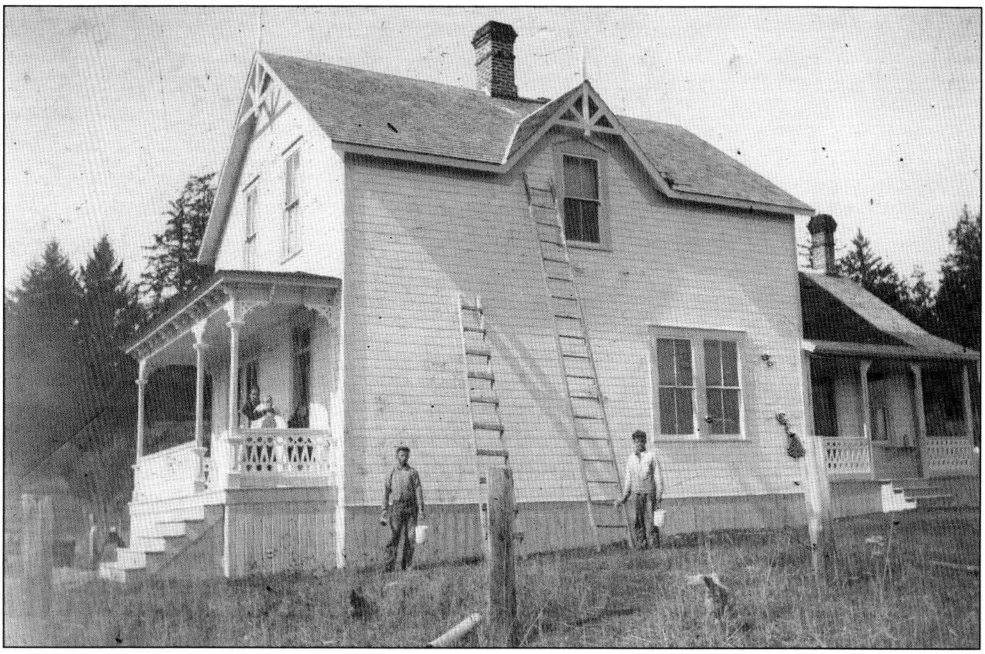

Alex Lightheart and Joe Cribbs use a pair of homemade ladders around 1900 to paint the Robert Sandwith home, which stood on 320 acres on Beaverton Valley Road and later burned down. This was not uncommon because water was scarce. By 1915, the town had 20 firefighters, a dam, water system, 29 fire hydrants, 3,000 feet of fire hose, three hose carts, lots of buckets, and a fire bell.

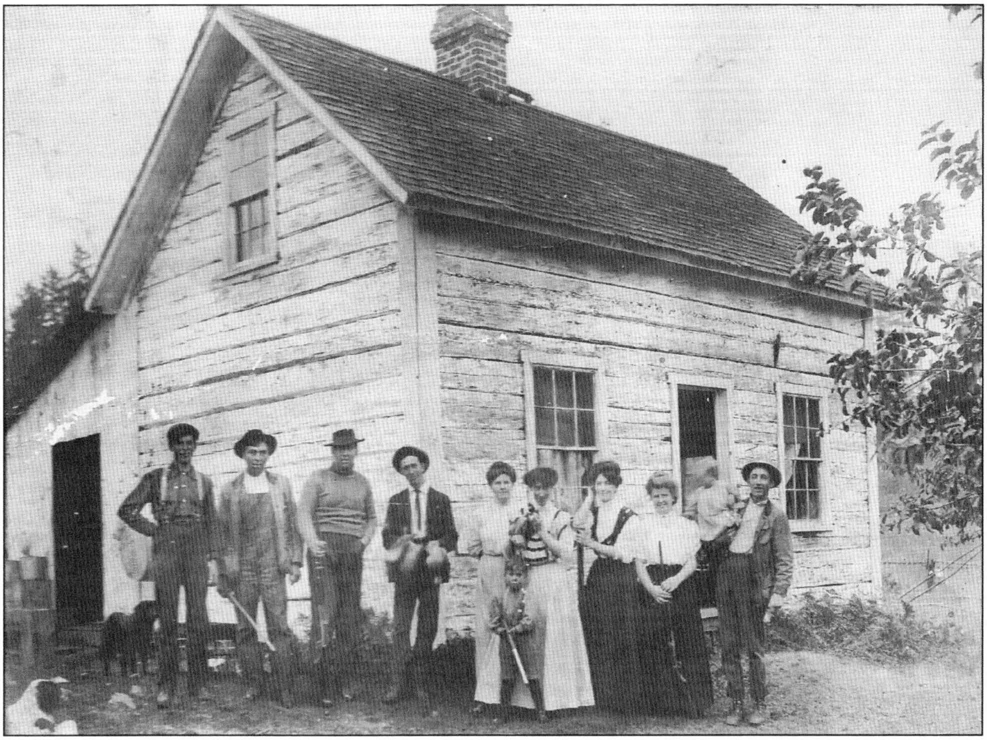

Friends gather for a bit of fun at John "Bigfoot" Johnson's house on Sutton Road. Included in the photograph are friends Warren Dightman, Bill Beigin, Arthur Erickson, Steve MacNurnee, Ella Erickson Dightman, Erica Erickson Wiley, and Joseph MacNurnee. Johnson, not pictured, was known for his mismatched feet—one larger than the other. Large-chested, ruddy-complected, and boisterous, he was a lifelong bachelor who horrified dinner hostesses by licking his butter knife.

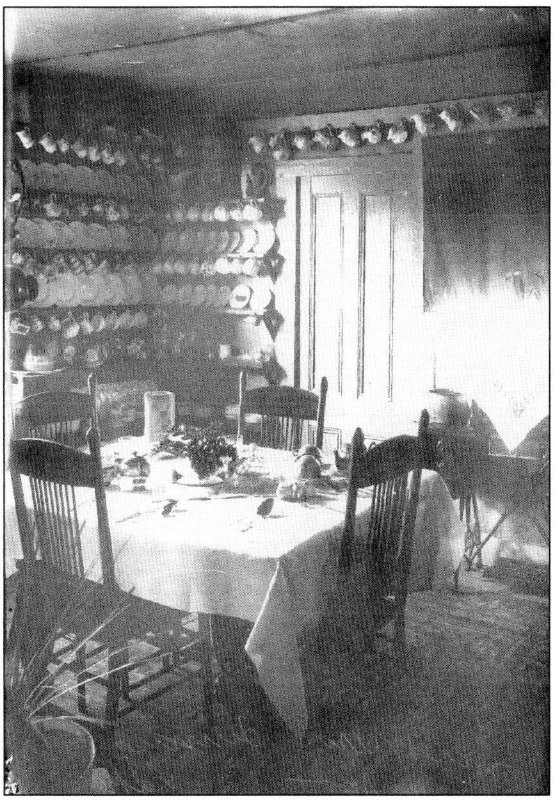

This image inside Frank Wilson's cabin at Sportsman's Lake offers a rare look at the interior of a modest home on the late frontier. The china displayed on the wall and sewing machine with foot treadle may have been ordered from a Sears, Roebuck, and Company catalog, which in the 1890s sold everything from watches and revolvers to cream separators and women's clothing, and later, automobiles and kit houses.

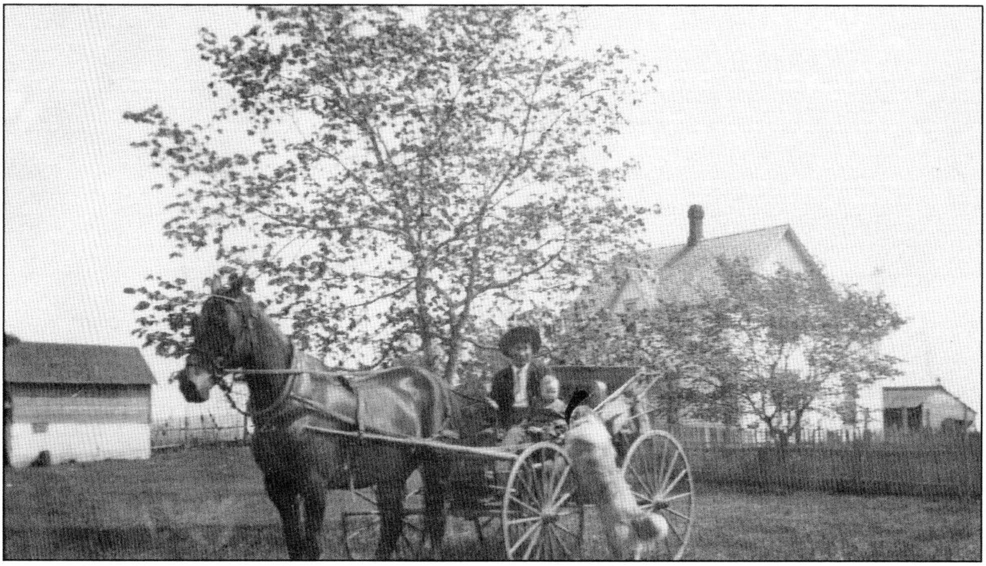

Bill Rosler and passenger pause for a greeting at the Rosler-Landahl farm, just off Cattle Point Road. When his parents, Christopher and Anna, homesteaded this property in 1861, they first built a root cellar, at left, out of stones and mortar with a second story out of wood. They lived here with a few of their nine children while building their first farmhouse and built this one in 1897.

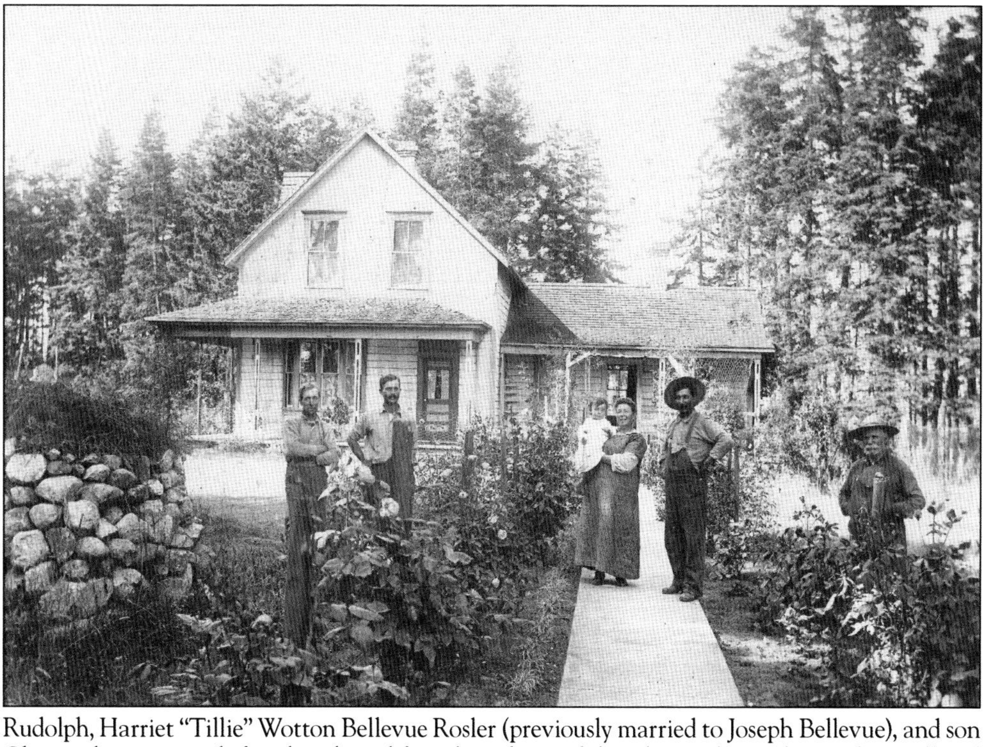

Rudolph, Harriet "Tillie" Wotton Bellevue Rosler (previously married to Joseph Bellevue), and son Christopher pose with farmhands and friends in front of their home, located near the trailhead at the American Camp visitor center. They built their farmhouse on a 160-acre claim deeded to Rudolph (born 1863) by his mother, Anna Pike Rosler. Tillie was known for her extensive garden as well as colorful metaphors when her temper was up.

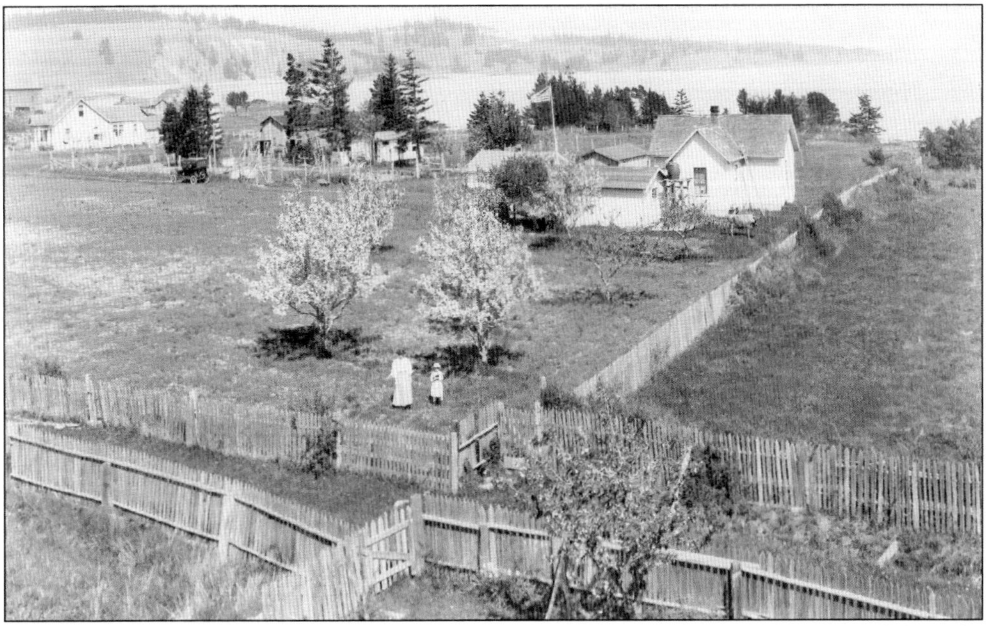

Fences crisscross properties in the village of Argyle around 1890. At the far upper left is the corner of the old grist (flour) mill, which was the only mill of its kind on the island. It warranted the building, by volunteer labor, of the Argyle Wagon Road, today known as Argyle Avenue in Friday Harbor. The U.S. post office here predated Friday Harbor's and was eventually moved to Madden's Corner.

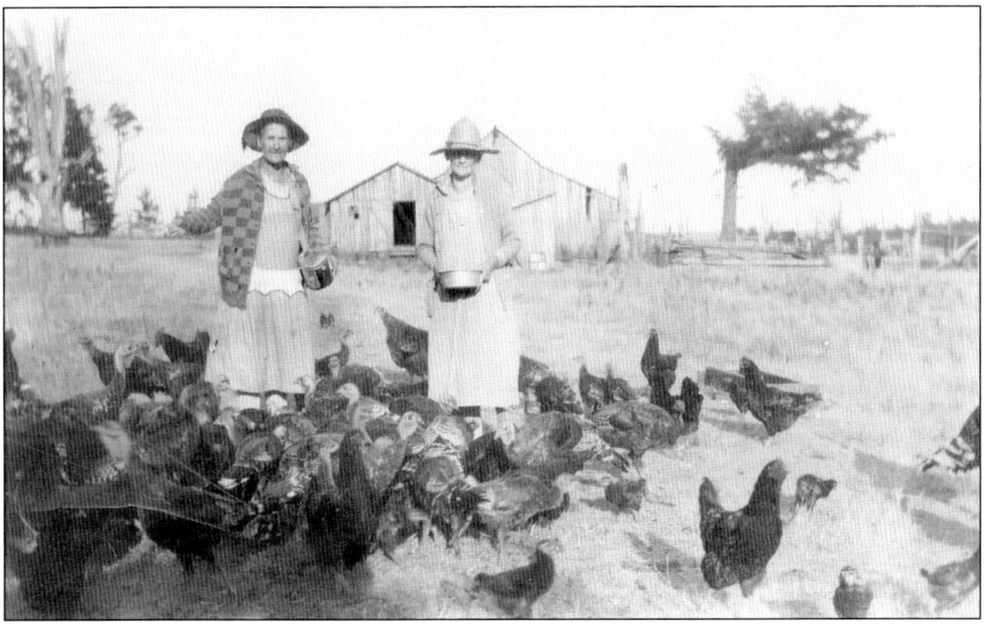

From left to right, sisters Almira Walter Boyce (married to John Henry Boyce, son of Stephen and Lucinda) and Mary Little feed chickens and turkeys on the Boyce farm near False Bay around 1916. Many women battled minks and raccoons to raise turkeys for extra income. Almira's daughter, Beryl Boyce Wade, recalled one mean old tom: "He'd chase us to the outhouse and circle for half an hour, making that crazy noise." (KR.)

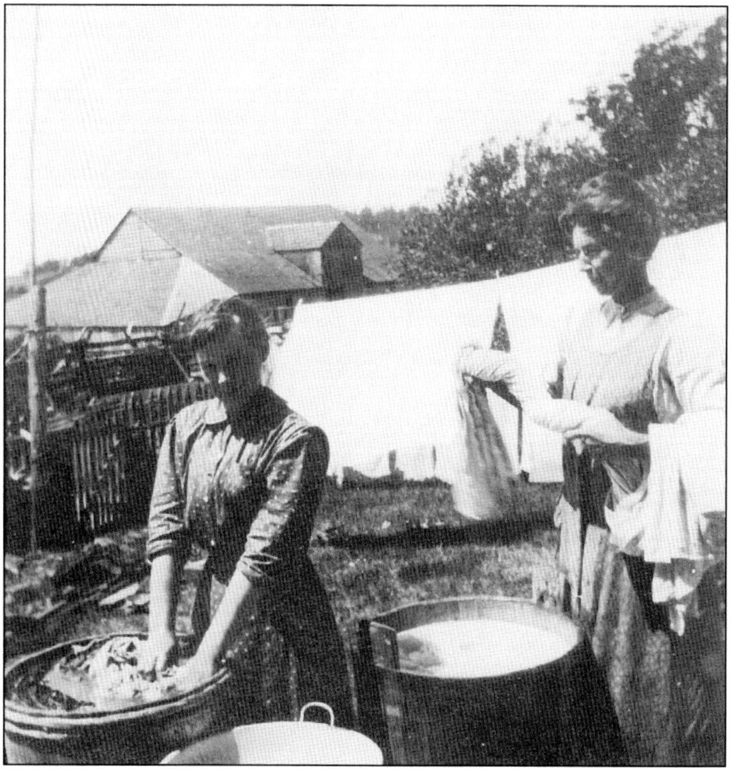

Etta Lightheart (left) and her aunt Lizzie Lawson share laundry duty—no easy task. Water had to be pumped or hauled from a well and boiled on a woodstove for the whitest whites, and clothes were scrubbed on a washboard using homemade soap. Woe to the woman who had a dozen children, for she would be out wringing laundry daily. It was a hard life, but Etta lived to be 105.

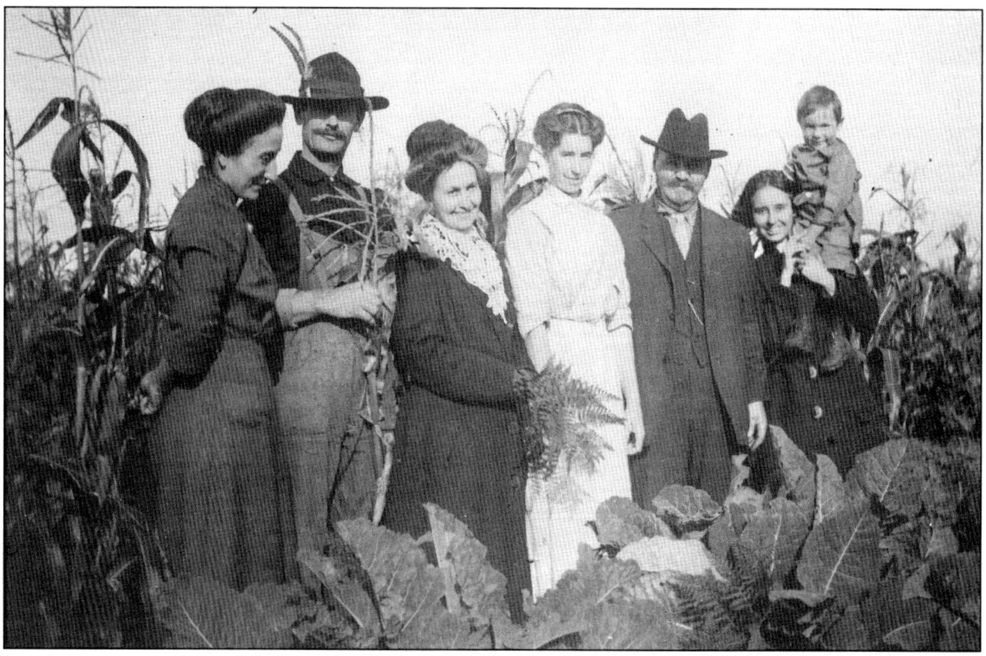

It is harvest time on south San Juan Island, around 1912, a good reason for neighbors to gather in the fields and enjoy the fruits of months of hard labor. From left to right are Adeline and Anton Thrones, Kate Rosler Merrifield, Lizzie Lawson, Mark Rosler, and possibly Laurena Rosler Landahl holding her son Vernie Frank. Note the enormous rhubarb leaves in the foreground.

Three

THE SALMON BANK

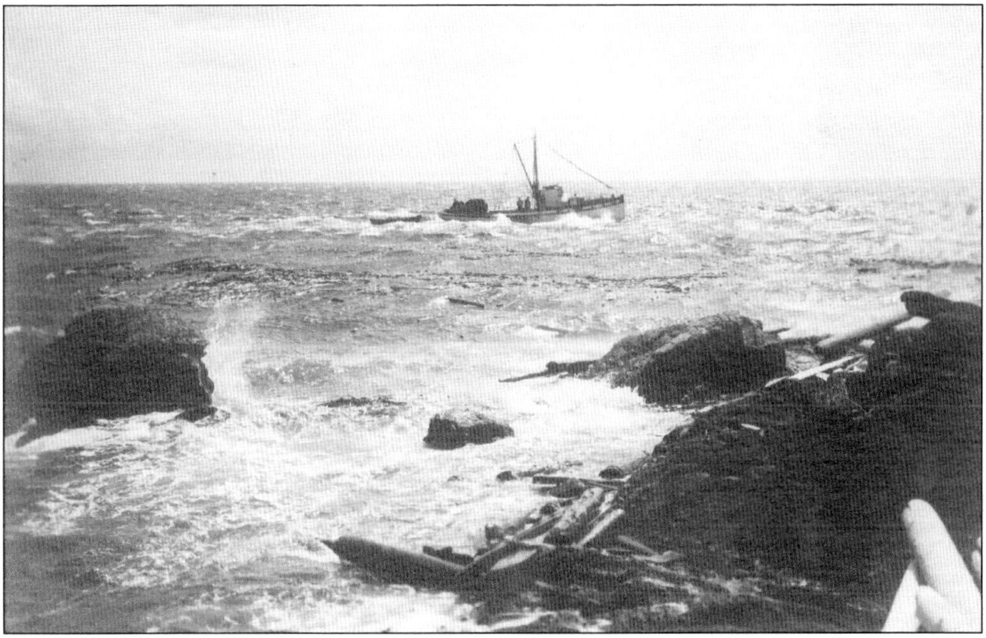

A 1915 purse seiner plows through the choppy seas of the Strait of Juan de Fuca on its way to the Salmon Bank off San Juan Island's southwestern shore. In 1858, Caleb Kennerly, a naturalist with the Northwest Boundary Survey, proclaimed the Salmon Bank as "perhaps the best fishing grounds on Puget Sound," where "numerous bands of Indians" seasonally encamped ashore. Those "with the proper appliances" for fishing could make money, he predicted. Geologically speaking, the bank is a submerged ridge formed by moraines left by the glacier that receded starting about 11,000 years ago. But its cultural and economic impact reverberates to this day. Kennerly's "appliances" were profoundly realized in 1892 with the introduction of fish traps, an adaptation of the Native American reef nets, which could trap thousands of sockeye salmon in a single season. Motorized purse seiners, heretofore powered by oars, and the rising sports fishing market soon rivaled the traps. The competition came to a head in 1934 when fish traps were banned and the job market slumped. By then, the old Native American fishery was a memory.

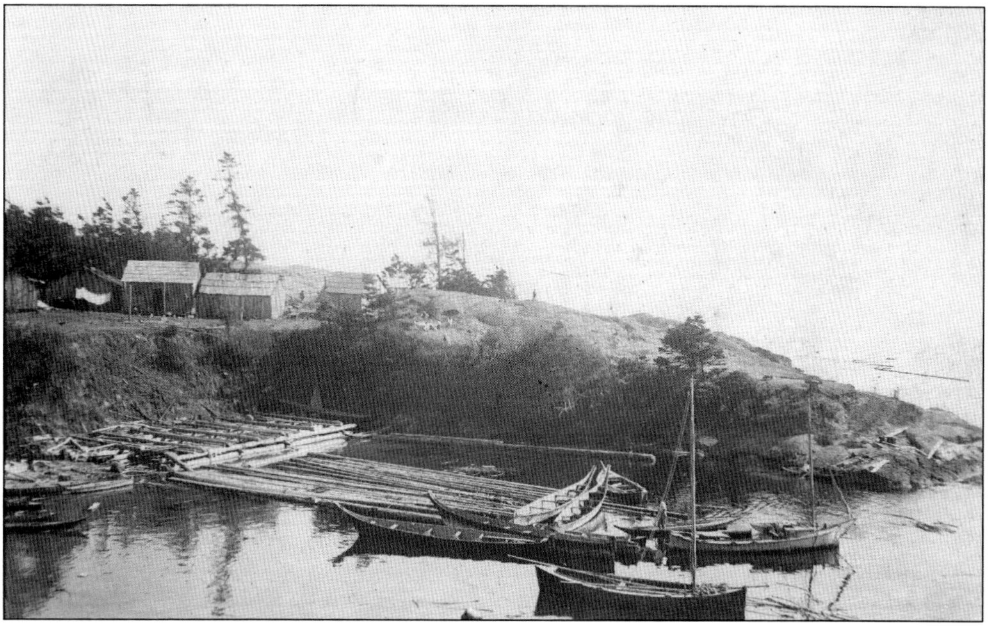

Coast Salish and Nootka canoes and "Columbia River" boats dock below the old Kanaka village (see page 19) on its namesake bay around 1897. The Coast Salish called it *ayalyex*, "good place" or "good spring water." Coast Salish from across the region reef-netted or trolled for salmon here for generations. By 1851, the Hudson's Bay Company paid one blanket for 60 fish, salting 2,000 to 3,000 barrels a season.

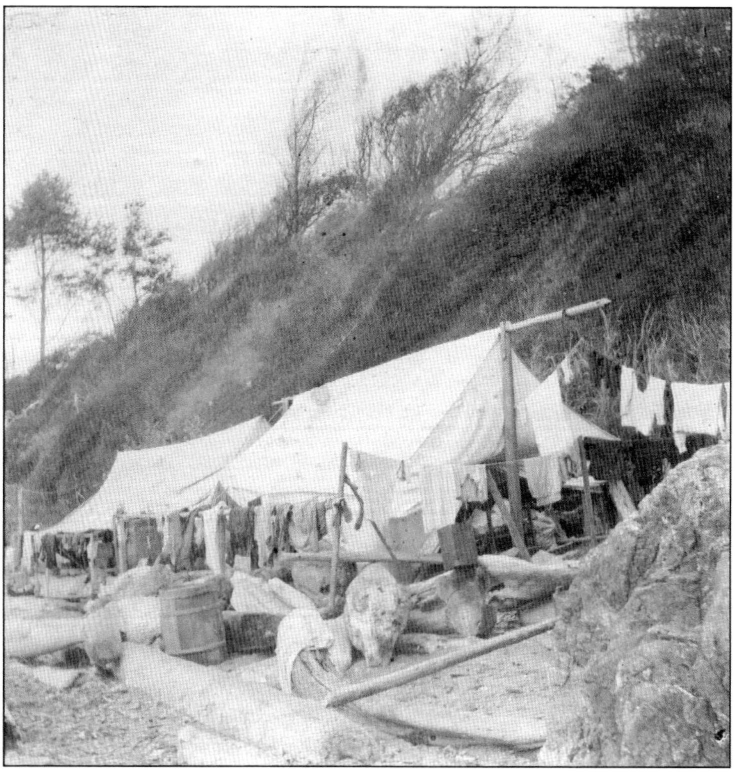

The John Ross Sr. family camp, festooned with laundry, clings to the bluff below the Peter Lawson farm around 1905. As with most of the purse seine fishermen, skipper Ross and sons Emmett and Johnnie arrived at the Salmon Bank each summer from their home in Gig Harbor and set up housekeeping on the beach alongside their Native American neighbors.

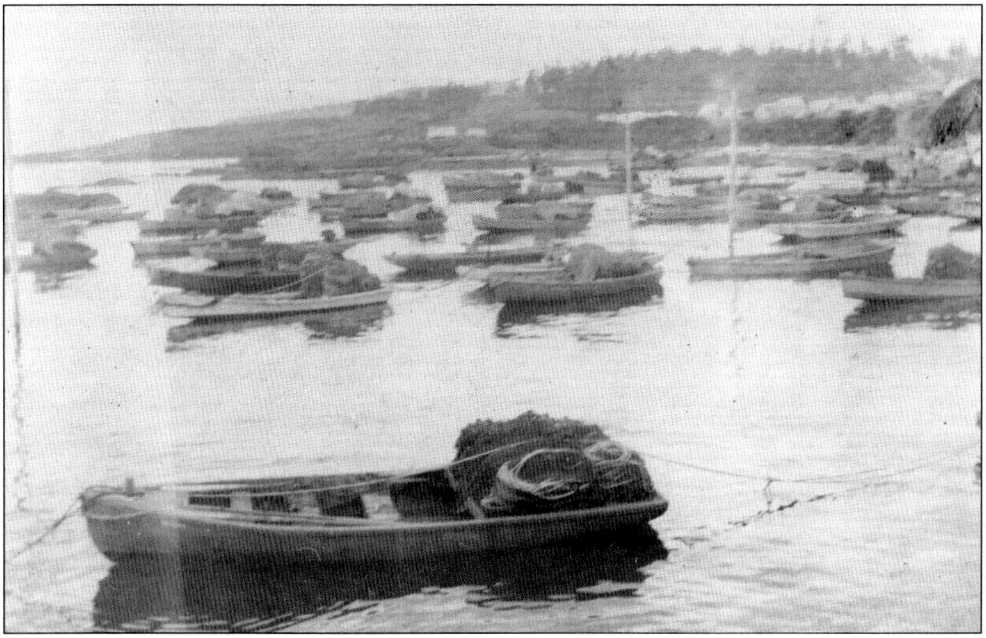

In the late 19th century, purse seine fishermen—Native American and non–Native American alike—were still rowing or sailing from shore in search of salmon schools to encircle with their nets. The work was arduous and the returns limited because of competition with fish traps, even with tugboats towing them to the fishing grounds. It was not uncommon to seine from the beach and haul in the net with horse teams.

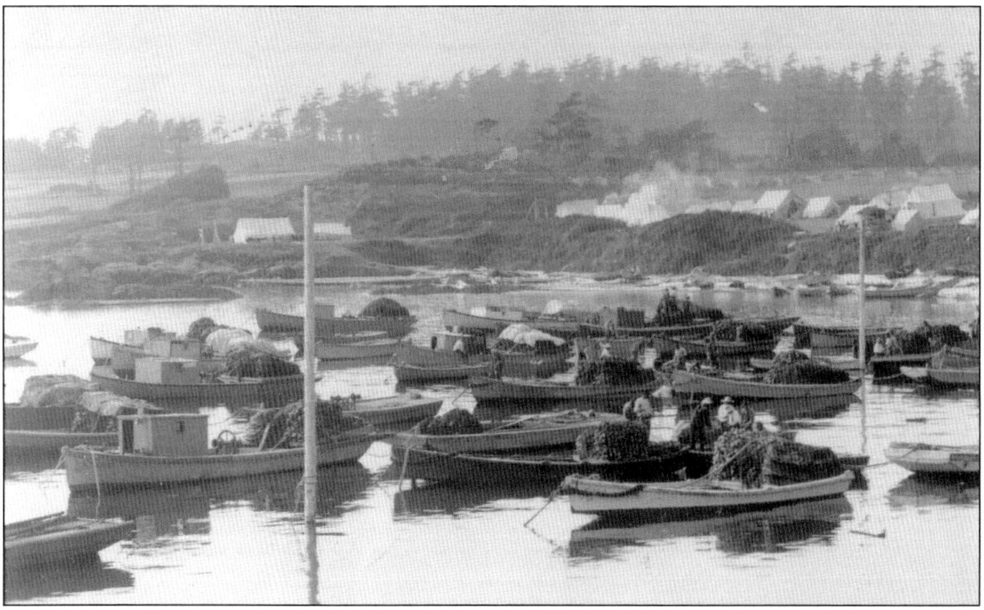

The transition from skiffs to vessels powered by 5-to-7-horsepower Frisco Standard gasoline engines is evident in this view of "Old Camp" below the Lawson farm around 1903–1904. As with all new technologies, the engines were temperamental and skilled mechanics scarce. Fishermen either converted or lost the race to the Salmon Banks. Engines aside, the catch still had to be hauled from the sea by hand. (SAJH.)

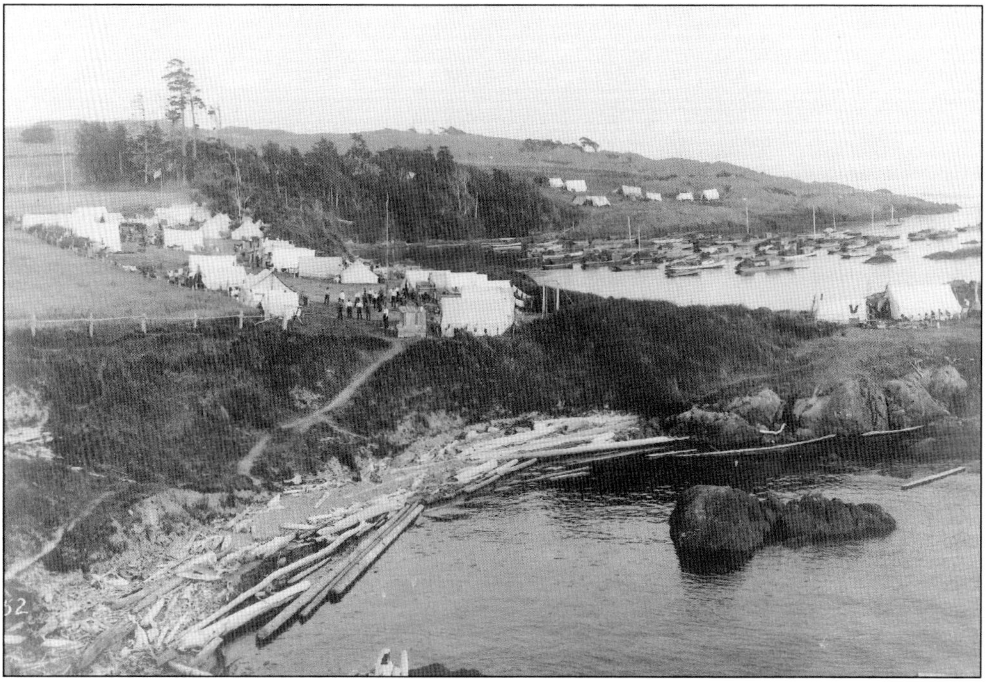

Purse seiners encamp around 1905 on the Peter Lawson and Ed McGeary farms while their vessels are secured to white mooring posts poking up like sailing masts. While a few brave souls, such as the Ross family (page 50), risked the flood tides on the beach, most crews pitched their tents on the uplands, where wells provided fresh water for drinking, cooking, and laundry. (SAJH.)

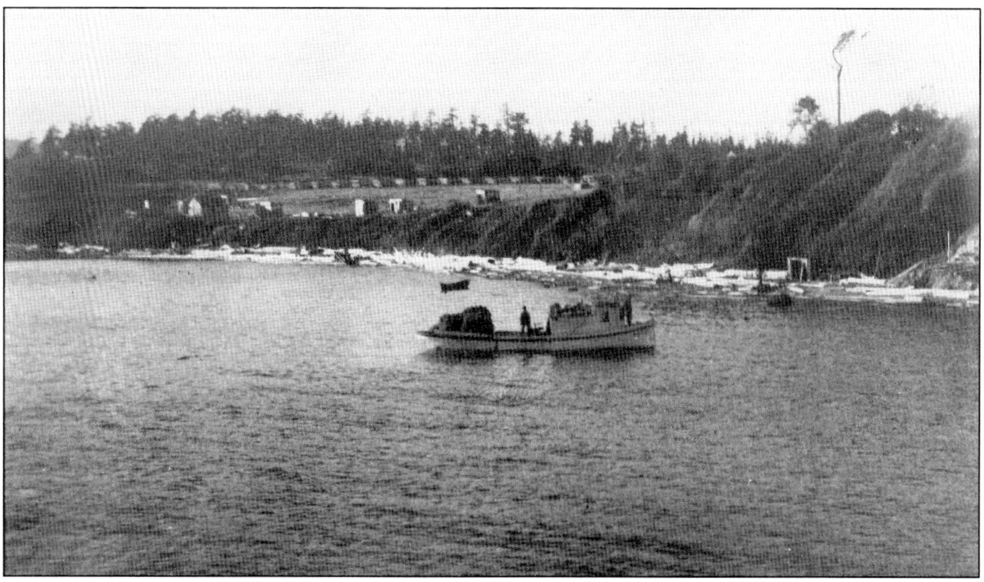

Fishermen's shacks line the bluff above the Salmon Bank around 1912 as a purse seiner motors by, presumably on its return from the fishing grounds. Islanders in the 1920s remembered such shacks, mainly occupied by Native Americans in nearly every cove along the Salmon Bank. In this photograph, a canoe is tied up just above the net on the stern of the seiner.

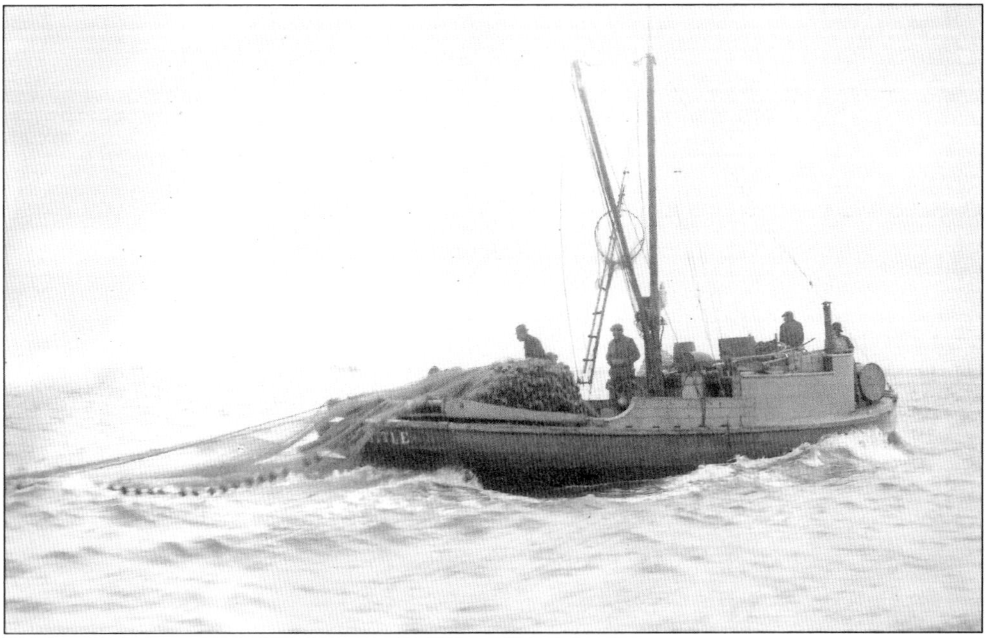

A seiner, around 1912, lays out a seine net while encircling a school of salmon. The skipper is at the wheel, looking aft to ensure that the net, stacked on the turntable astern, slips over the roller and into the water. The cork line at the top of the net floats on the surface, while the lead line sinks toward the bottom, creating a bowl-like purse that snares the salmon.

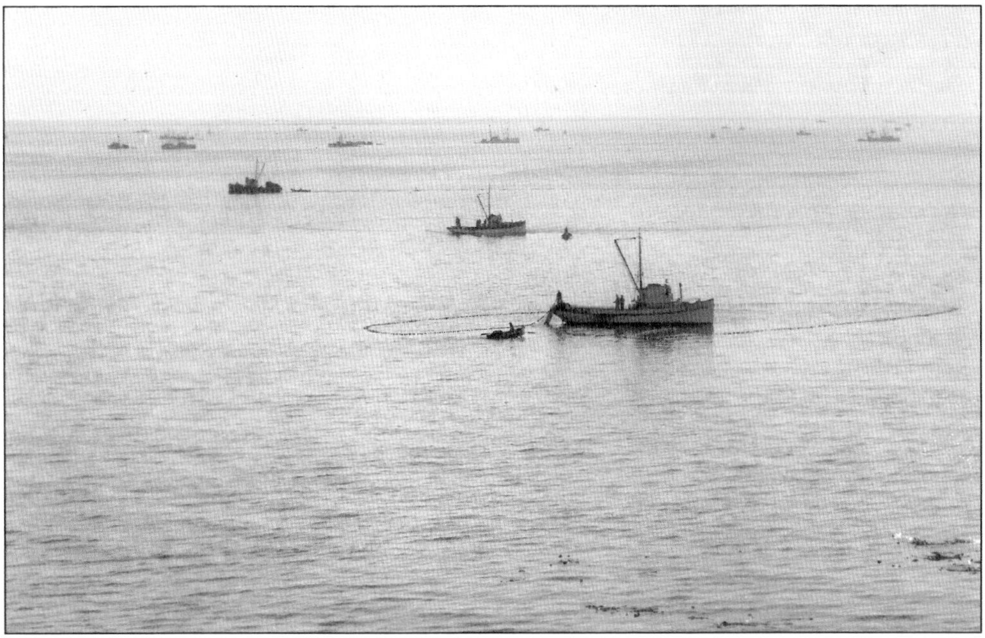

In laying out a net, each vessel above is making a "set" that hopefully will snare a boatload of fish to sell to a tender from the cannery. The vessels operated from dawn to dusk, with the best fishing in the morning, the poorest at mid-afternoon. This image dates around 1920, as the vessels have pilothouses. The engines by then were rated at 50 horsepower.

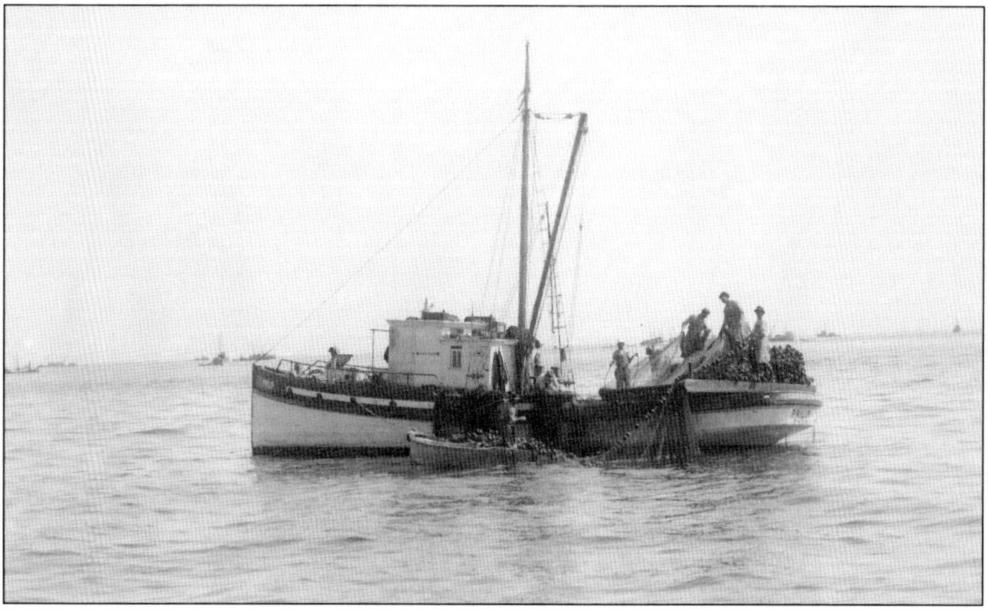

The purse line here has been pulled, cinching up the net. Deck hands scramble to haul in the net, while the crewman bending over the rail at center prepares to scoop or "brail" the fish out of the net and into the hold. The turntable has been shifted abeam to receive the net. By the late 1920s, the rollers were powered.

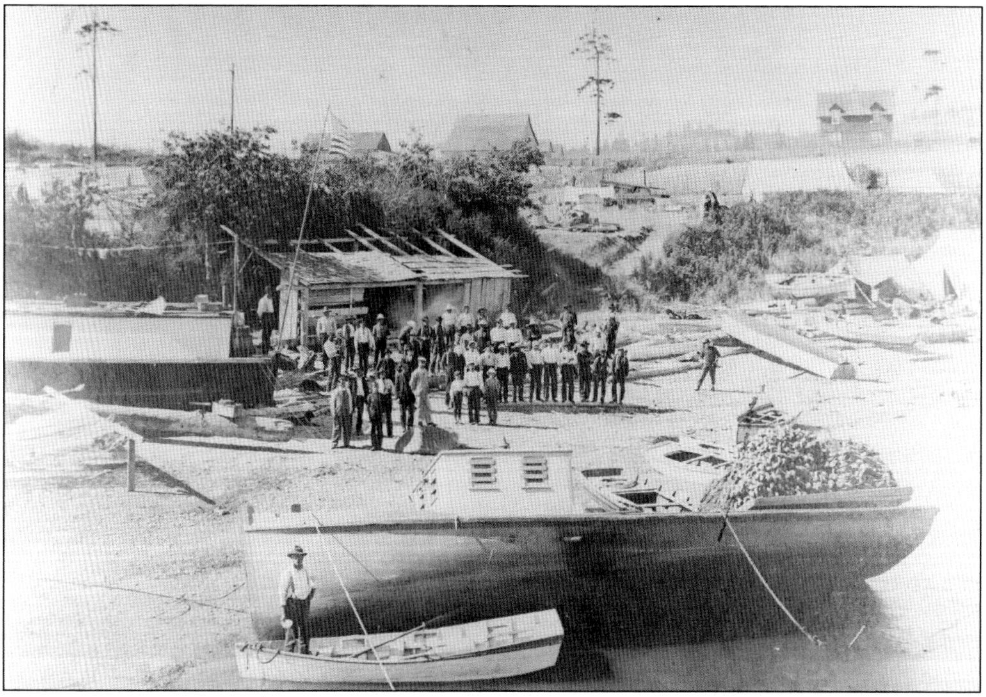

A purse seiner is careened on the beach at low tide at Kanaka Bay around 1912 to accommodate repairs or offload the net for mending and tarring. This net remains in place on the turntable, leading one to believe that the man in the skiff is not punting for pleasure, but inspecting and possibly making repairs to the hull.

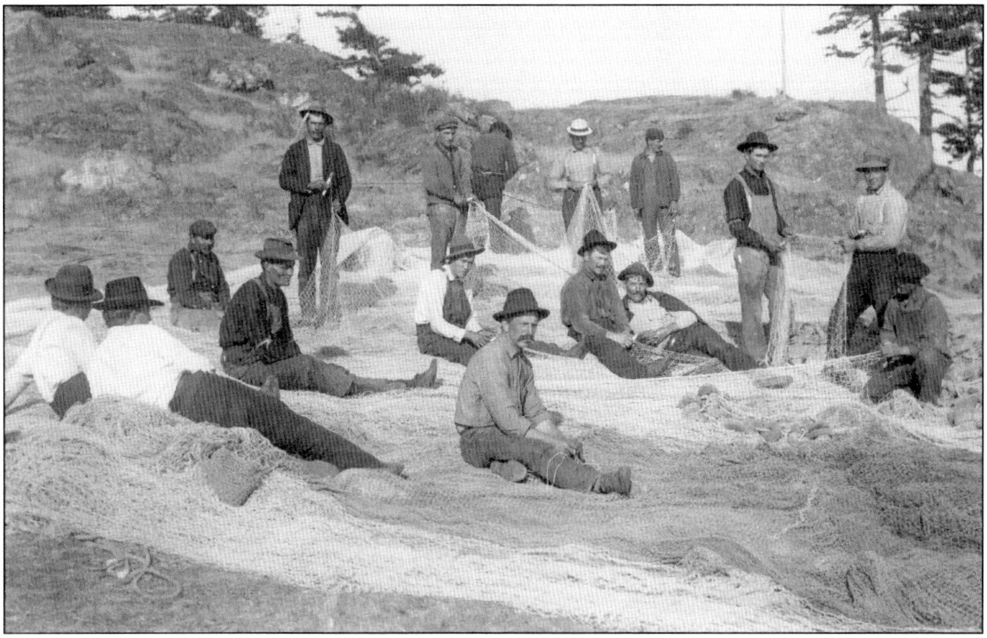

Native American and non–Native American fishermen at Kanaka Bay use mending needles to rework the knots that form the web of the seine net. The nets were fashioned from cotton and ranged from 900 to 1,200 feet in length and 25 to 40 feet in depth. To avoid stretching the new cotton webbing, the net was dipped in tar or other preservatives.

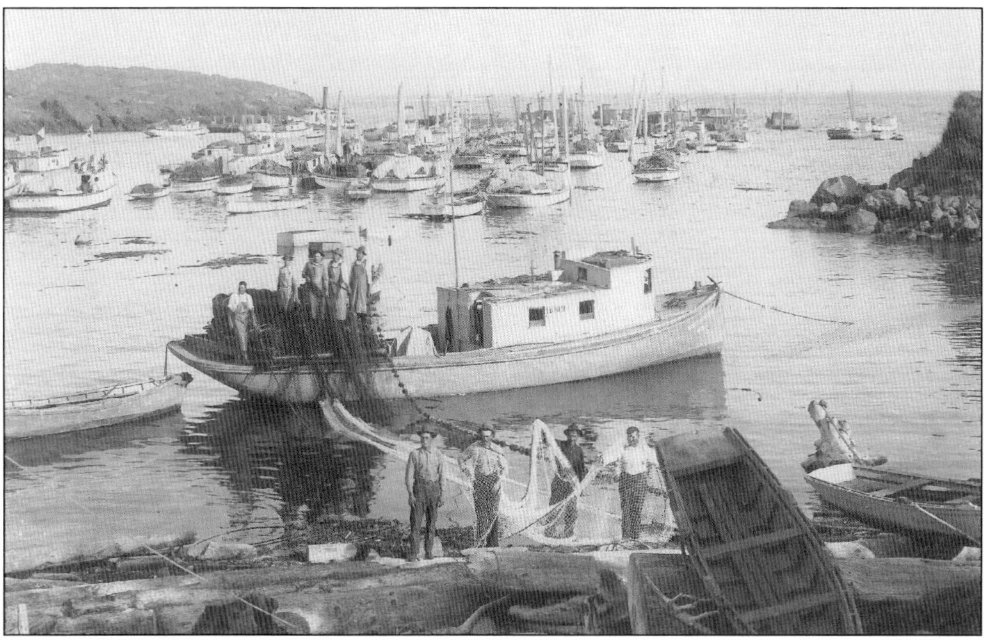

A purse seine crew, around 1910, loads a mended net aboard their vessel in Kanaka Bay. The skiffs tied to the stern of this and other vessels would be rowed out from the seiner with one end of the net, while the seiner circled the school of fish and made the "wrap." Today the skiffs, powered by marine engines, do the circling and reconnect with the seiner.

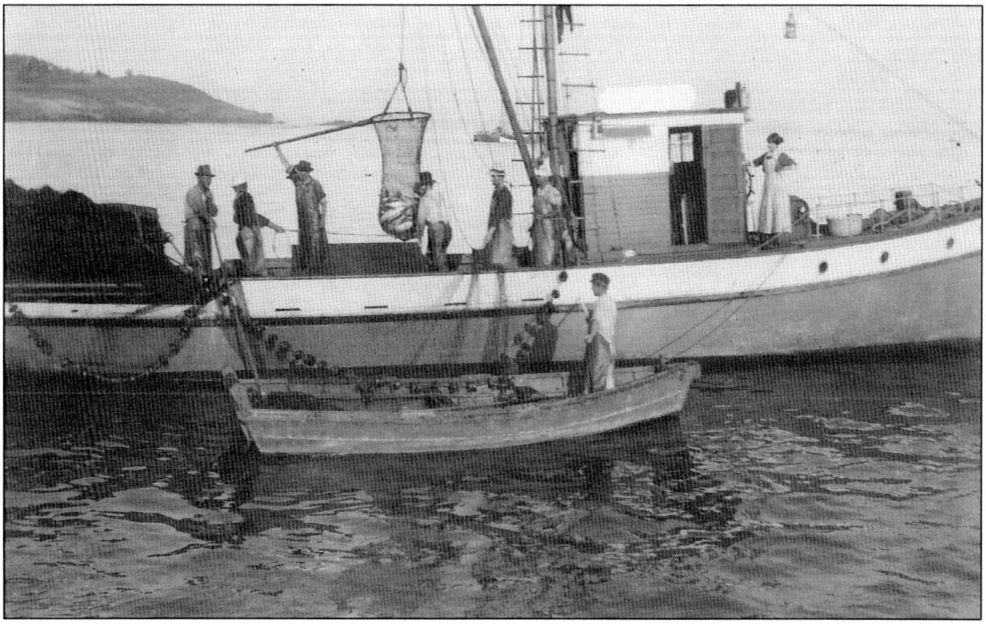

Fishermen employ a "stocking brail" to dip fish out of the net and into the hold of the tender/seiner *Wamega*, while Esther Nordland stands by at the bow deck wheel. Before the advent of the bridge atop the pilothouse, the bow deck wheel provided greater visibility to the helmsman during operations.

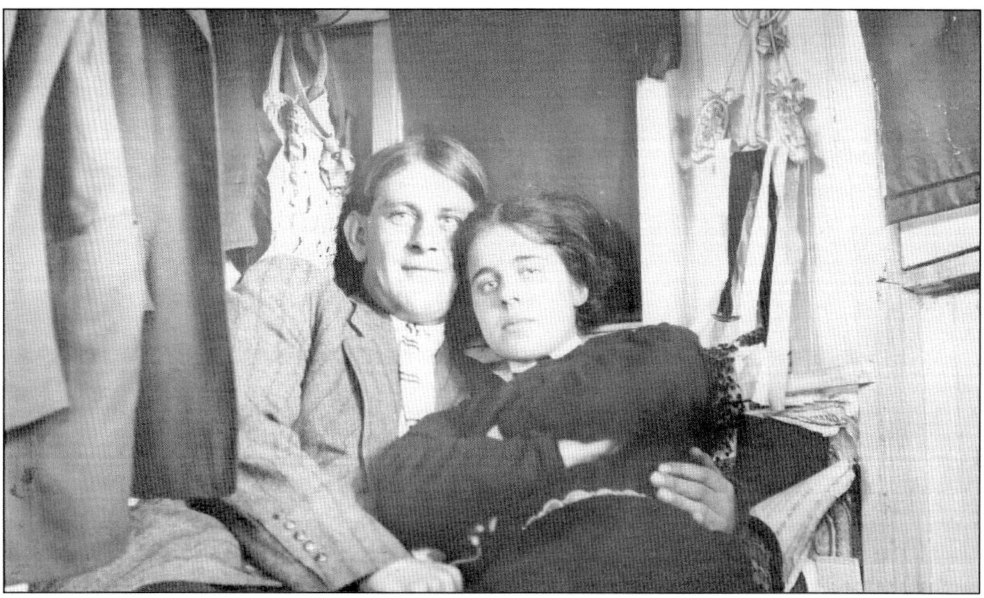

Frank and Esther Nordland cuddle in the cabin of their live-aboard vessel *Grizzly*. Although trained as a milliner, Esther plied the Salmon Bank with Frank aboard *Wamega*. In July 1914, she suffered severe stomach cramps and died that night. Fifteen purse seiners paid their respects by circling the harbor on the day of her funeral.

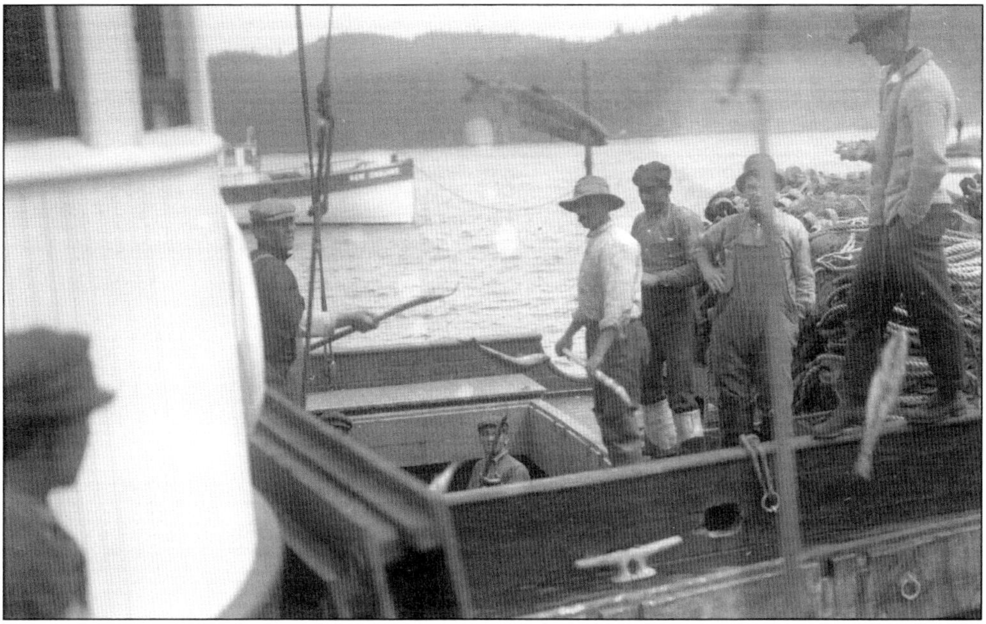

A fisherman employs a "pew" to pierce the fish and pitch them from the hold of his boat onto the deck of the fish-buying tender. The tender then transported the catch to the cannery in Friday Harbor. Pews are no longer used in the industry because they leave blood spots in the flesh.

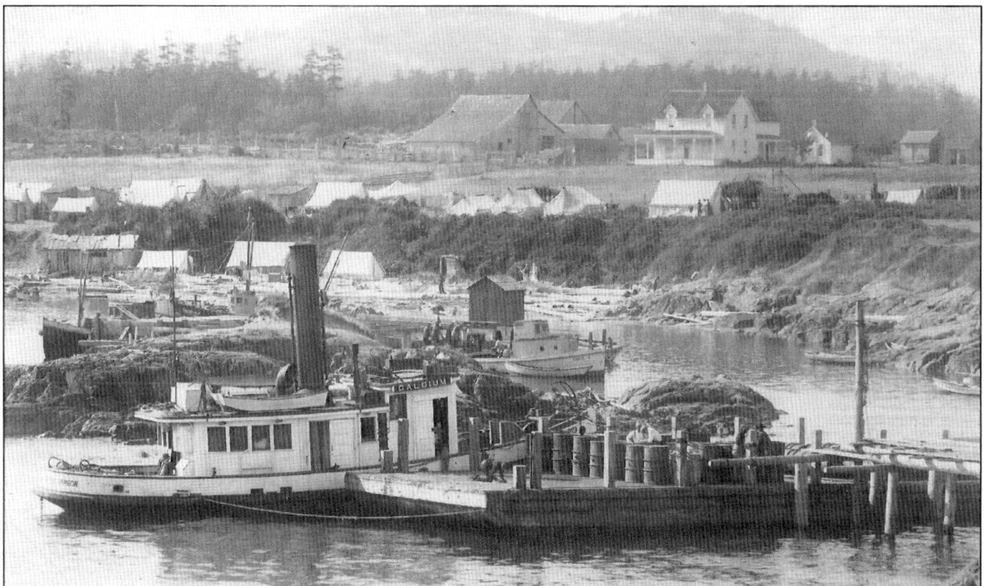

The James Fleming farmhouse and barn overlook purse seine fishery operations at Kanaka Bay around 1912–1915. The house was built around 1890 by Fleming and passed to Art Clement, who was related by marriage. By 1910, the *Friday Harbor Journal* reported that the camp had a store, a fuel dock, and nearly 500 fishermen camped on its uplands. The site closed in the 1940s and is now private property.

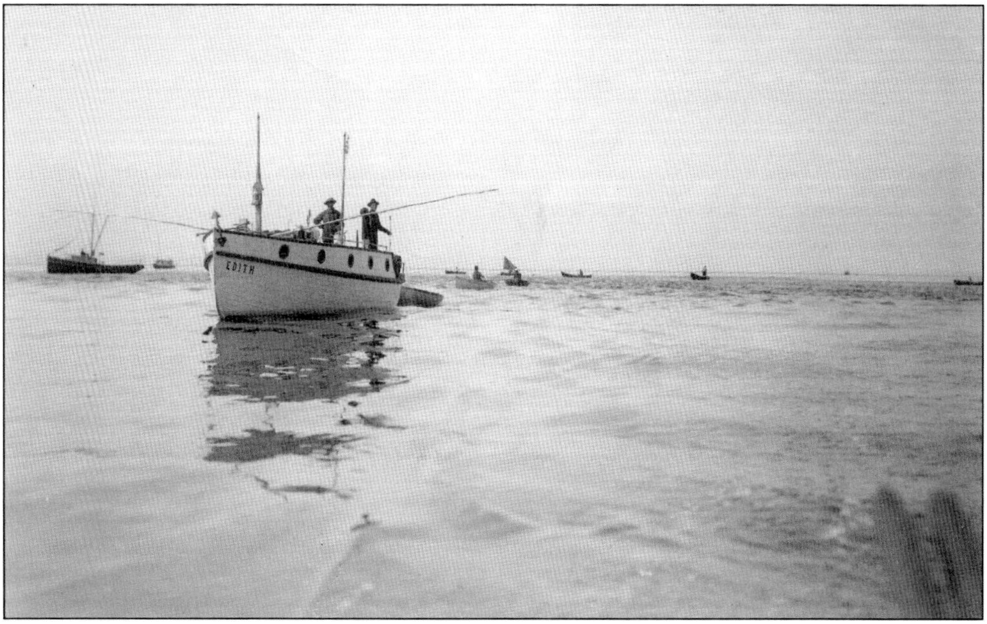

A mix of purse seiners, canoes, and skiffs join the trim powerboat in the foreground to troll on the Salmon Bank around 1915. Of the three methods of fishing—hook and line, entrapment, and encirclement—only trolling, again adapting timeless Native American methods, was done in deep water in quest of King and Silver salmon for the fresh fish market.

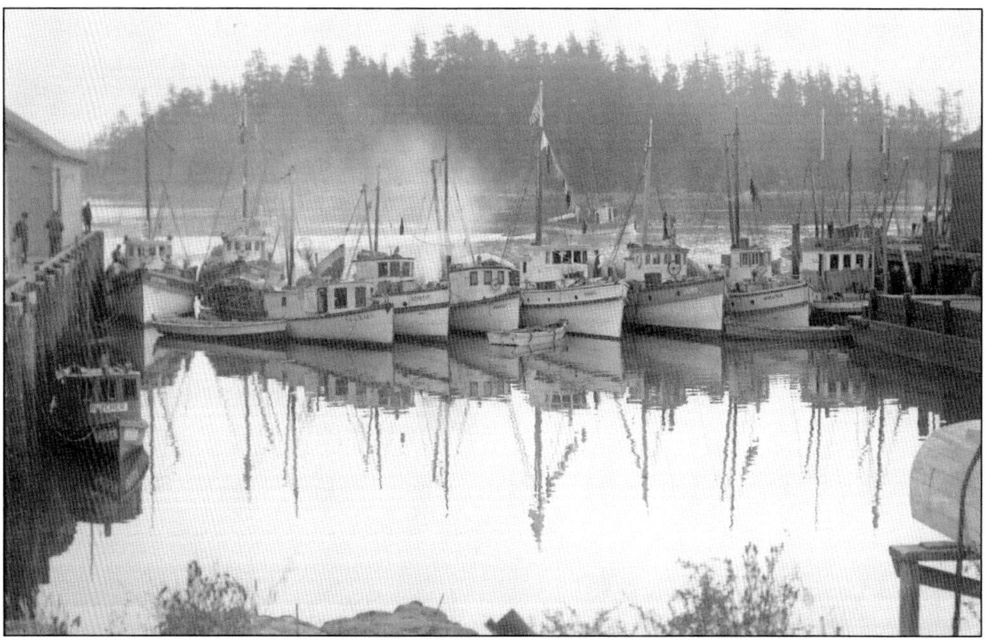

In the 1920s and 1930s, independent purse seine boats tied up at the cannery on Friday evenings. The fishermen made their way to the barber in the old Blue Front store and to the bathtubs for a soak out back. Then they drank or went to the dance at the Moose Hall, or both. Some of the boats pictured are the *Astorian*, *Comet*, *Sea King*, *Rondont*, and *Monarch*.

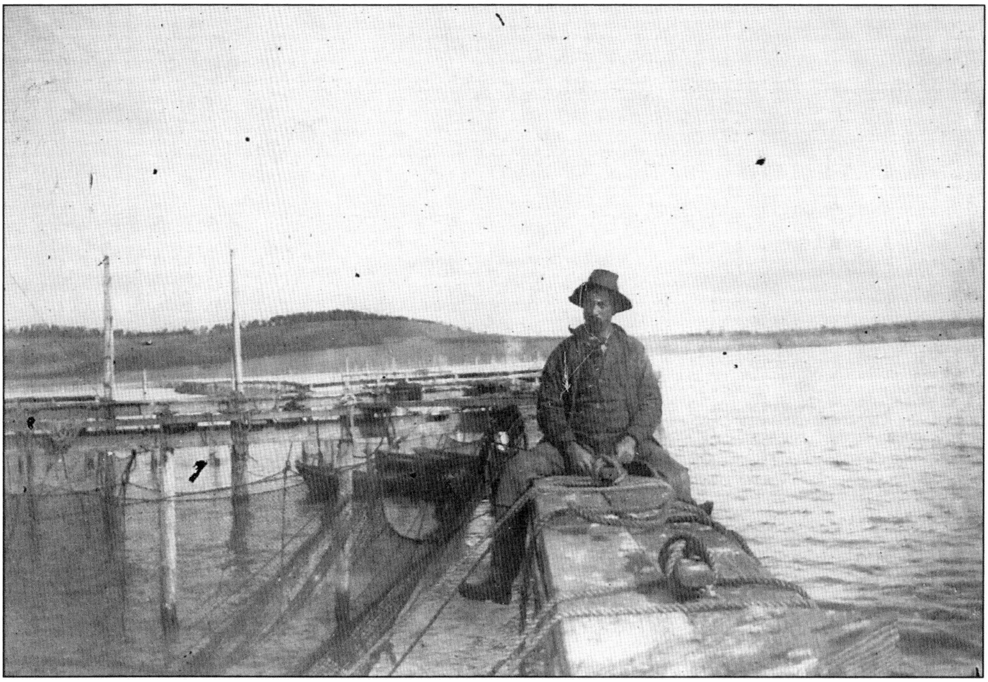

A fish trap worker straddles a heavy beam while adjusting the rigging on one of 12 traps located off South Beach. Corralling thousands of fish per day, the traps were the lifeblood of the island economy from 1894 until the state banned them in 1934. "Lifting crews" brailed fish out of the traps and into the scows destined for the cannery.

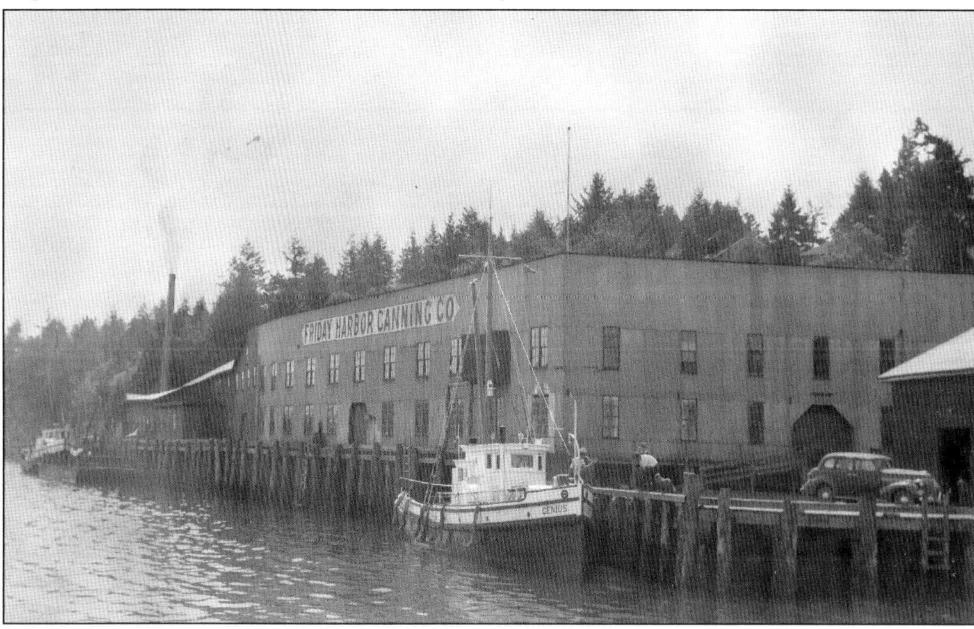

The Friday Harbor Canning Company was still in business in this 1930s view of the company dock. The fish trap closure in 1934 was a blow to the island. As purse seiners became more competitive with the fish traps, animosity grew, the seiners believing that the canneries dominated from "trap to can" and cared little about conservation. (KR.)

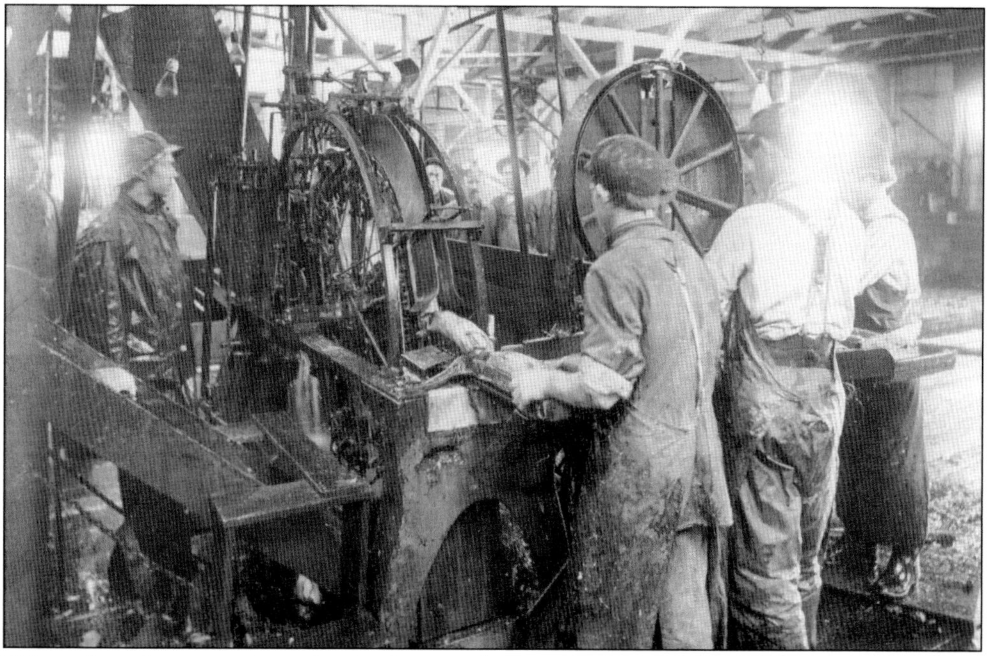

Fish-packing lines accelerated with the introduction of the "Iron Chink" in 1901–1902. The machine replaced employees, mostly Chinese immigrants, who chopped off heads and tails and gutted fish before tossing them to the "slimers" for washing. While such a racial slur would never be tolerated today, it was widely accepted then among whites.

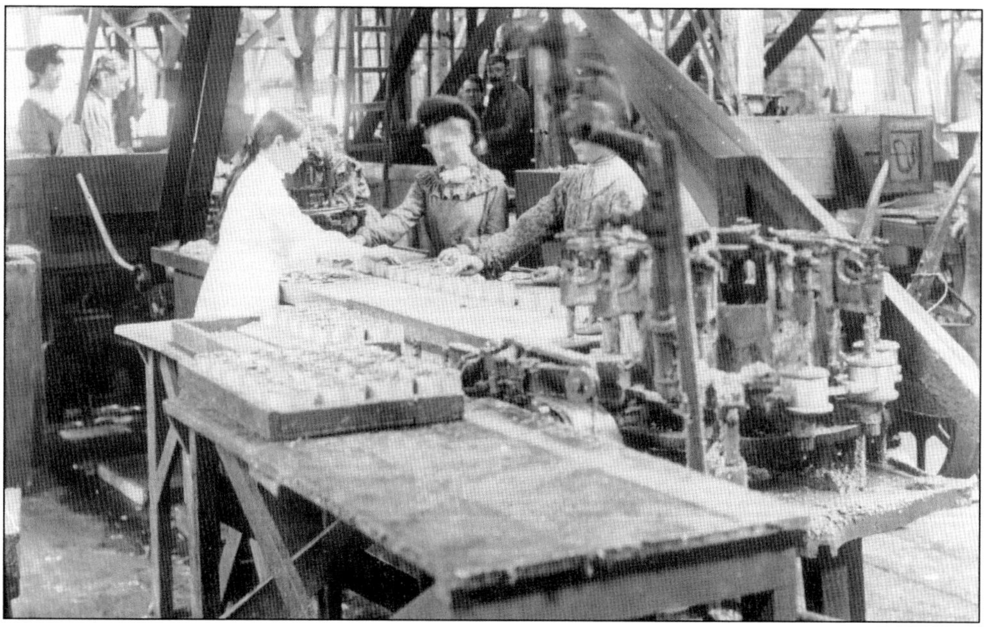

For more than 40 years, the cannery provided seasonal work to anyone who wanted to work, such as these young women on the packing line. However, with the 65-percent passage of Washington State Initiative 77 in 1934, the traps were gone and jobs reduced dramatically. Many cannery workers returned to family farms, raising crops for the pea cannery begun in 1922. Others who could afford to bought purse seiners.

Four

A Vanished Commerce

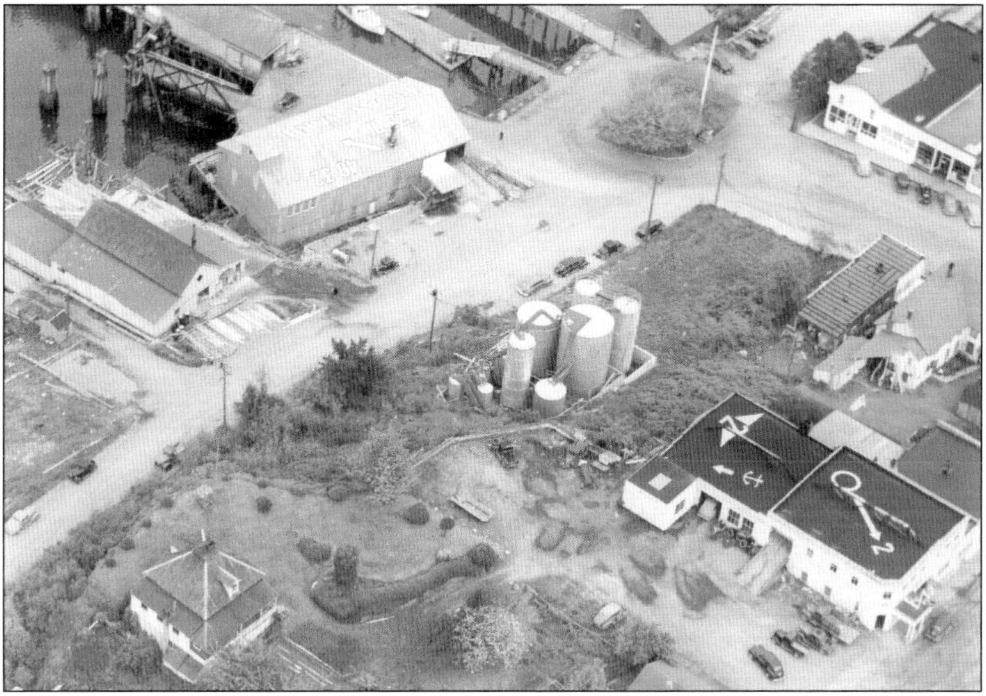

This 1940s aerial view of Friday Harbor's waterfront reveals what community planners today call a "transportation hub," a mix of elements designed to build and expand on commerce. By this date in San Juan Island history, the old extraction economy geared to fish canning, cash-crop farming, and lime mining and production was already in decline. Encompassed within a city block are, clockwise from left, the H. H. Davis Lumber Company in the old creamery with dimension lumber stacked and strewn about; the San Juan Agricultural Company warehouse, which functioned as a mini-hardware, customs, and ferry ticket office downstairs, with sacks of grain and cleaning machine upstairs; the MacKenzie dock, which accommodated cargo ships and the island ferry slip; the City Float and Carter's dock; the ferry holding area that circled Memorial Park; gasoline and oil storage tanks; and the Ford dealership featuring a showroom and maintenance bays and, on the roof, directions for aviators to the old airport in San Juan Valley. In a matter of decades, this way of life, except for the ferry, was gone from the waterfront.

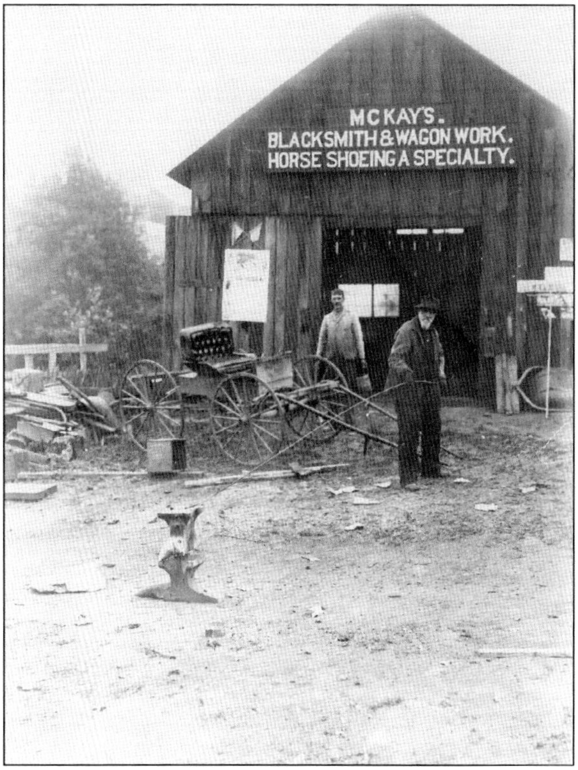

Charles McKay sets a length of hot iron on an anvil in front of his smithy, which was behind his First Street house where the ferry lines are now situated. McKay claimed he rowed to Whatcom (Bellingham) to obtain the American flag that was raised in defiance of the British during the 1859 Pig War crisis. Leaning against the building at right is a rake, as shown on page 33.

Friday Harbor's Dr. George S. Wright was still driving this horse and buggy to make house calls in the county in 1909. Wright purchased the Friday Harbor Drug in 1902, which was next door to his house on Spring Street. He then turned the operation over to his wife, Laura, and cousin Leon Little, who, after World War I, bought the business in partnership with Albert Nash Sr.

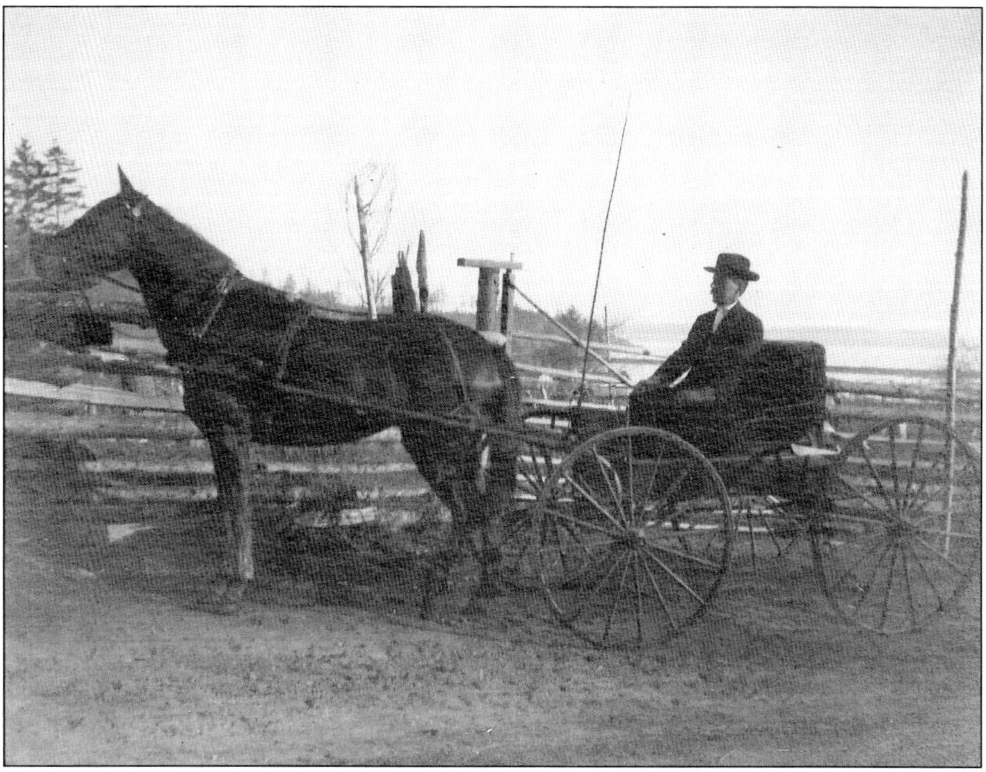

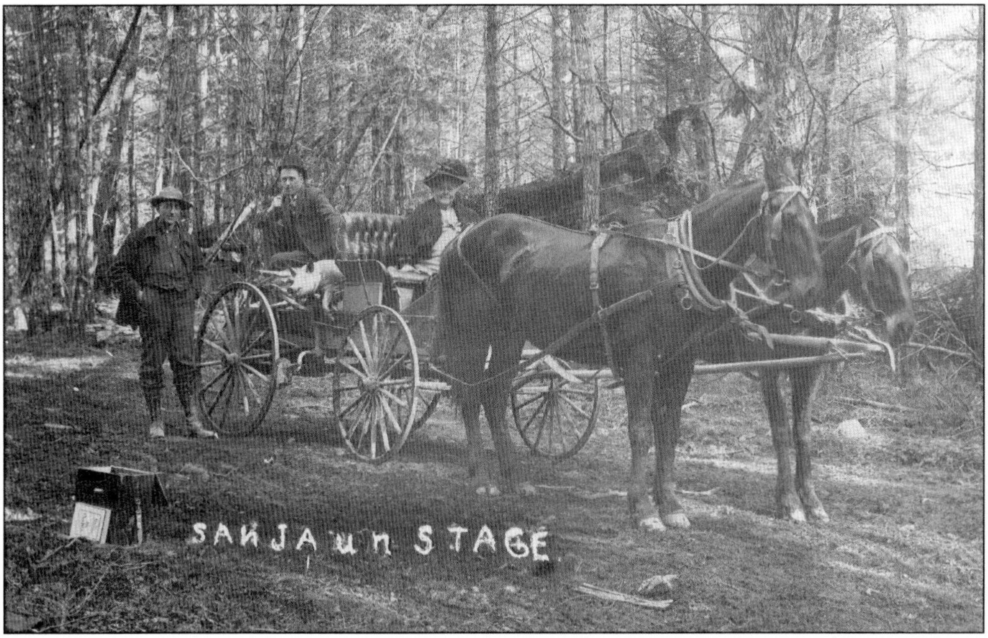

Belle McKenzie Erickson beams from the passenger seat of the San Island stage either on the way to market in Friday Harbor or on the homeward leg, depending on the origin of the dead pig in the back. The box in left foreground is J. A. McCormick's photography kit, which contains Stanley Dry Plates. The inscription on this postcard reads as follows: "You will be pleased to get this postcard of our stage."

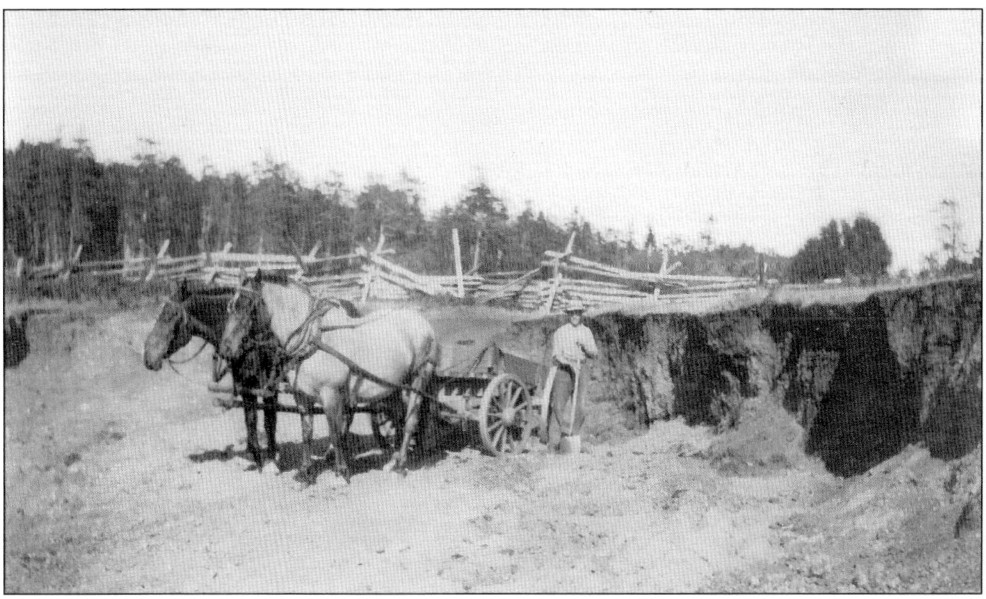

An islander pauses from his labors, excavating gravel from a small quarry situated along a county road. In the days of the horse and wagon, the weight of a load of gravel made it prohibitive to haul around the island as dump trucks do today. Therefore, small quarries were located conveniently near various crossroads to fill potholes or repair washouts.

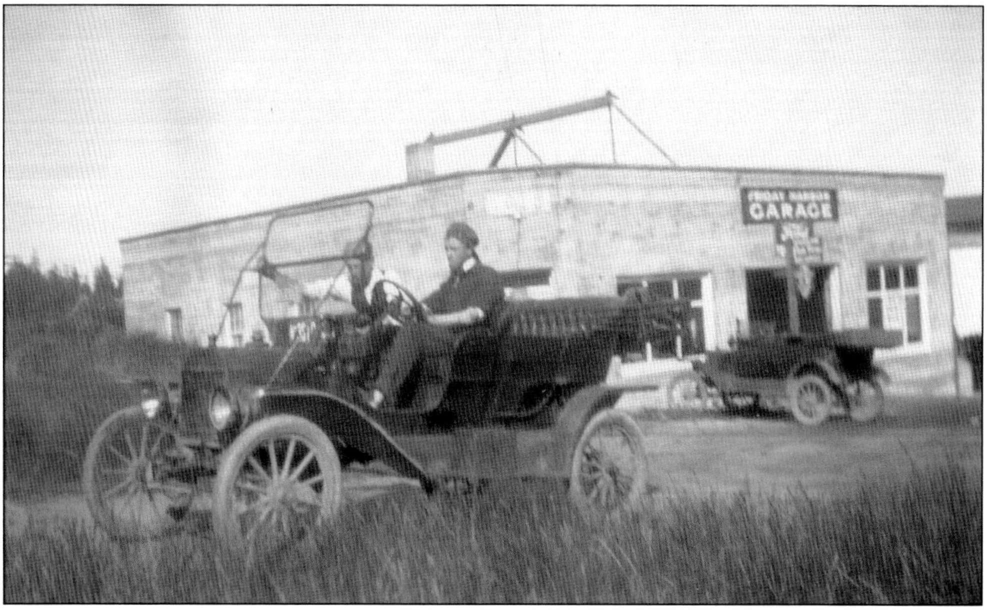

In 1906, Calvin Lightheart and George Franck Sr. embraced the future and launched the island's first automobile dealership in this concrete structure at the corner of First and West streets. At first they sold and maintained Overlands, a forerunner of Willys Jeeps and Studebakers. Lightheart dropped out and Franck offered the irrepressible Model T, built from 1908 to 1927. A sign over the garage door read, "Drive slow."

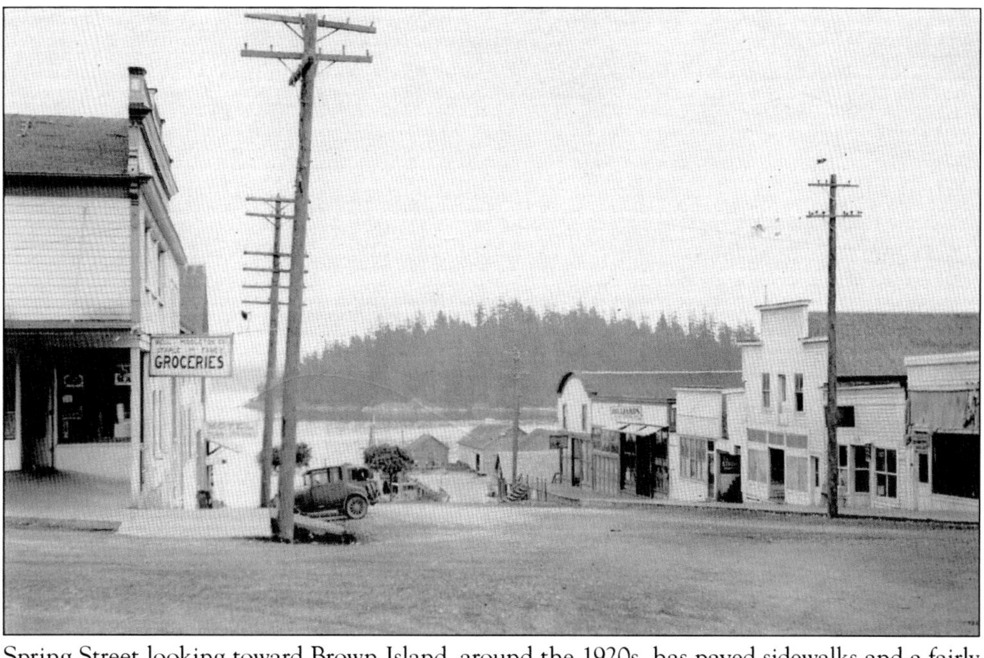

Spring Street looking toward Brown Island, around the 1920s, has paved sidewalks and a fairly smooth road surface to accommodate automobiles such as the coupe parked in front of Hotel San Juan, founded by William Douglas in the 1880s and then the oldest hotel in town. The Moose Hall, once the famous Saloon Best, continued to anchor the boulevard along with Memorial Park, as it does today.

San Juan County roads boss Mark Lunsford snaps the shutter on the edge of the Westside Road near Deadman's Bay in 1927. The automobile is a 1927 Chevrolet with disk wheels that belonged to Agnes Madden. The sign is not promising motorists a "Dance," but instead proclaims "Danger" from oncoming vehicles. Drivers blew their horns and waited five minutes, because the road narrowed around the bluff.

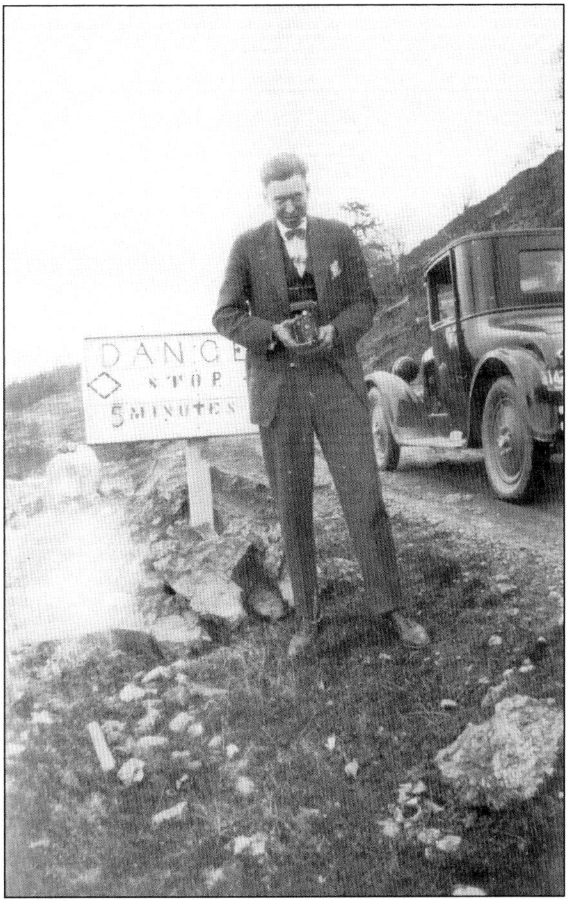

The Westside Road remained a primitive track at mid-20th century, with two plank bridges along the route. Portions were built for the lime quarries, but when the county park was developed in the 1930s, the road was barely improved. By 1957, the road had widened to its current width. One powder monkey looked over at Victoria across the strait and said, "Hey, great, I can use as much as I want!"

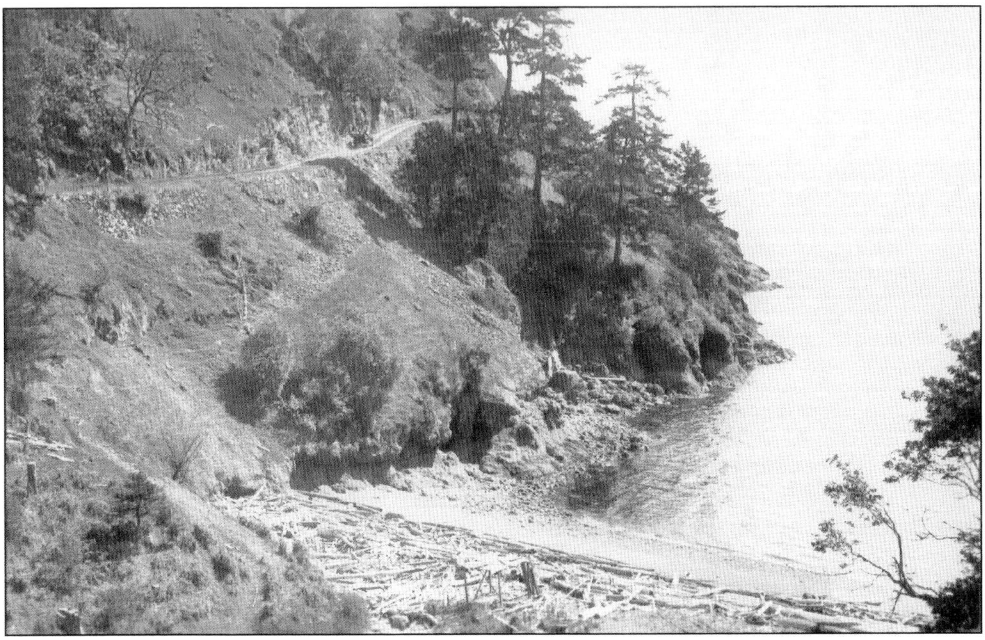

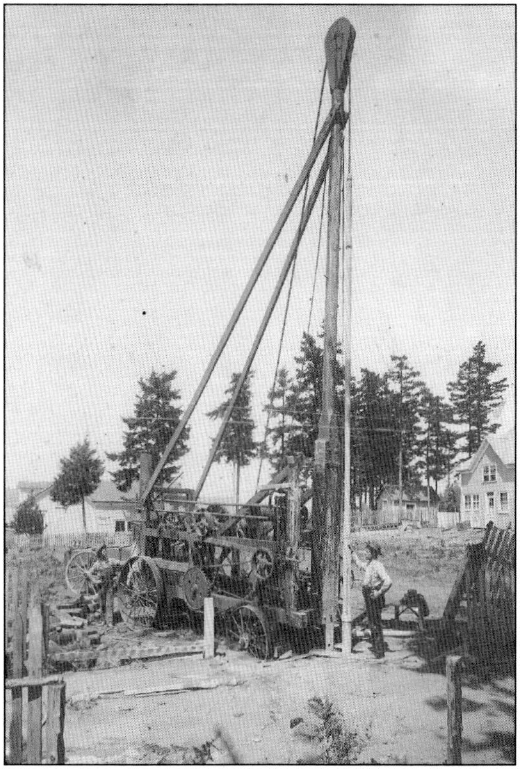

Warren Dightman monitors his steam drill while searching for water at the home of A. H. Culver, president of the Friday Harbor School Board. The house was located just across the street from today's Harrison House. Note the network of chains and pulleys on the engine, as well as the steel wheels buried deep in the soil. This rig disintegrated after decades in a lot on Carter Avenue.

A teamster pulls up with a load of cedar bolts destined for the shingle mill. For decades island forests were logged, sectioned, and hauled to the mill in Friday Harbor by horse and wagon. The wagons also transported cordwood to town to fuel the boilers of Mosquito Fleet vessels and the furnaces of government buildings, homes, and the lime kilns at Roche Harbor and on the island's west side.

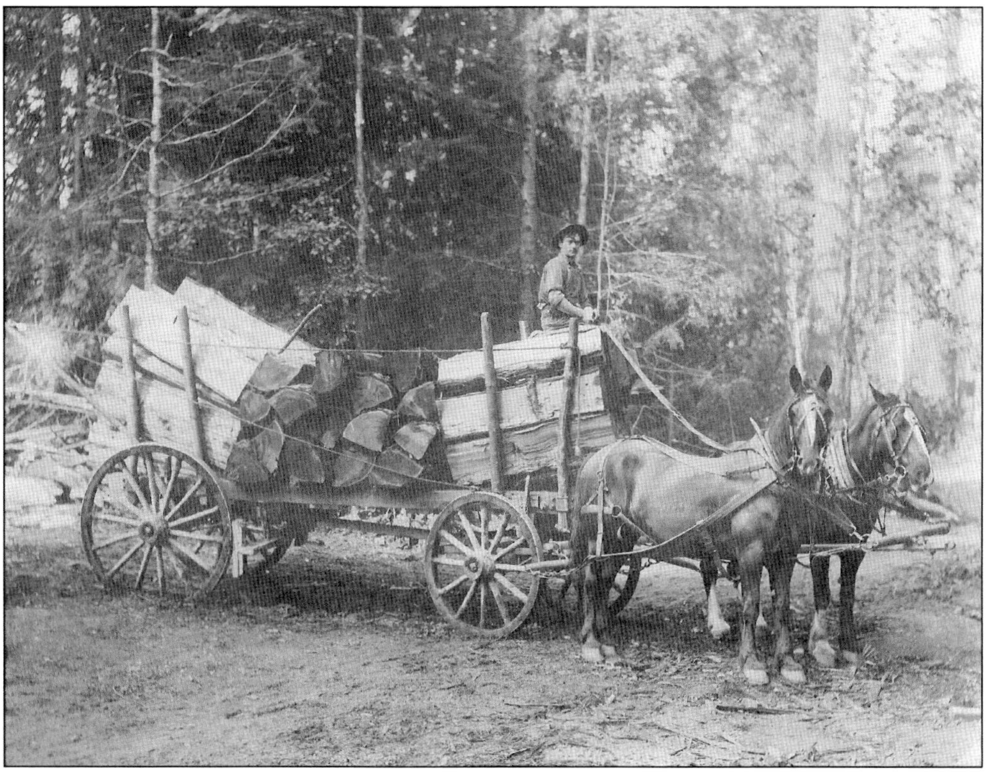

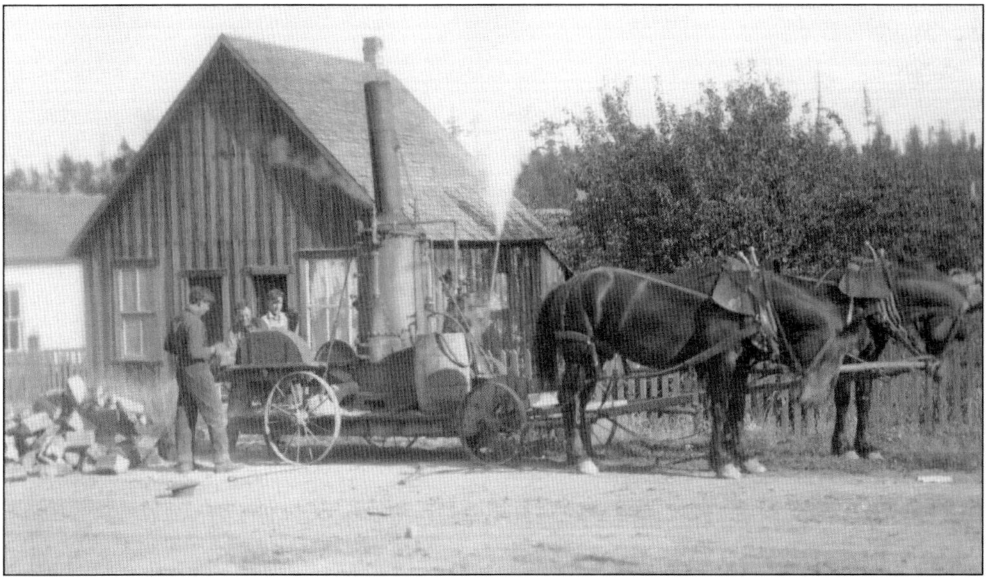

A crew using a steam-powered circular saw dices cordwood into "rickwood" for a Friday Harbor residence. The wood was usually cut in four-foot sections. The circular "buzz" saw would cut your wood into threes (16-inch lengths), just right for your stove or boiler. In this instance, the crew cuts the wood on a rear-mounted carriage. Note the water barrel, as well as the ever-patient horses.

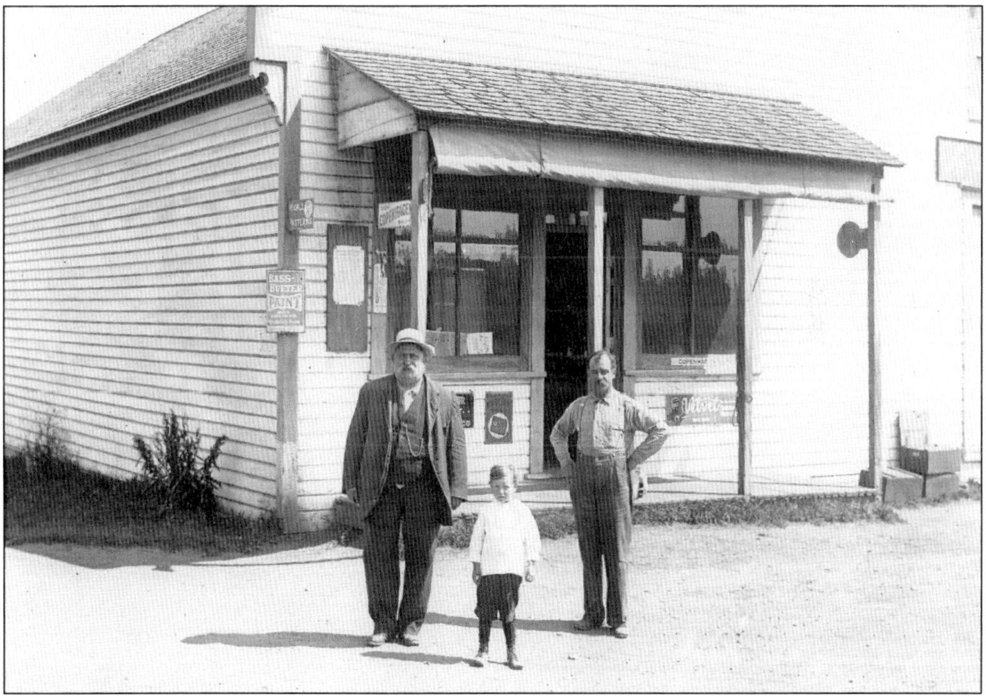

J. O. Bergman, left, founded the Corner Store at Madden's Corner in 1890 after moving from Port Townsend to run the store in Argyle. He is joined by his son J. O. Bergman Jr., right, and grandson Daniel (named for his other grandfather, Daniel Madden). J. O. Jr. continued to extend credit during the Depression, which was the ruin of the store. Asked why, he replied, "People have to eat."

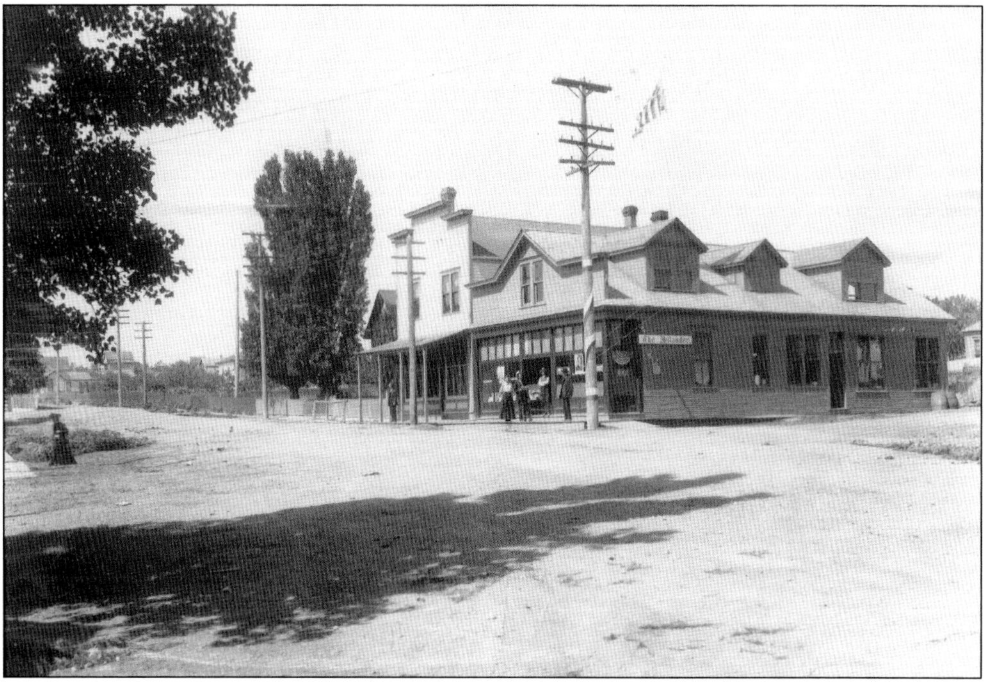

San Juan Island's rural character was still evident around 1900, when poplars mixed with telephone poles at the corner of Second and Spring streets in Friday Harbor. On the corner was the second home of *The Islander*, Friday Harbor's first newspaper, which did not shy away from objectivity by posting its favorite candidate's poster in the window. Next door is the two-story, first iteration of Friday Harbor Drug (still standing).

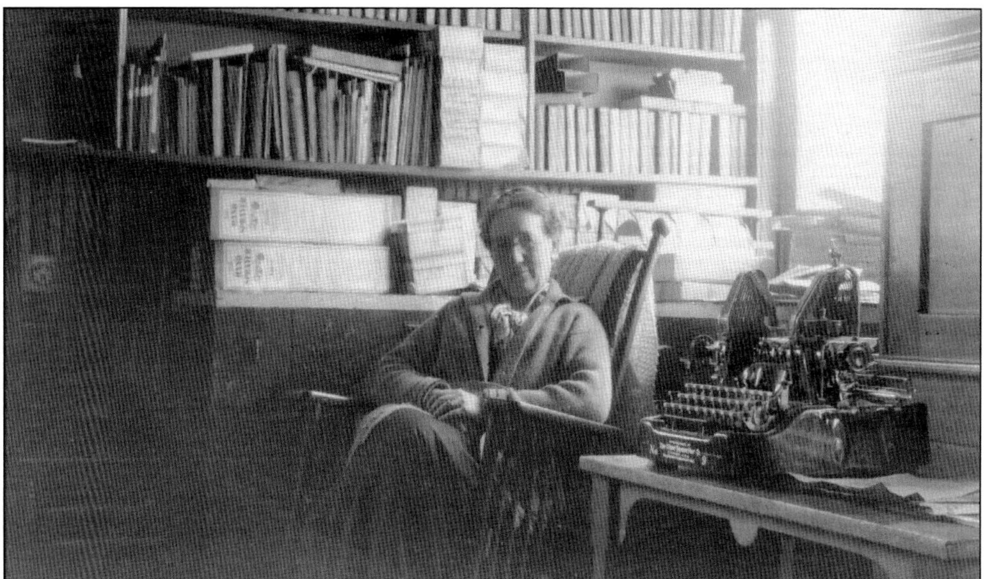

Laura Tenney Wright, wife of Dr. George Wright, relaxes in her office at Friday Harbor Drug, where she kept the books and helped supervise operations in addition to running her household and raising daughters Agnes and Louise. She was an avid volunteer in the community and active in the Women's Christian Temperance Union.

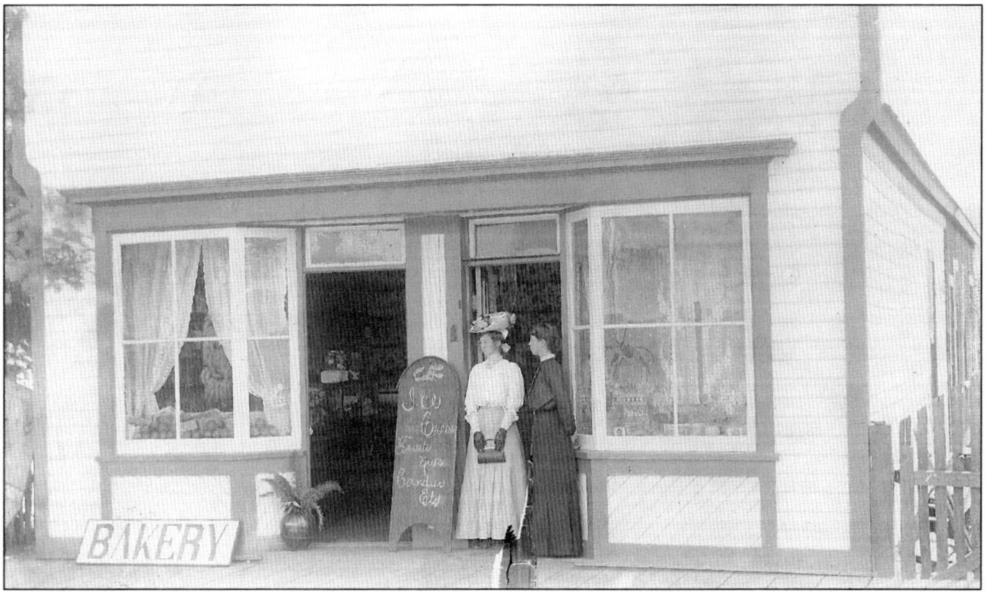

Alta (left) and Myra Nordyke pause for a photograph in front of their Spring Street bakery, which was located across the alley from today's Palace Theater. The space later became a meat market and then a restaurant under various owners until it burned down when a coffee urn was left connected.

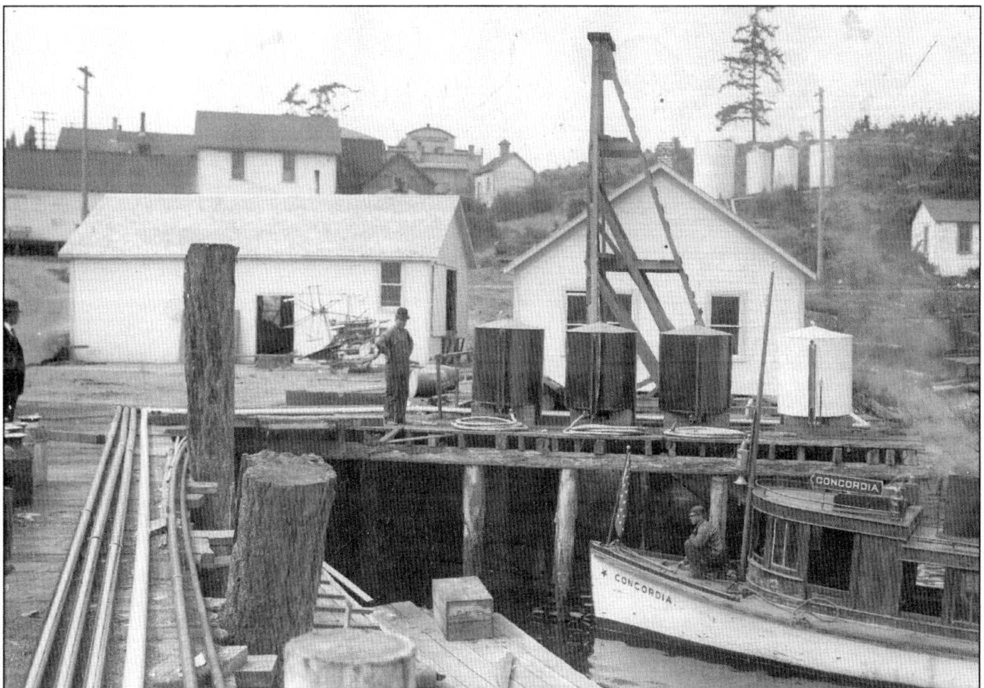

The *Concordia* slips up to the MacKenzie dock in Friday Harbor for fueling around 1900. Piping runs from foreground to storage tanks on the hillside and back to the four dockside dispensing tanks above the vessel. The apparatus behind the man wearing the derby appears to be a piece of agricultural machinery. The man almost out of the image at left is identified as John "Jack" Douglas.

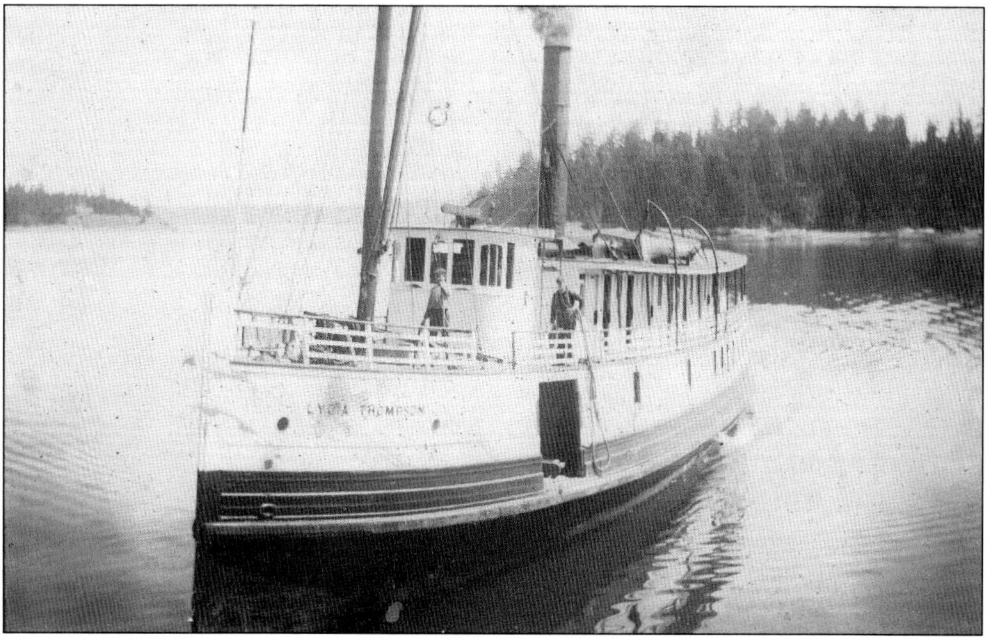

The *Lydia Thompson*, a mid-sized steamer for the Puget Sound Navigation Company, was a regular caller to Friday Harbor from 1893 to 1907, when she sank in Hood Canal. Mosquito Fleet vessels almost always ran at night from Friday Harbor, arriving in Seattle in time for breakfast. If you got cold, you would go topside and curl up next to the smokestack, the warmest place on the ship.

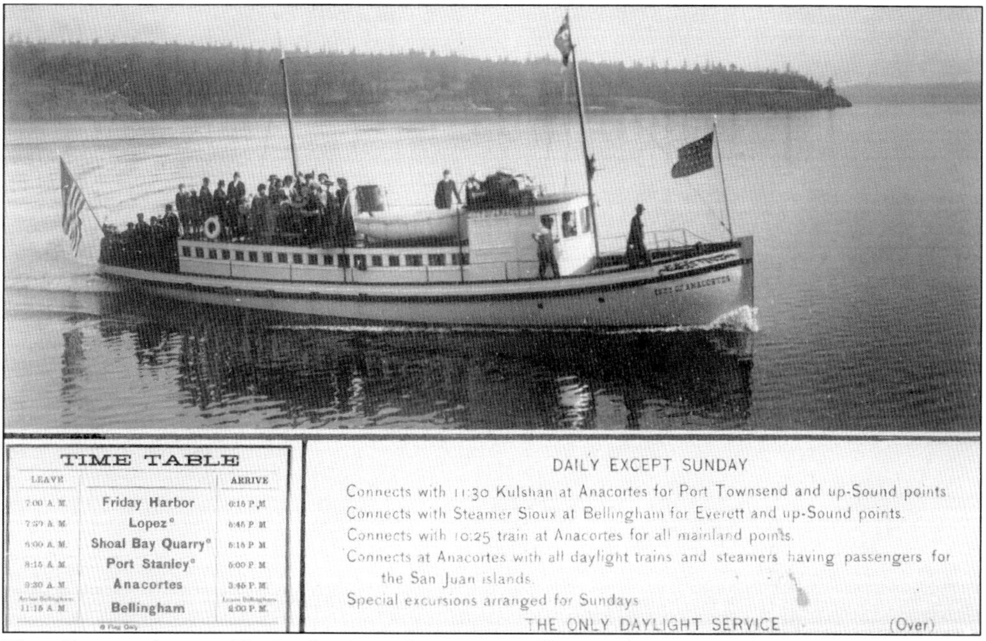

TIME TABLE

LEAVE		ARRIVE
7:00 A. M.	Friday Harbor	6:15 P. M.
7:30 A. M.	Lopez*	5:45 P. M.
8:00 A. M.	Shoal Bay Quarry*	5:15 P. M.
8:15 A. M.	Port Stanley*	5:00 P. M.
9:30 A. M.	Anacortes	3:45 P. M.
Arrive Bellingham 11:15 A. M.	Bellingham	Leave Bellingham 2:00 P. M.

* Flag Only

DAILY EXCEPT SUNDAY

Connects with 11:30 Kulshan at Anacortes for Port Townsend and up-Sound points.
Connects with Steamer Sioux at Bellingham for Everett and up-Sound points.
Connects with 10:25 train at Anacortes for all mainland points.
Connects at Anacortes with all daylight trains and steamers having passengers for the San Juan islands.
Special excursions arranged for Sundays.

THE ONLY DAYLIGHT SERVICE (Over)

This illustrated timetable for the *City of Anacortes* offers guidance for making connections with Puget Sound liners and passenger trains, as well as the inter-island trade and Bellingham-Anacortes run. Note that the timetable boasts the line as the "Only Daylight Service" because of the railroad connection. Church and fraternal organizations or extended families often chartered these smaller vessels for Sunday excursions and picnics.

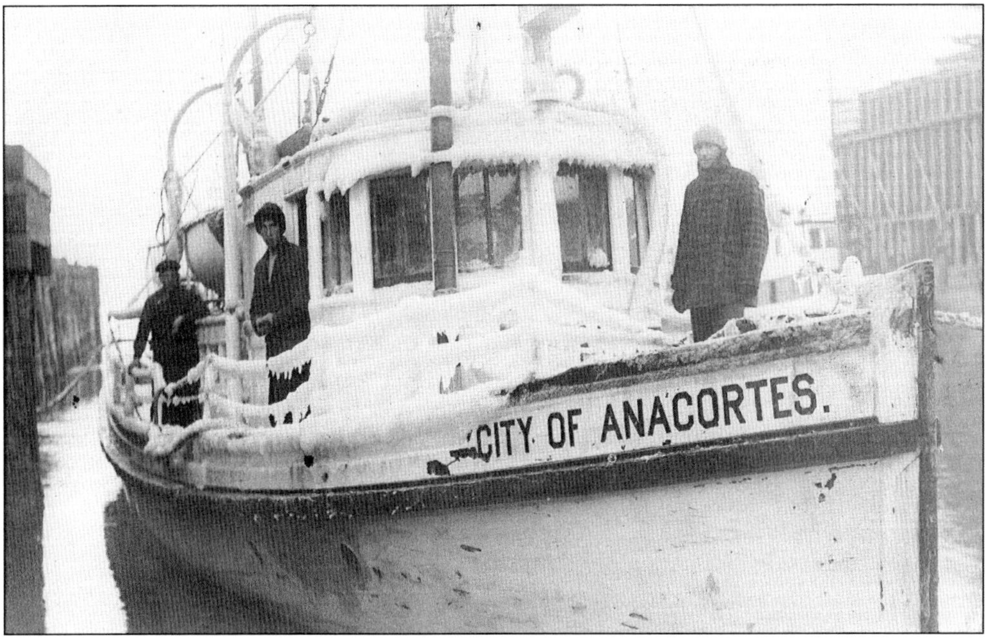

A northeaster frosts the *City of Anacortes,* tied up in Friday Harbor during the severe winter of 1909. "I believe the climate of this State of Washington is a delusion and a snare," Bert Coffin wrote about the mercurial island weather. When the steamer *Evangel* arrived late one winter, "she was covered with ice about an inch thick, all over her. The thermometer is down to two degrees."

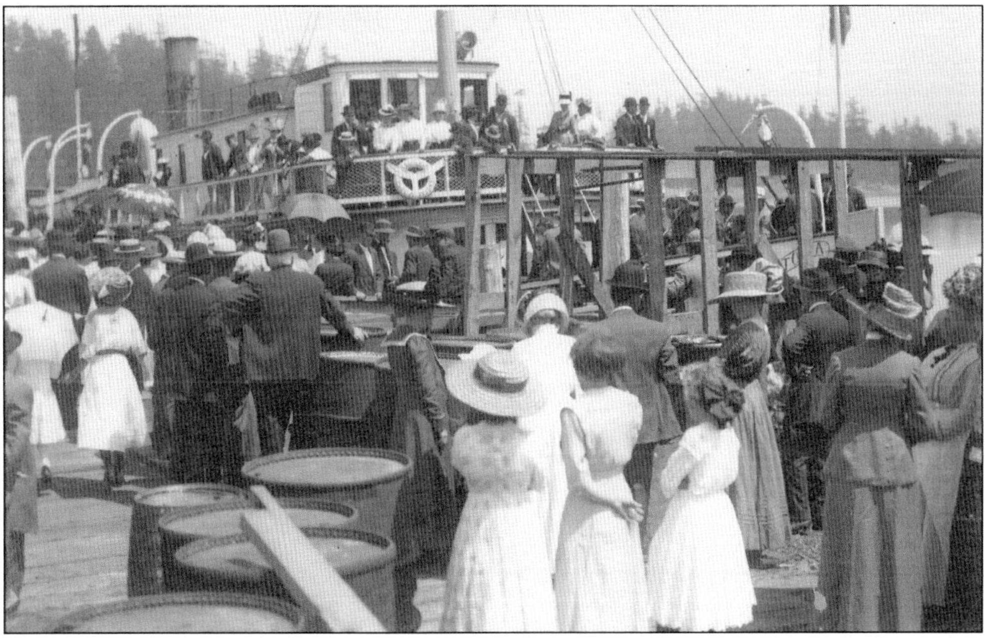

The Mosquito Fleet steamer *Utopia,* out of Port Angeles, loads passengers from the Friday Harbor dock around 1899. Built in 1893, she was considered "chubby" at 123 feet and proved it when she plowed into the Great Northern Dock in Anacortes and knocked it into the bay. But she was burly enough to survive the Alaska run until abandoned in 1922. The wooden frames on the dock are cordwood cribs.

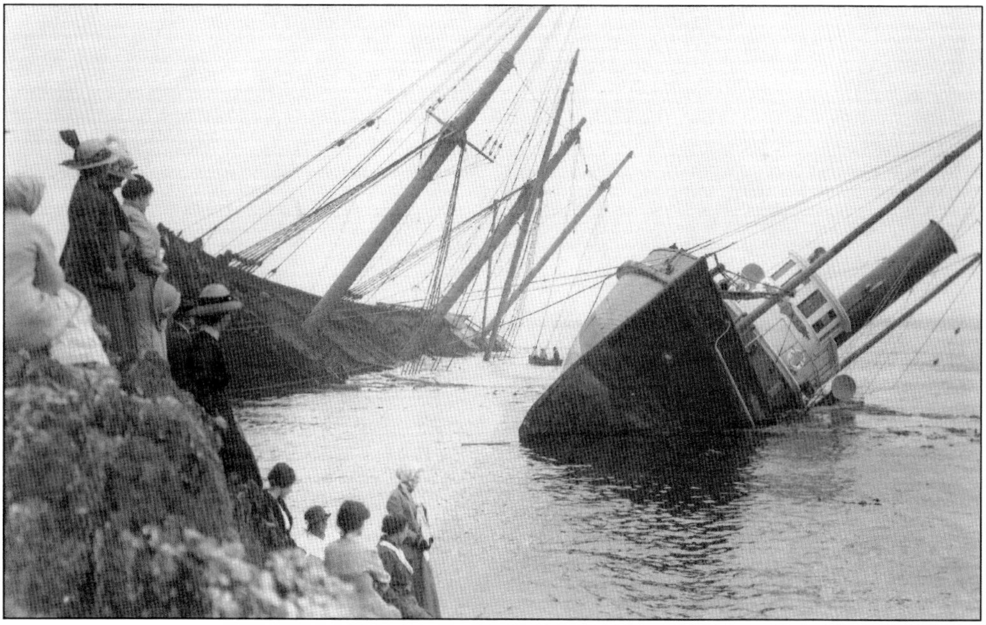

The 223-foot, 1,908-ton former Downeaster *America* and her tug *Lorne* went hard aground below Hannah Heights on the island's west side on a foggy Sunday afternoon, August 20, 1914. Built in 1874, she had circumnavigated the world before being relegated to a coal barge. The tug was floated off in a matter of days, while the *America* sank off Pile Point where she remains an attraction to sport divers.

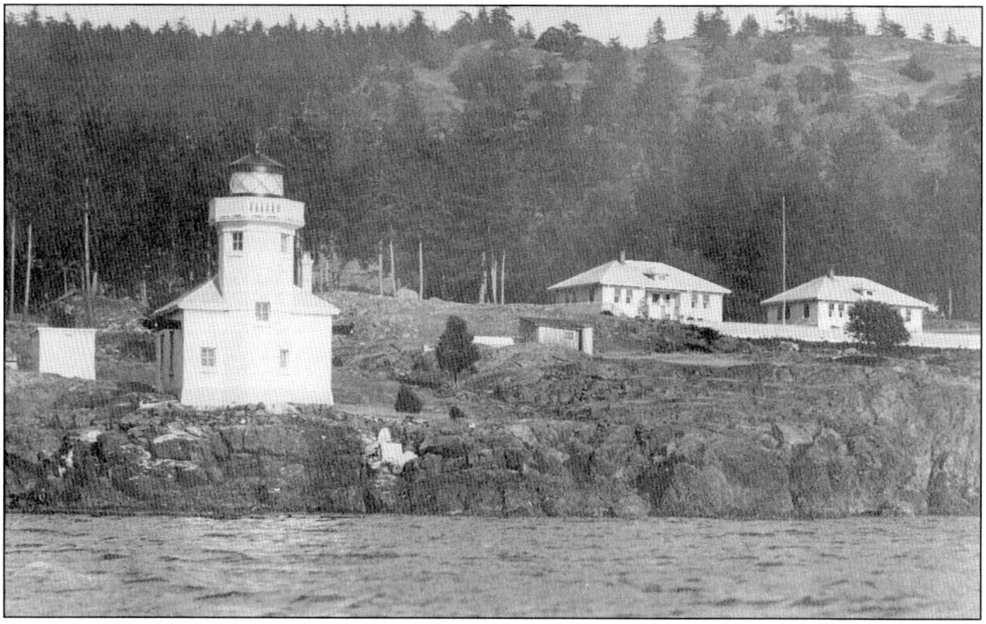

Established in 1914 and operational by 1919 on Deadman's Bay, the Lime Kiln lighthouse, with its light keepers' quarters and new Fresnel lens, was emplaced to ensure against repetition of the *America* wreck further down the coast. In addition to this location, lighthouses were also designated in 1875 for Cattle Point on San Juan and Stuart and Patos islands. The Lime Kiln light has been automated since 1962. (KR.)

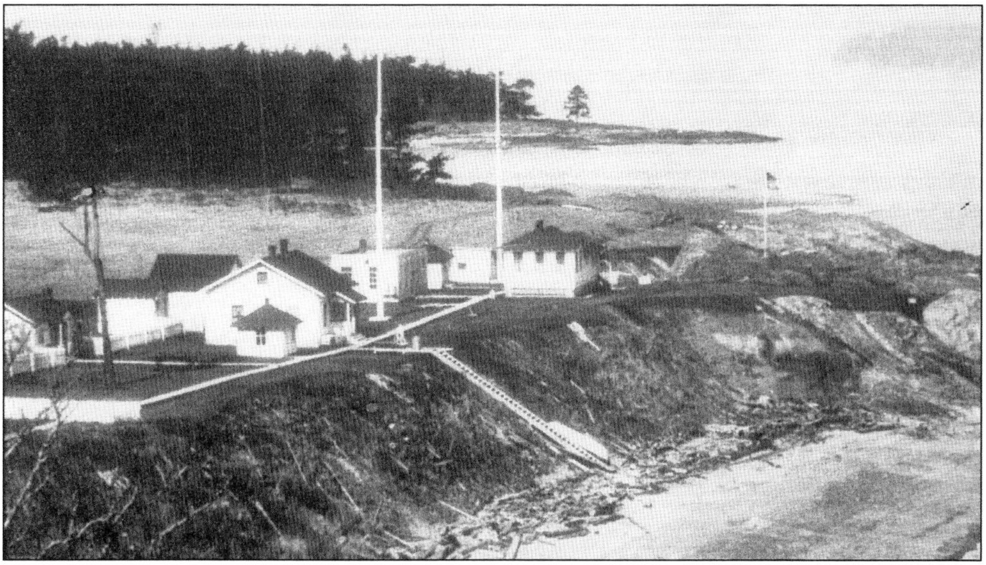

From the first lens lantern hung on a pole in the 1880s, Cattle Point on the island's southern tip has featured progressive navigational aids. A quantum leap was this radio compass station established in 1921 by the U.S. Navy. The station plotted radio transmissions using Morse code from ships and coordinated with stations at Smith Island and New Dungeness Spit. Closed in 1935, the site is now a park. (KR.)

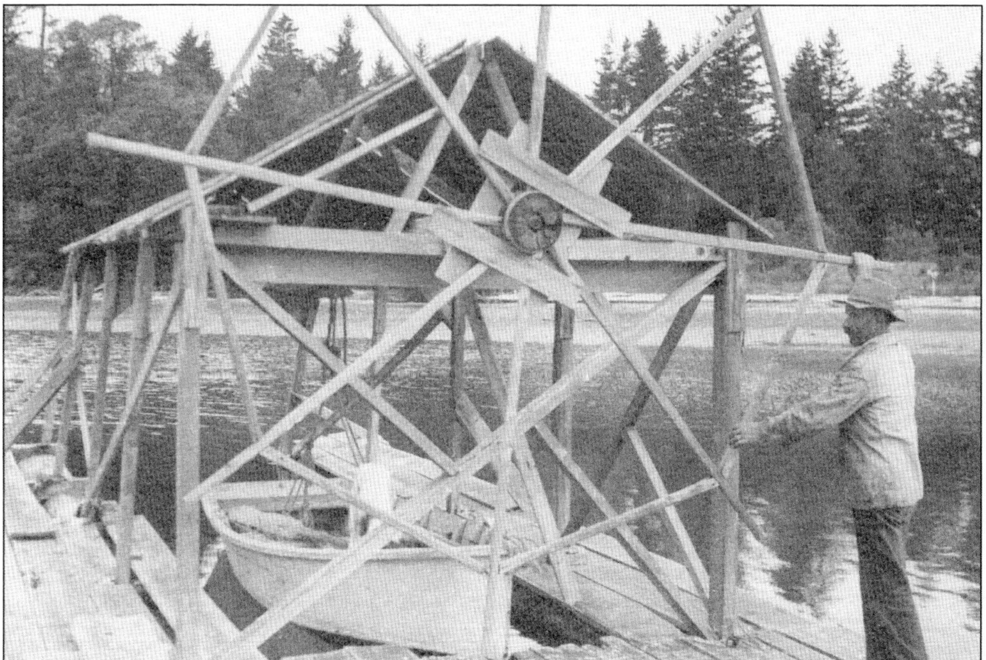

Renaissance man Jim Crook never failed to delight his neighbors with an intriguing new invention. Pictured here is a boat hoist operable with one hand. Another was a machine that made his bed—mandatory for a lifelong bachelor. He was frustrated upon learning the Wright Brothers had flown the first heavier-than-air machine, he told visitors in later years, because he had had similar plans on the drawing board.

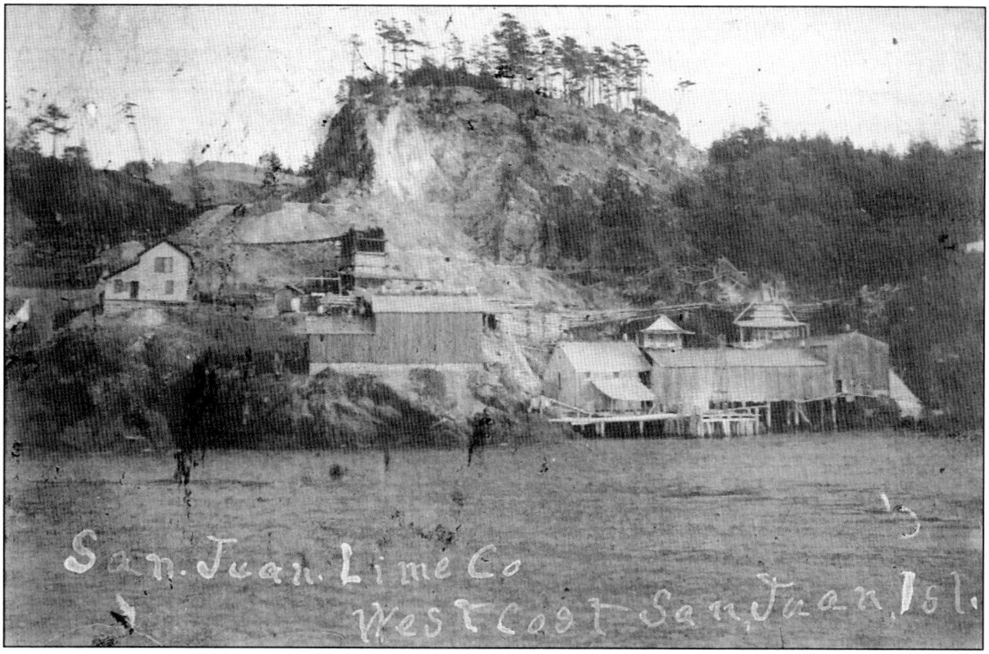

The San Juan Lime Company was founded on the island's west side in 1860 by a partnership that included pig-killer Lyman Cutlar. After premature deaths of two of the partners (one was murdered) and legal troubles, the operation settled down by 1892 under the ownership of Ernest Cowell. He ran it as a lime works and quarry until it shut down in 1955, when the commercial value of lime plunged.

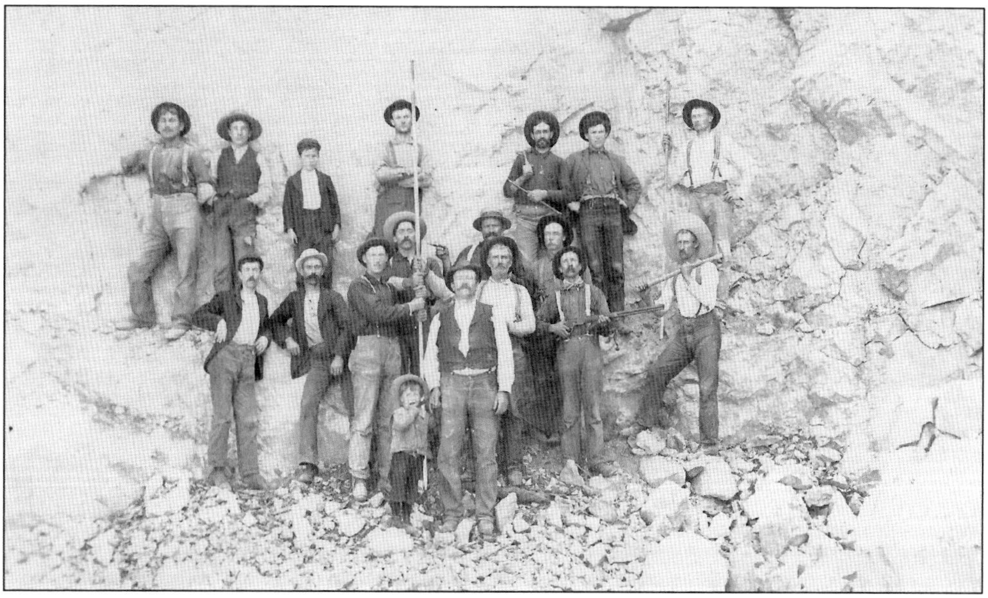

Nine limestone sites were mined on the island since the mid-19th century, but none had the "Deadwood" reputation of Lime Kiln Point. In 1870, for example, a disgruntled employee killed co-owner August Hibbard—no lily liver himself, having sold toxic liquor to Native Americans. At one point, the U.S. Army posted guards. In this *c.* 1900 view, miners display blasting drills and a rifle to maintain appearances.

Alex Lightheart rides the brake as he guides a load of cordwood down Mt. Dallas on the west side, while his brother-in-law Joe Lawson whoops it up as a rodeo cowboy. The horse teams were trained to be sure-footed on the slope. The wood was unloaded in the wood yard on a flat close to the bank facing the Haro and Juan de Fuca straits, and from there, hauled to the Cowell's Lime Kilns.

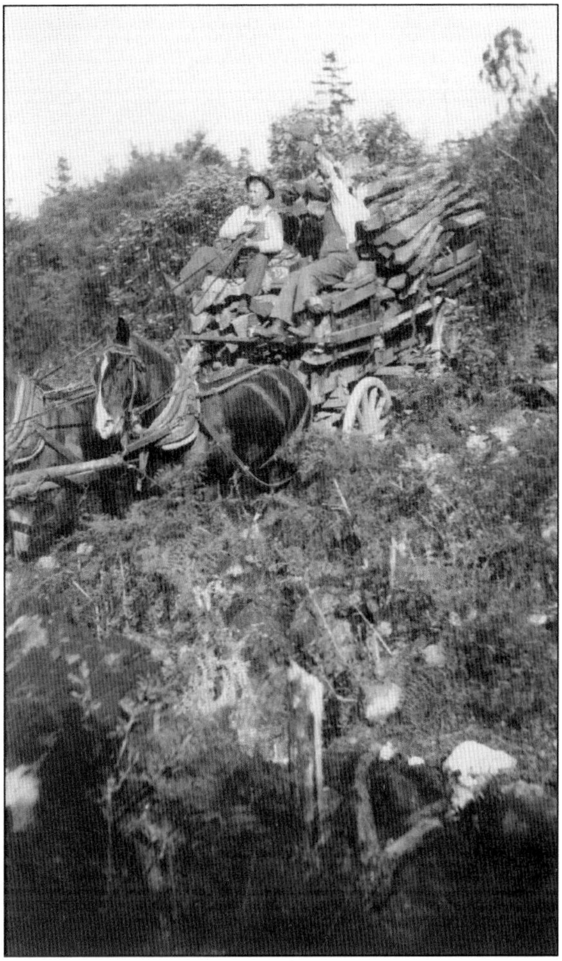

In contrast to the Cowell operation, Roche Harbor Lime and Cement Company boomed with all the trappings of a company town of the gilded age with its private railroad dumping lime into a bank of kilns. At its height in the 1890s, the company boasted the lime works, a barrel-making plant, church, school, company store, homes, piers, ships, shipyard, and offices. But company script was encouraged in the store.

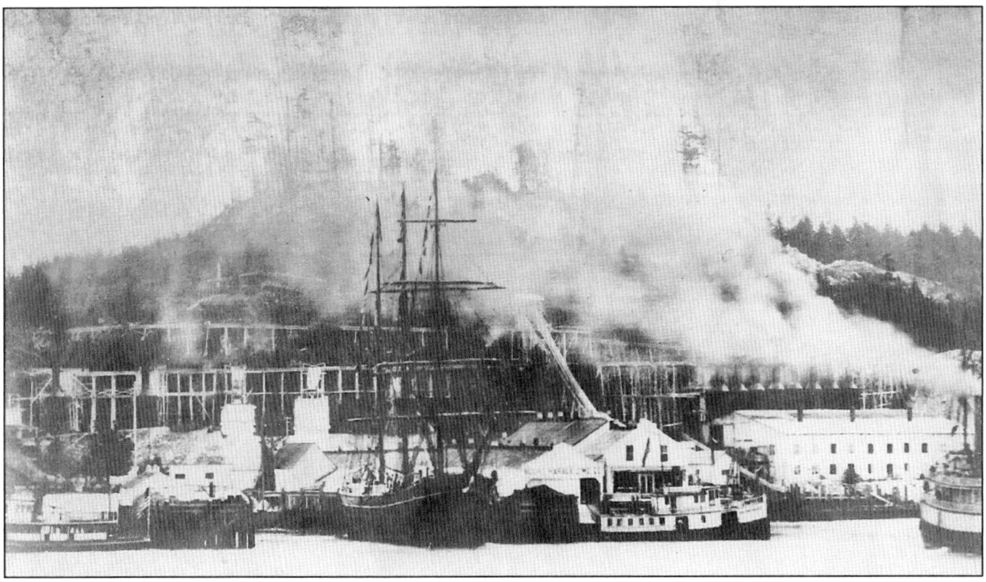

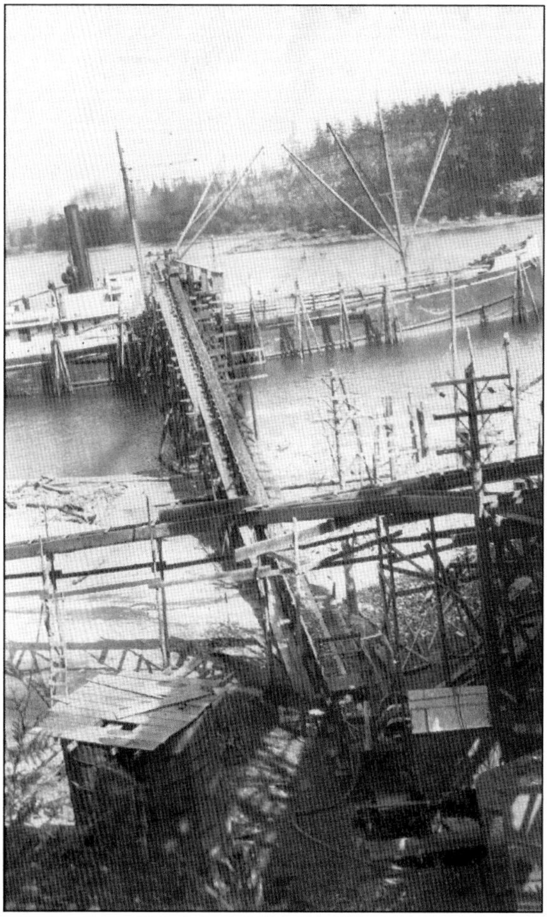

A cargo ship takes on a load of gravel from the conveyor of the Superior Sand and Gravel Company at the south end of Friday Harbor around 1926. Bunkers were constructed on the shoreline in 1924, just north of the Jensen Shipyard. Saltwater was pumped to the north slope of the once gravel-rich Bald Hill to wash and sort the gravel, which was then sent down the hill. The operation was shut down in 1935, along with the Friday Harbor Sand and Gravel Company, also established in the 1920s on the Griffin Bay side of the hill. The tunnels under the abandoned bunkers were magnets for island children until the Griffin Bay pit reopened in the 1950s, providing employment for more than 40 years before shutting down in February 1999. The hill now attracts joggers and dog-walkers.

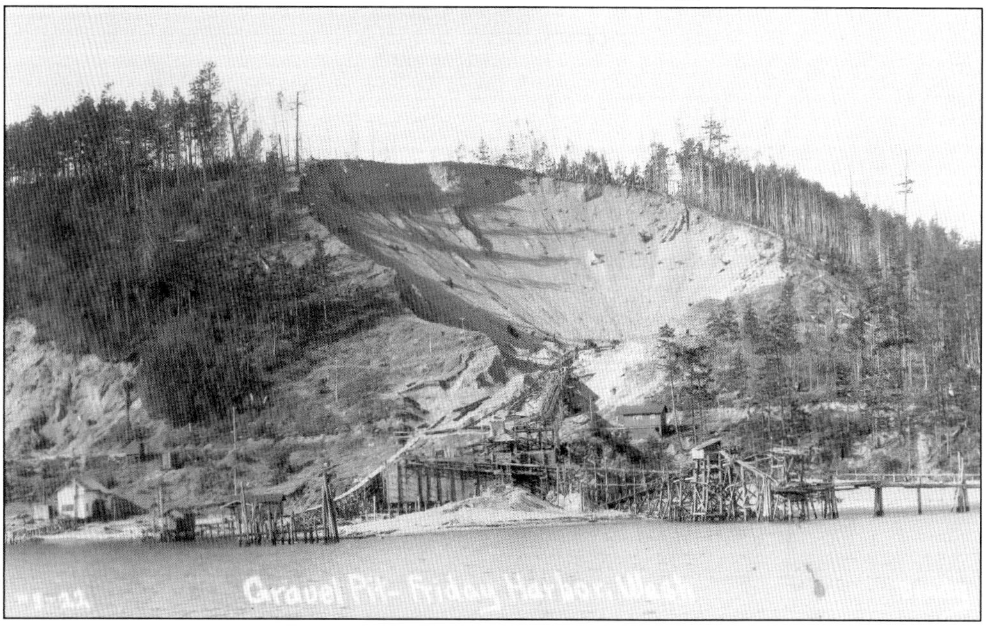

Five

Hearth and Home

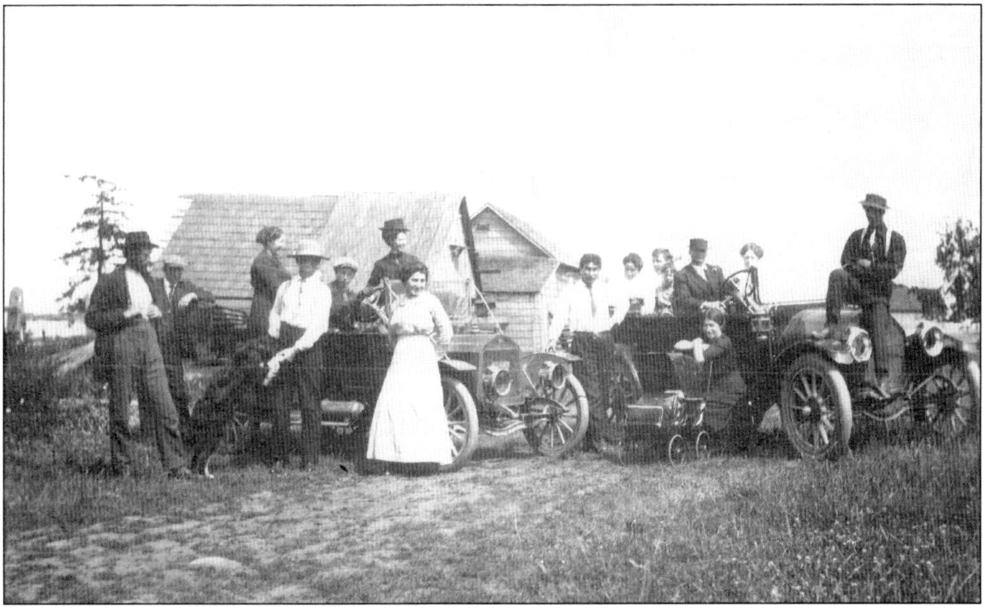

The Lawsons, Roslers, Lighthearts, Landahls, and Thrones gather for yet another party at the Thrones farm on the southern end of the island off Cattle Point Road. Lizzie Lawson wears the pork pie hat at center left, Adeline Thrones is at center, and her brother Bill Rosler leans on a fender center right. Adeline frequently battled wills with her equally stubborn niece, Sylvia Landahl. They shared electricity, and when Adeline got angry, she would flip it off, hopefully interrupting Sylvia as she separated cream in an electric creamer. Gatherings of multiple families from around the island were common (although islanders from the north and south mingled only occasionally during special events), which explains why many islanders today can trace their heritage back through a long line of two or three pioneer families. Bill Rosler's connections were especially unique. He married Louise Bellevue, who was his brother Rudolph's wife's daughter. Thus Louise was Tillie's sister-in-law as well as her daughter, and Bill was not only Tillie's brother-in-law, but also her son-in-law.

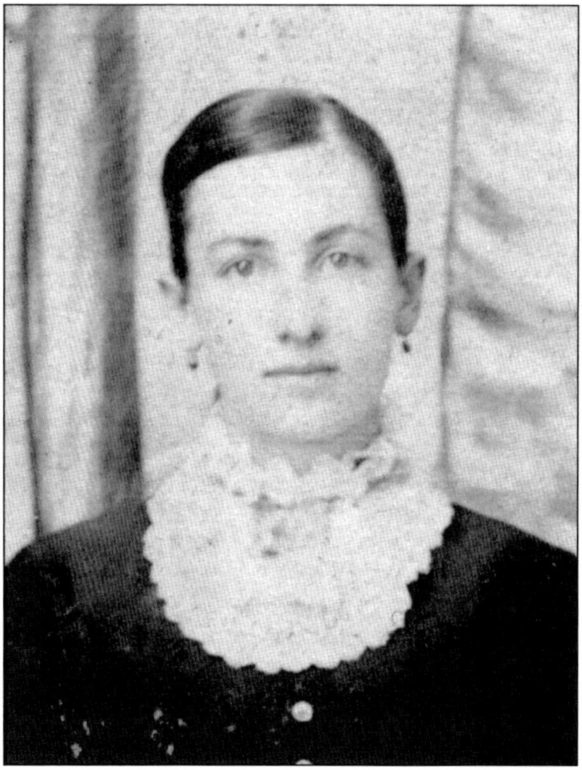

Lila Hannah, born to James and Manerva in 1865, married Robert Firth Jr., son of pioneers Robert and Jessie, in 1882. They ran a sheep ranch until 1901, then moved to Seattle. Lila was smitten with Robert from a young age, when he would gallop past their farm on his little sorrel horse, herding sheep to the Hudson's Bay Company on the south end of the island, where they were shipped to Victoria. "We could hear them coming for miles down the mountainside, bleating and the shepherds' whips popping like distant guns going off. Robert always wore a scotch cap with two black ribbon tails that fluttered back in the wind." They would circle the sheep, whirl the long whip around their shoulders, then give it a jerk, creating a loud snap that "made the sheep dance." (Both, SAJH.)

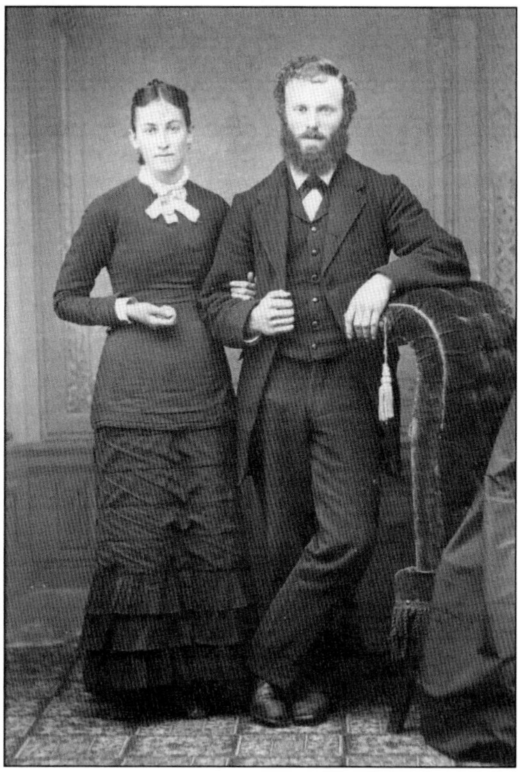

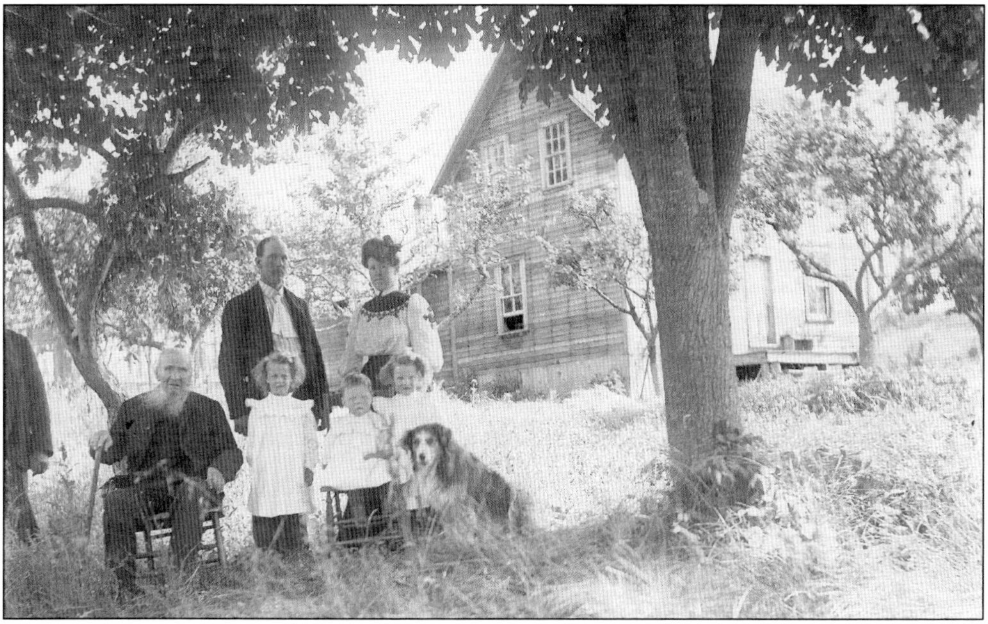

The Ben King family dragged the dining room furniture outdoors and under the old maple tree in 1906 to capture this portrait with the family patriarch, Francis King, the father of James, John, and Ben. Ben and Ida Mae Little King stand behind their children, from left to right, Mary, William "Bill," and Elizabeth "Bessie." The original house burned down, and Ben rebuilt it. It is still standing near Halvorsen Road.

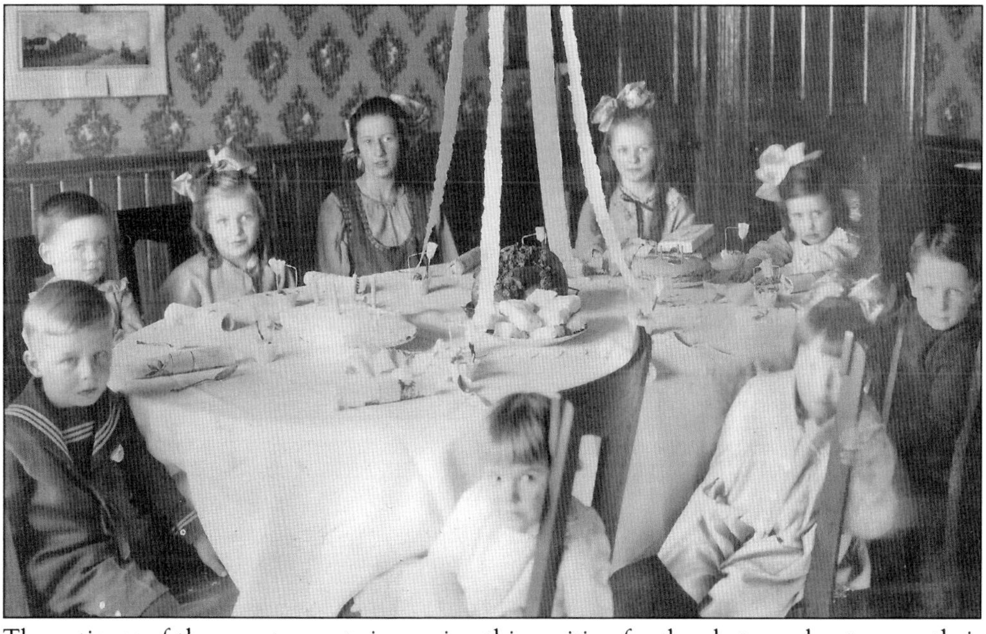

The patience of these party guests is wearing thin waiting for the photographer to snap their picture. This *c.* 1920 birthday party for Kathryn Madden was at her Grandma Agnes Madden's house, which still stands directly across from the corner store. Clockwise, from left, are Arnold Guard, Frank Douglas, Marjorie Jensen, May Bergman, Audrey Jensen, Kathryn Madden, Paul Guard, Margaret Guard, and Edythe Guard.

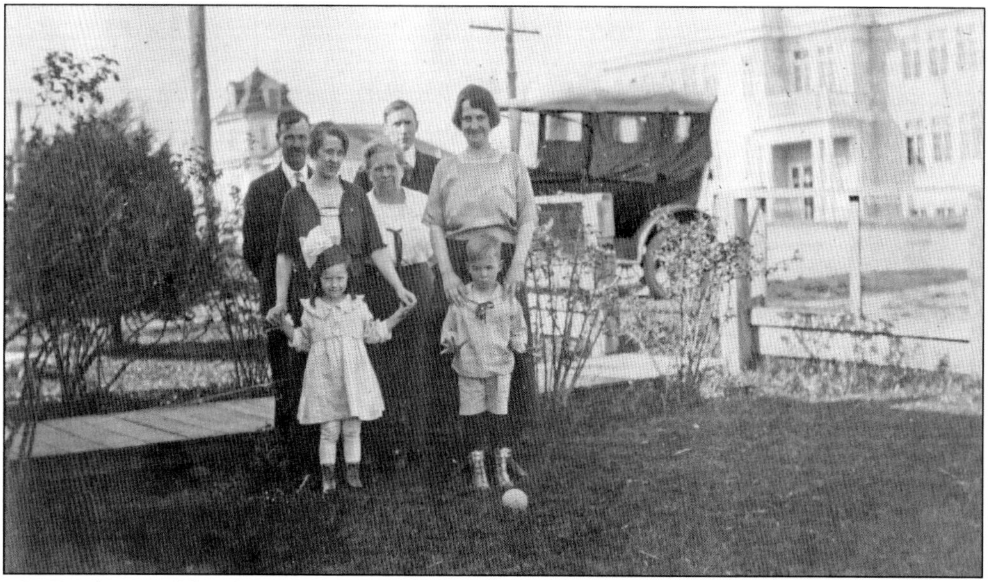

The Frank Guard family poses at the home of their daughter, Florence Guard Douglas, on Second Street in Friday Harbor around 1921. The high school and old belfry school stand at rear. The family members are, from left to right, (first row) Kathryn Madden and Frank Douglas; (second row) Gladys Guard Madden, Alice First Guard, and Florence Guard Douglas; (third row) Frank Guard and Raymond Madden. John Douglas Jr. probably took the photograph. (SH.)

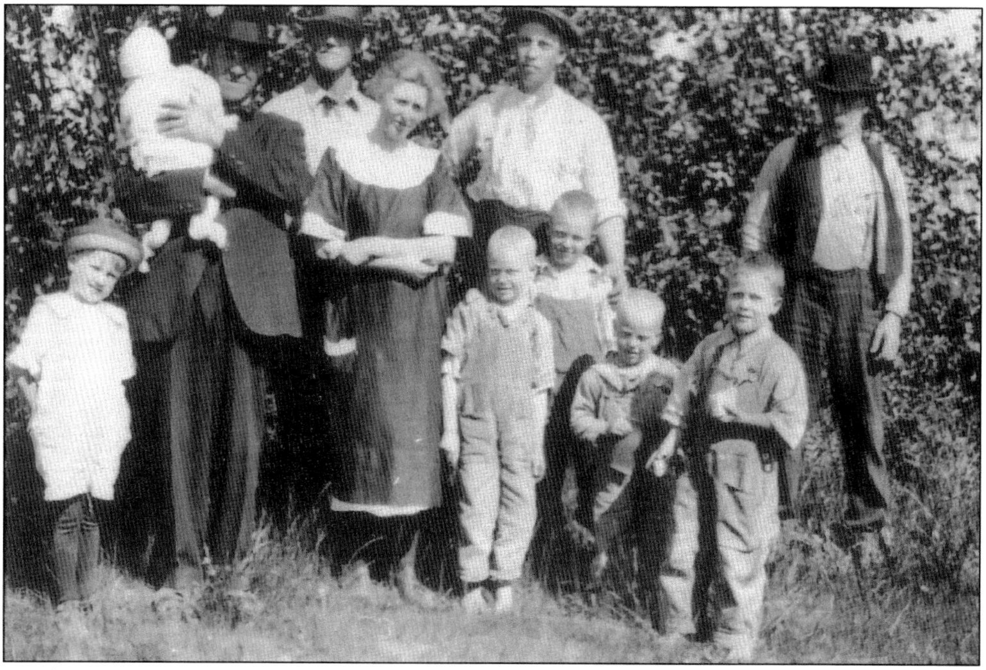

Sundstroms and friends are, from left to right, Eldon Halverson; Gunder Halverson holding Lenore Sundstrom (born 1925); John and Josie Madden Sundstrom; Ernest Sundstrom; the Sundstrom boys: Dave, Clyde, Wade, and Al (Lindy and Fred not pictured); and Josie's grandfather, Pete Gorman. Many islanders remember Josie for her kitchen—open to all—and good humor, even when being "snowballed all the way to the hog pen" by her sons.

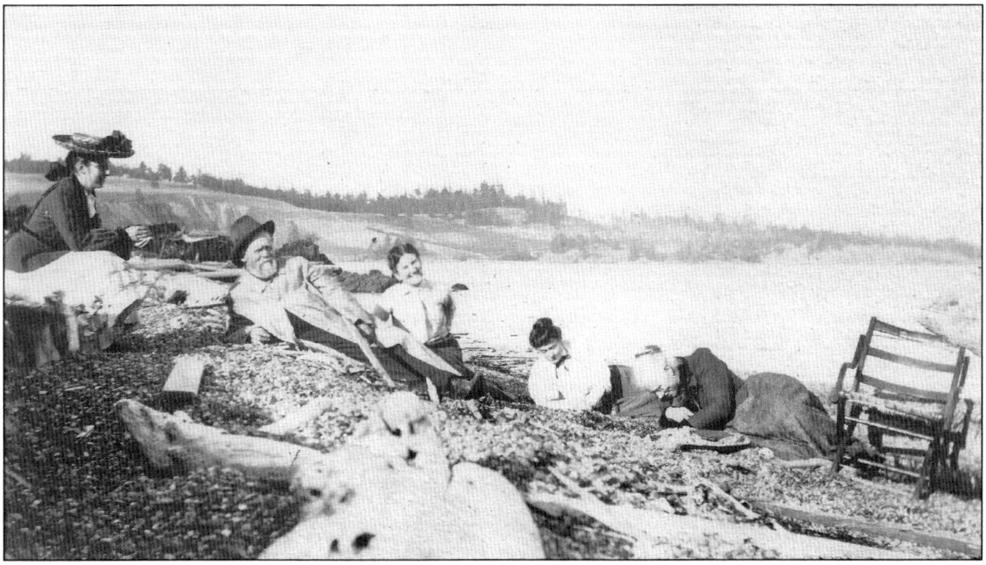

Sprawled left to right are Louise Wright Little, John Blair, Agnes Wright King, unidentified, and Harriet Whittlesey Wright Blair. John, who married Harriett in 1902, was born in 1834 in New York, joined General Sherman's army during the famous march across Georgia, and in 1891, bought a home in Friday Harbor. In 1906, he was elected state senator. He practiced law but preferred farming and took pride in his orchard.

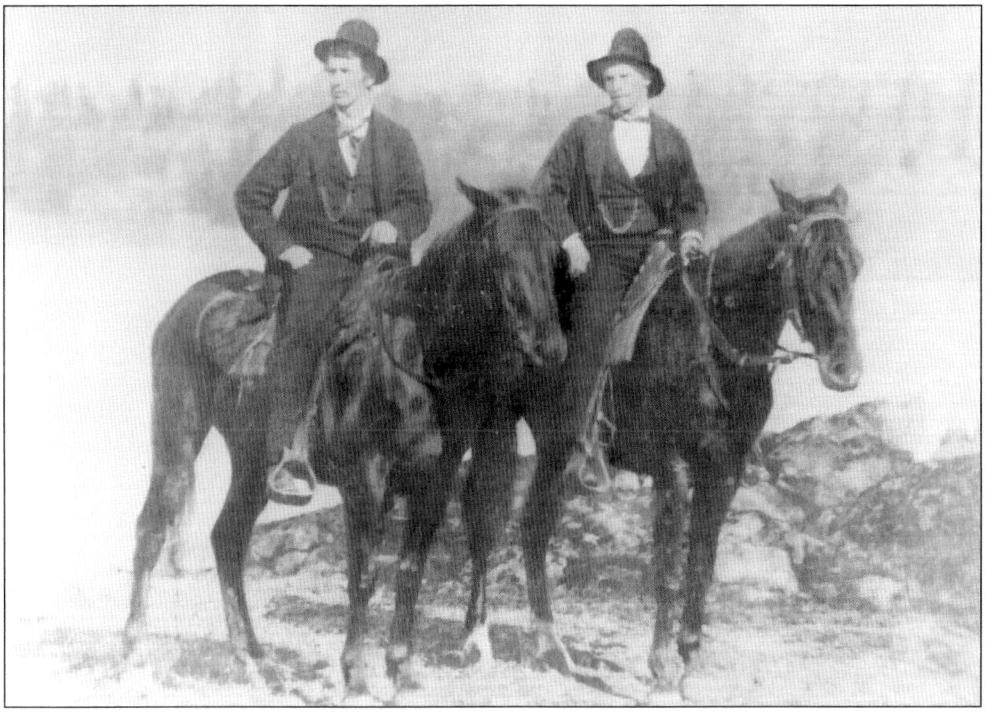

James King (left), 20, and John King, 17, looked a bit like the Earp brothers while on a ride along the primitive Friday Harbor waterfront in 1877. The sons of island pioneer Francis King, James farmed more than 400 acres on San Juan Island and built the house that eventually became the San Juan Historical Museum. John's son Lyle founded King's Market.

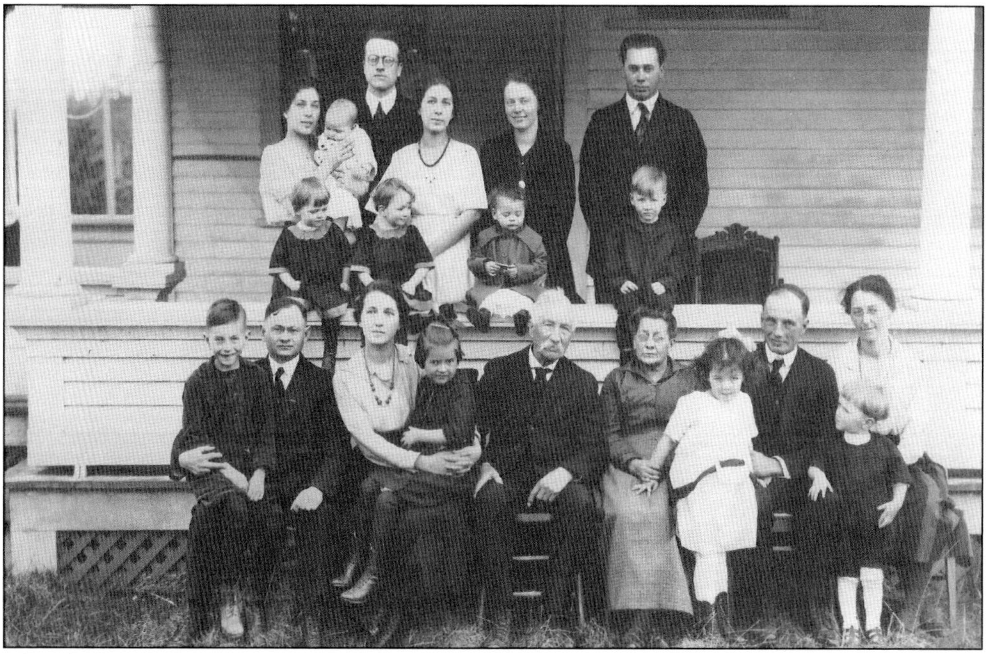

The Shulls (Daniel and Emma sit center front) and Carters pose at the Shulls' Beaverton Valley farmhouse in 1923. The Shulls were struggling by this time, competing against larger farms. Their son, Howard, second from right, died in a tractor accident in 1925, and when Daniel died three years later, the family left the island. The 1902 house, 6,000-square-foot barn, and other outbuildings have been renewed by Synergy Farm.

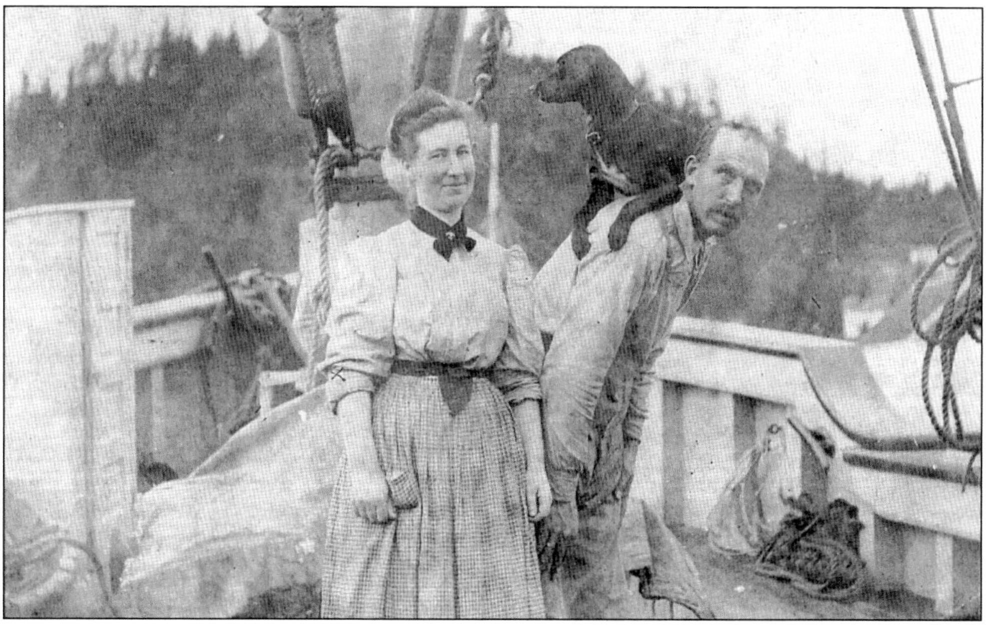

In 1900, Rhoda Crook, William and Mary Forrest Crook's third child, married Fred Anderson in Seattle. He was the chief engineer of the steamer *Lydia Thompson*, which regularly called in Friday Harbor. They remained in Puget Sound for more than 30 years while Fred continued in the maritime trade. Here they—and their dog—pose aboard their boat, presumably in Garrison Bay.

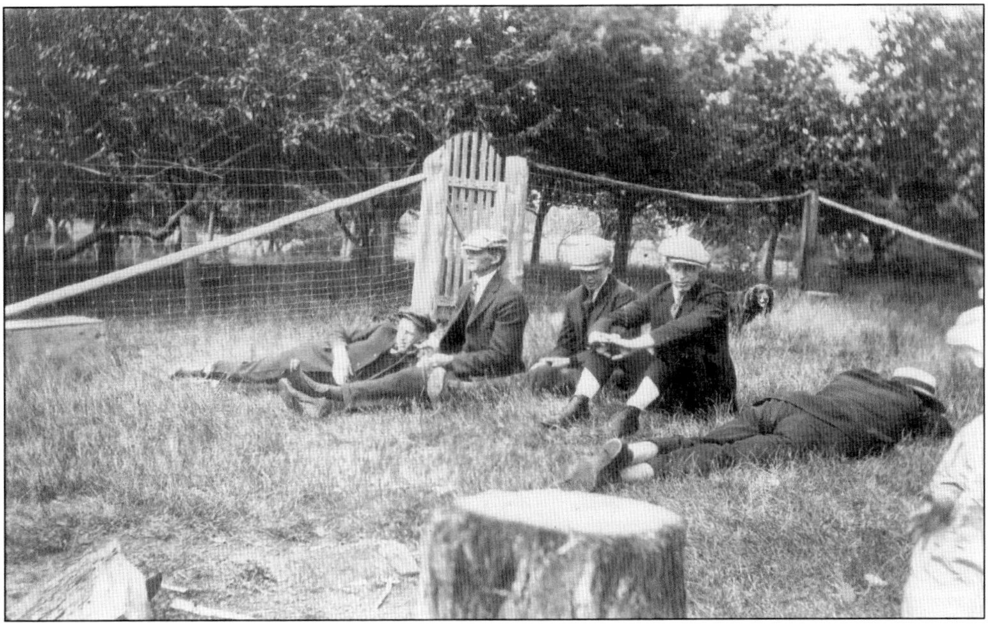

The early days on San Juan Island required hard work six days a week, but Sundays were still considered days of rest. Here friends lounge after supper at Lizzie Lawson's farm around 1910. From left to right are Harold Lightheart, George Lawson, Ben Dennison, and Joe Lawson. George and his brother Peter's North End Farm on the slopes of Mount Dallas and Cady Mountain eventually encompassed 1,200 acres.

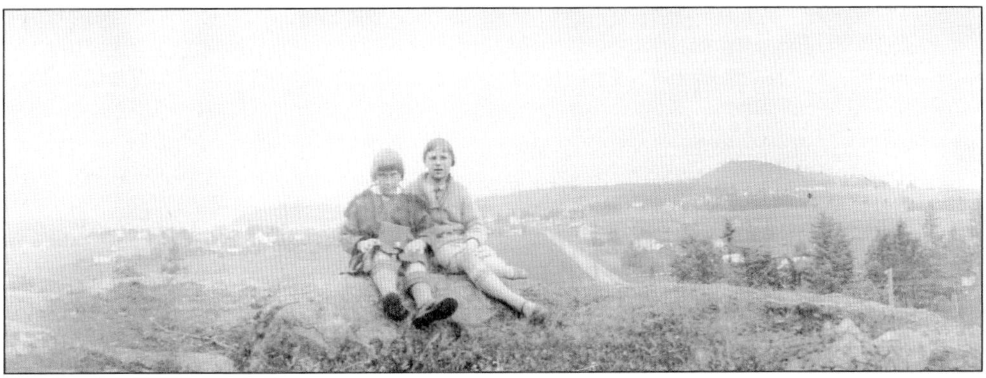

Juanita Rouleau, left, and Mildred Swenson view Friday Harbor from King Mountain around 1926–1928. Juanita, born in 1916 to Harry and Etta Egeland, married Wilfred Rouleau in 1940. She taught school for 17 years—piloting a skiff for two years to Stuart Island—and went reef-netting with Wilfred. Her son, Ed, said his Norwegian grandfather, Harry, "just raised hell, because white women didn't go out commercial fishing in those days."

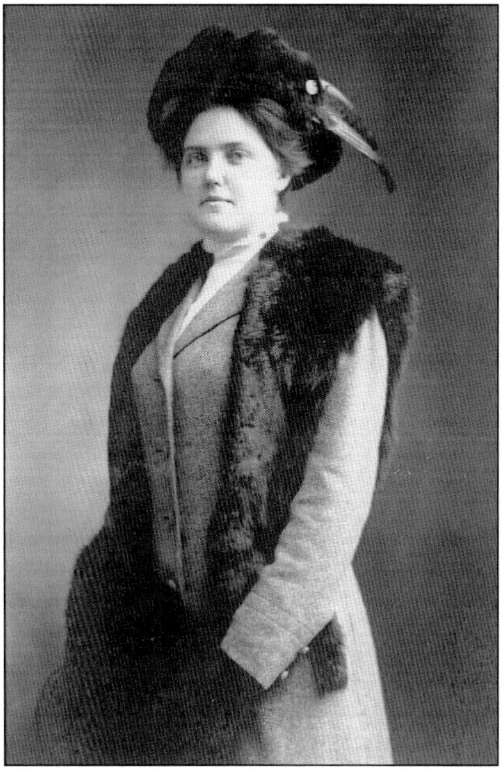

In 1910, Belle Wallace married Frank Mullis, son of George and Ella Mullis of England. They raised four children in the still-standing Mullis House on Argyle, built by master craftsman George in 1905. In 1923, they moved to Los Angeles. After nine months, they returned. Said Frank, "People may rave about glorious California, but they are uninformed and have no knowledge of the San Juan Islands." (PM.)

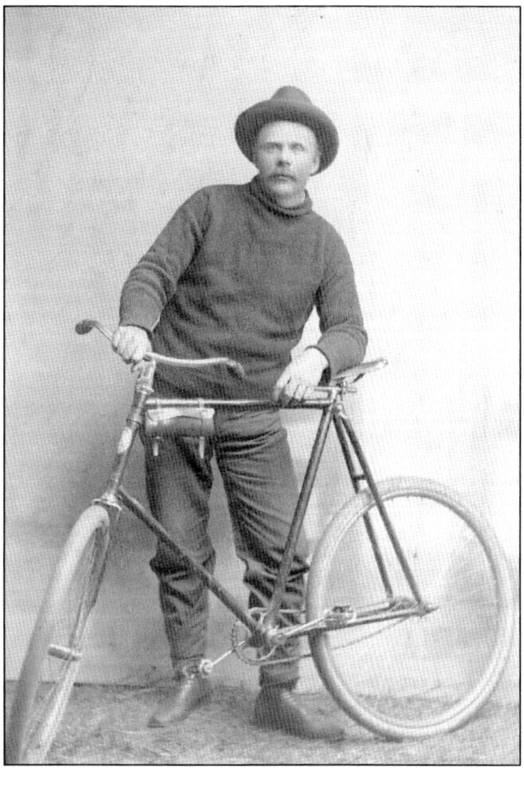

John W. Firth was elected San Juan County sheriff during a Republican sweep of county offices in 1898. He was born on San Juan Island in 1864 to Robert and Jesse Firth, and in 1900 married Iowan Frances "Ella" Warren, who ran a successful millinery store. They moved to Seattle in 1910. His bicycle was likely from Sears, Roebuck, and Company, which sold 100,000 in just one year.

Hattie Rosler Merrifield, eldest child (born 1862) of Anna Pike and Christopher Rosler, and her husband, Stafford, farmed where the golf course is located today. Like many islanders, they were known for their hospitality. One friend, Argyle storekeeper Bert Coffin, tells of visiting one Sunday, and when he found them away at church, let himself in to fix breakfast. When they returned, he was invited to supper.

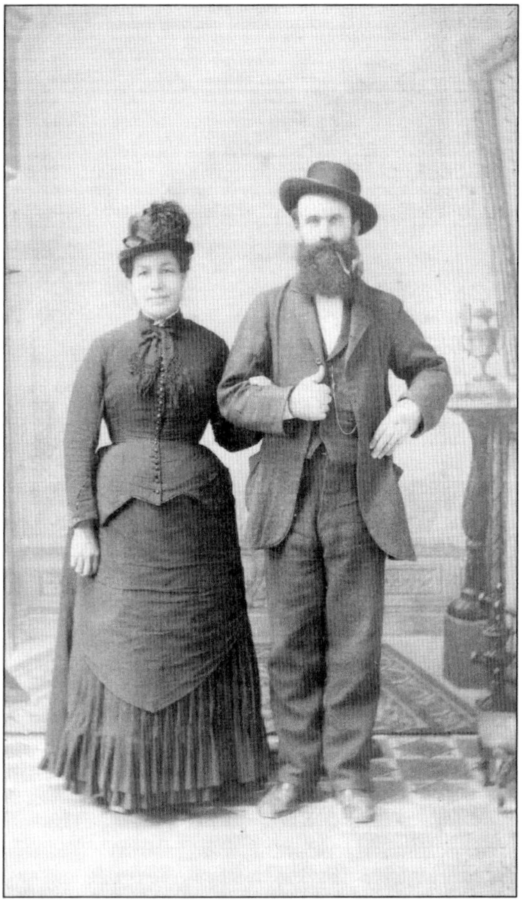

Mary Forrest Crook, left, and daughter Rhoda, born in 1880, rest in their English Camp garden in 1897. After Rhoda's husband, Fred, and her sister, Mary, died, she returned to the island at age 80 to care for her brother Jim. After he died, a demolition crew found their father William's treasure of currency and gold coins hidden in the old barracks. Jim had been searching for it for 60 years.

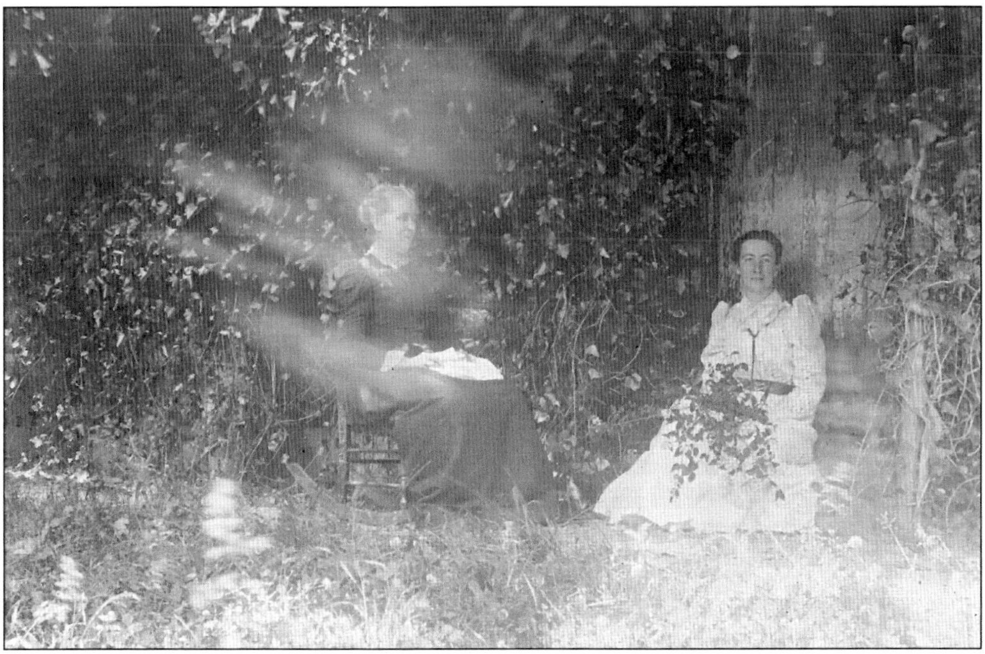

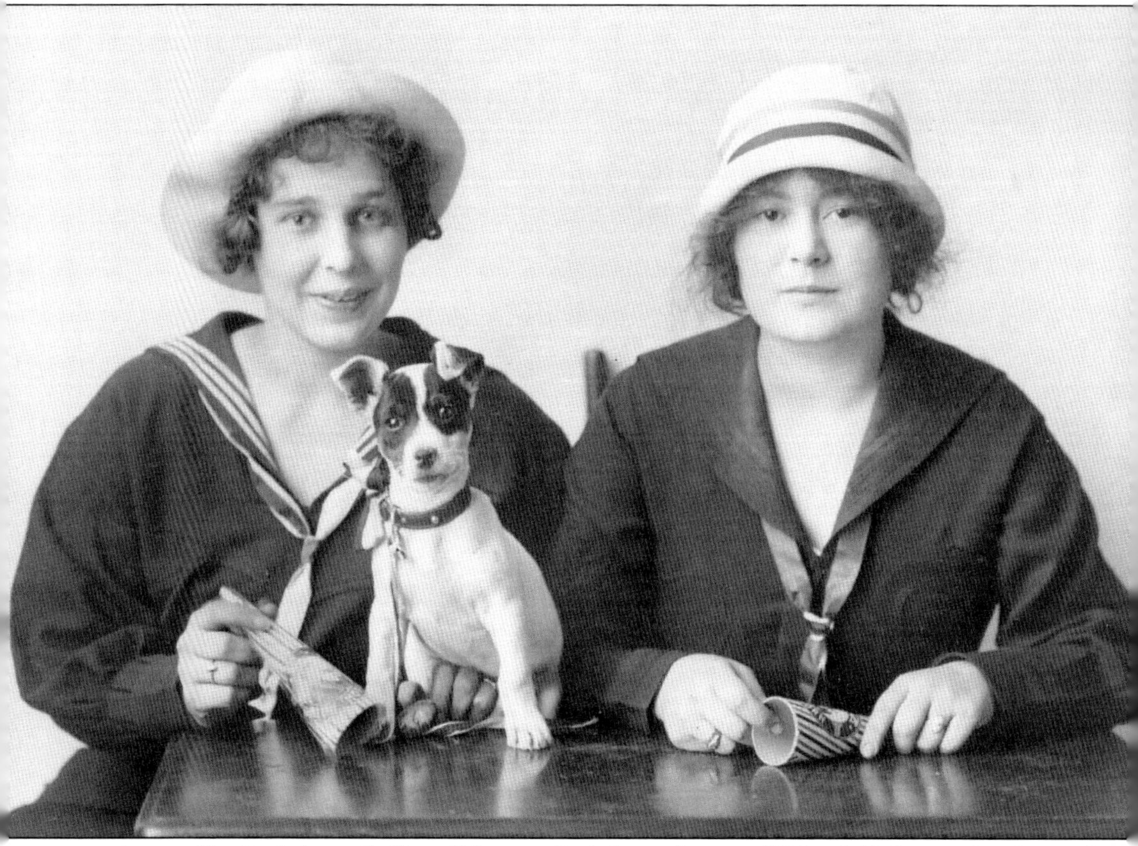

Cousins Etta Lightheart (left) and Margaret Lightheart, born in 1896 and 1894, were daughters of Alex and Annie Lightheart and Frederick and Alice Lightheart, respectively. Etta, who married Henry "Harry" Egeland, was founder of the San Juan Island Historical Society and Museum. She was also a born leader. At age 20, she shocked the community by bobbing her hair in imitation of her idol, the famous dancer Irene Castle.

Jessie Firth, pictured at right at age 17, was born in 1862 to Robert and Jessie Firth. In 1883, she married Canadian-born John Douglas, who started Saloon Best in the cellar of a house in Argyle that once served as the commanding officers' quarters at American Camp (see pages 21 and 22). The saloon eventually moved to Spring Street, where it thrived until liquor sales were banned within town limits in 1910. Douglas continued to make money on his real estate holdings and also captained boats for hire. Below, the steely, slightly dazed expression on Jessie's face may be testament to a woman's life in these early days. These were not ladies of leisure, but hardworking women who had little in the way of conveniences. (Right, SAJH; below, SH.)

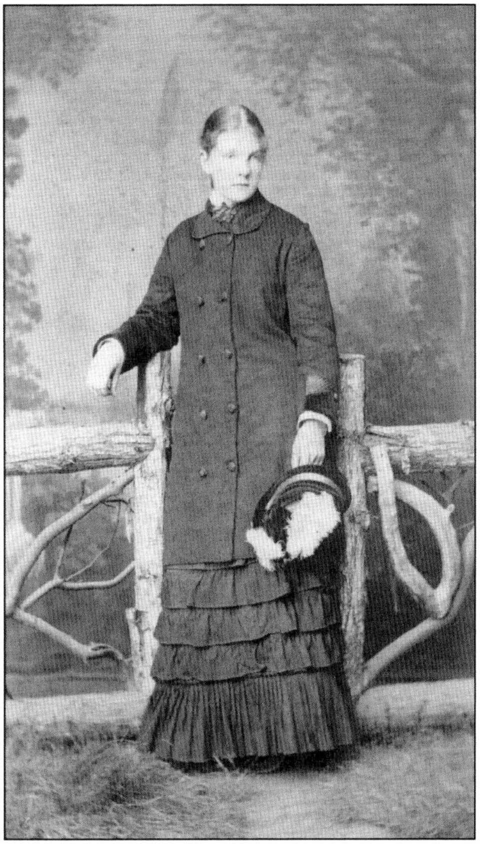

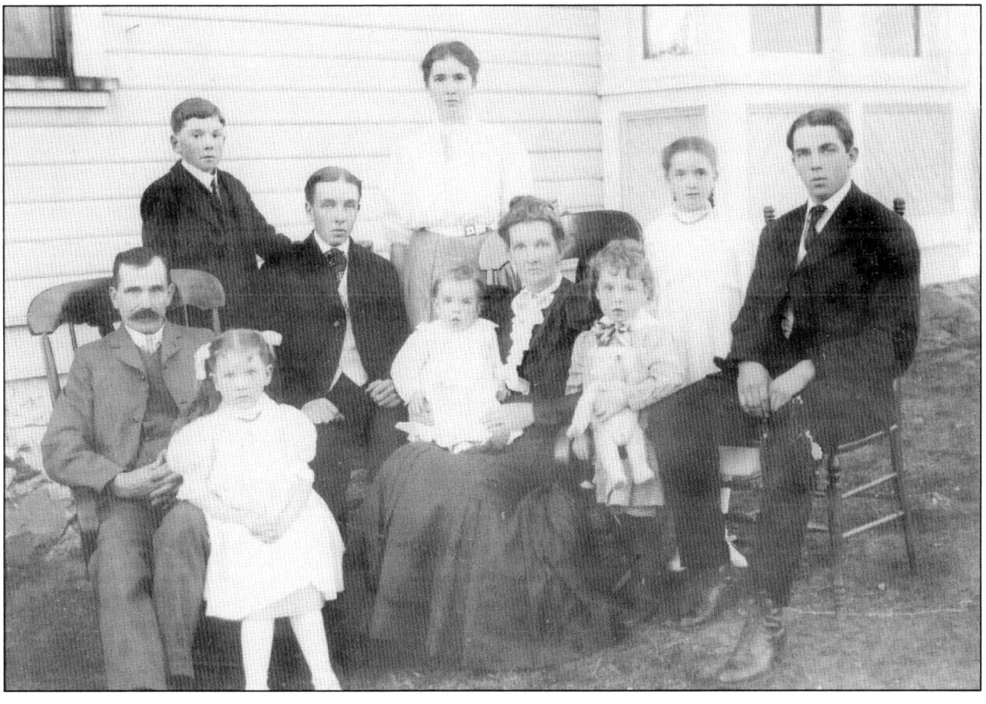

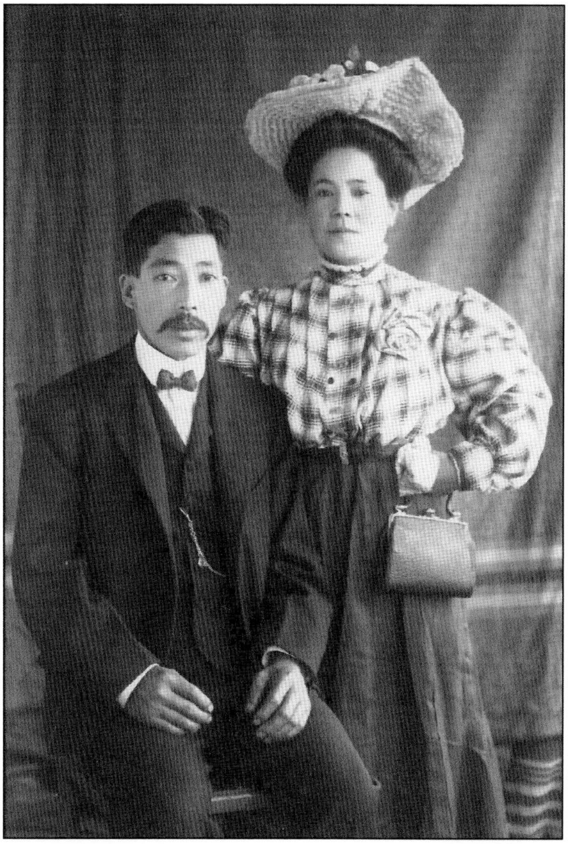

At left, Jack and Fuji Saoka, *issei,* or native Japanese, moved to the island in 1917. Jack found work at the cannery, was promoted to supervisor, and eventually opened a florist and nursery. Fuji died in 1920 in the influenza pandemic, and their daughter, Fumiko, graduated from Friday Harbor High School in 1933. Below from left to right, Edna Nash, Beryl Wade, Jack Saoka, John Nash, and Yuki Saoka—Jack's second wife—gather on the eve of the Saokas departure for internment at Camp Minidoka in Idaho. Even remote San Juan Island was not exempt from President Roosevelt's Executive Order 9066, when all persons of Japanese ancestry were banished from the West Coast of the United States. Jack returned in 1945 to settle his affairs, then left and never returned. However, he, Fuji, and Yuki are all buried in the Protestant cemetery on Madden Lane. (Below, KR.)

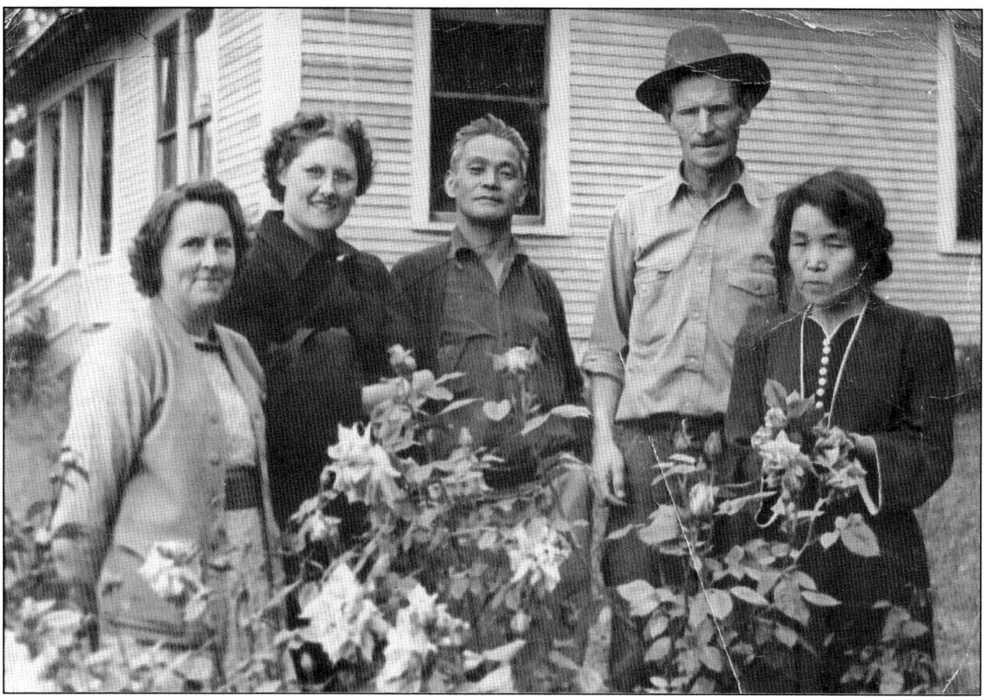

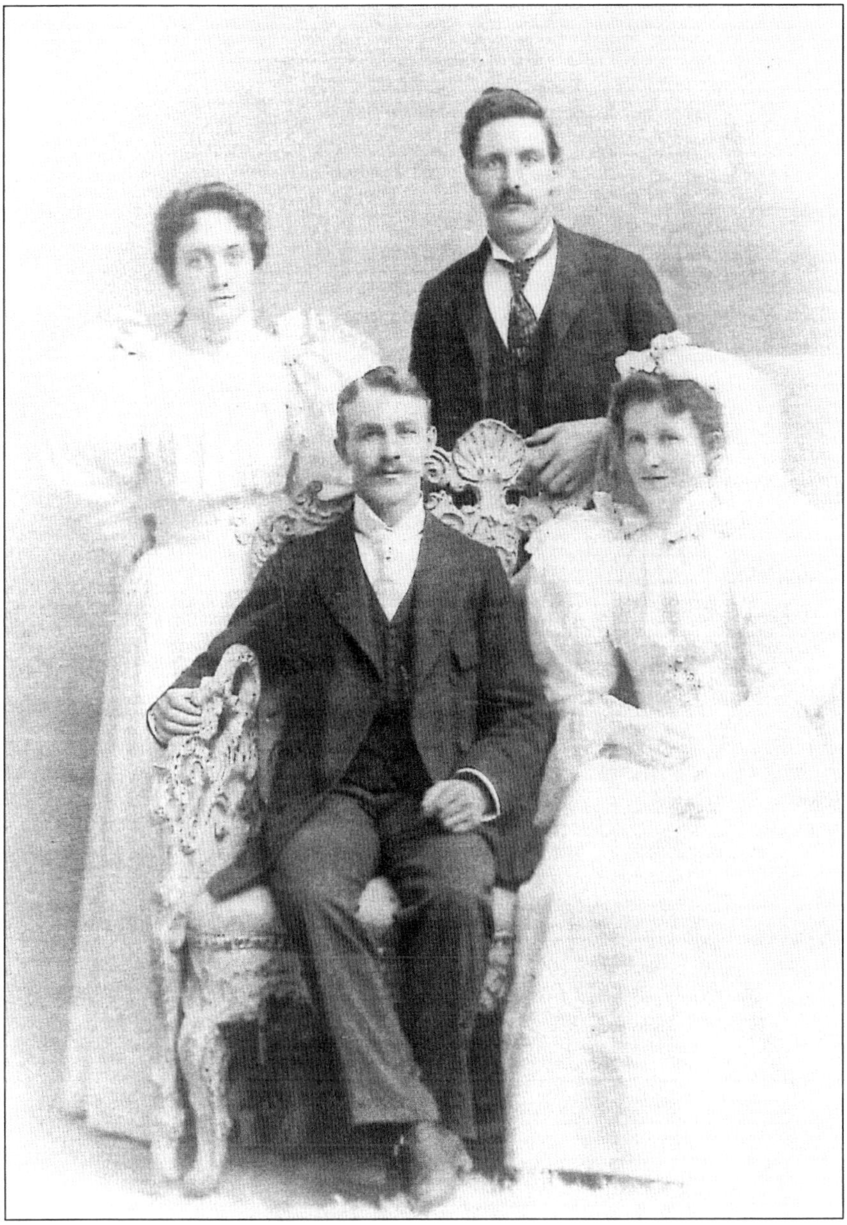

Elijah Hamlin Nash (front) and his friend Bert Coffin (rear) found love as well as permanent homes on San Juan Island after landing in Argyle in 1893 (see page 21). Here they are at Nash's wedding in February 1896 to Deborah Julia Kelly (front), who was born on the island in 1877 to John and Mary Ellen Kelly. John Kelly was a former American Camp soldier, as was Mary Ellen's father, John Hankinson (whose stepson was John Dougherty). Coffin would later marry the matron of honor on his right, Florence Hankinson Labar, Deborah's young aunt. Although Nash hailed from hearty stock (his father, a retired sea captain in Maine, would sit on his porch and bellow orders to children on a megaphone), he came west in 1890 at age 18 due to his delicate health but was stalwart enough to serve three terms in the legislature. A quiet man, Nash frustrated diarist Coffin when, on returning from the Chicago World's Fair, he barely spoke of it. "If it had been me . . . I shouldn't have been done talking about things I saw . . . to this day."

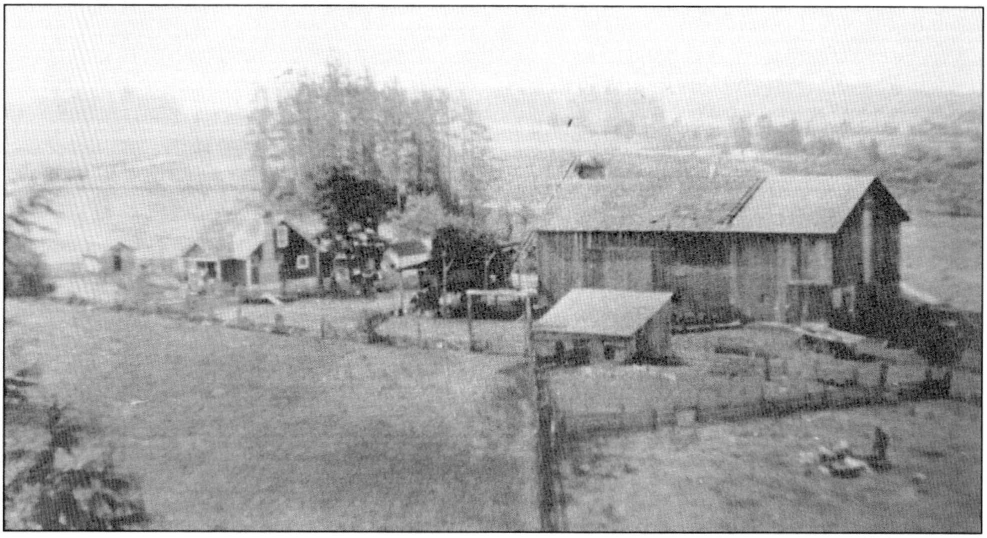

The John Sundstrom farm, captured here in the 1920s looking south from the branches of a Western red cedar tree on the property, was one of the few that remained independent when "Pea" Henry bought up the valley (page 41). Sundstrom bought the farm in 1918, and when the original house burned down, he converted the grainery, then under construction, into the home at far left (still standing). (GS.)

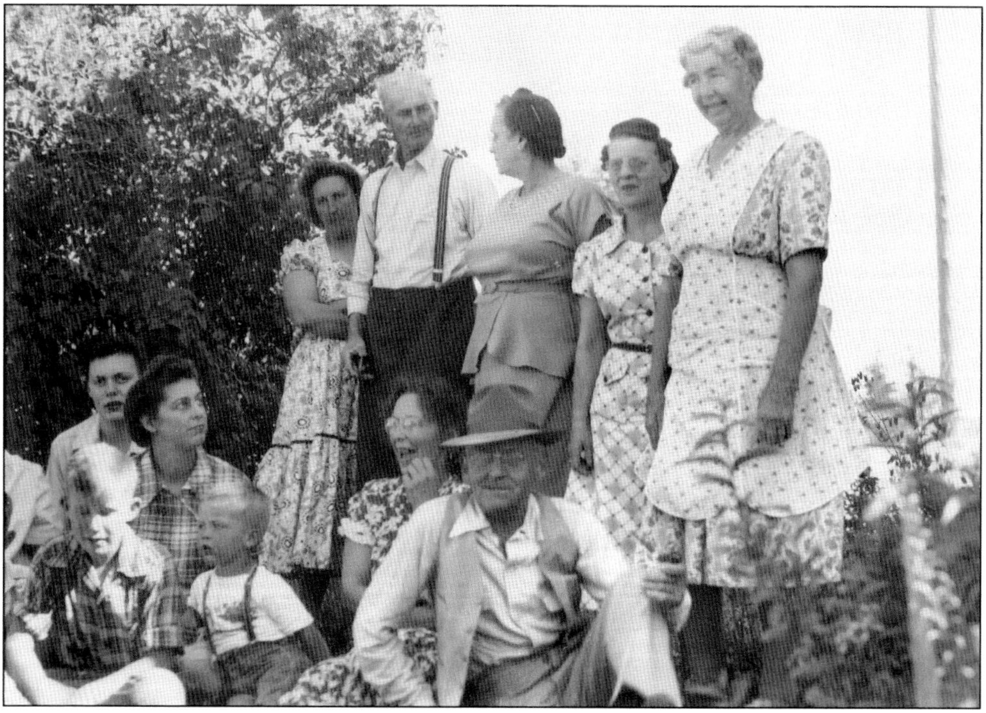

Longtime friends gather at Lizzie Lawson's farm in the summer of 1950. From left to right are (seated) an unidentified boy, Jackie Lightheart, Ulebell Lawson Wold, Donald Crosby, Etta Egeland, and Harry Egeland; (standing) Juanita Egeland Rouleau, George Lawson, Ella Lightheart, unidentified, and Lizzie Lawson. Lizzie was close to her nieces and nephews; her niece Etta lived with her off and on over the years (see page 48).

Friends Joe Lawson, left, and Lawrence Bellevue pose around 1900. Joe and his father, Peter Lawson, were both daredevils. Peter once walked across False Bay at low tide and was slogging through chest-high water by the time he reached the other side. Joe's story is more sobering. He drove over the bluff on West Side Road one night in 1927 and was found under the waters of Haro Strait.

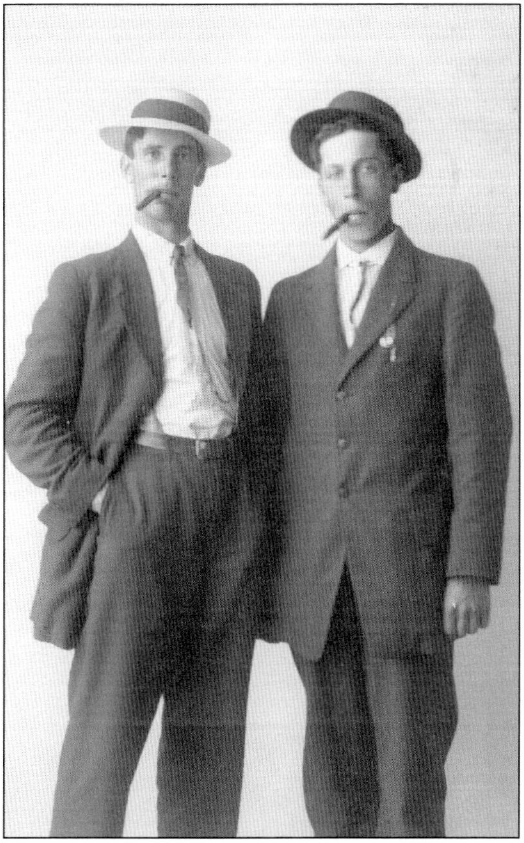

The Patrick Beigin family and friends gather at the farmhouse for a quilting party on Bailer Hill Road around 1917. Irish-born Patrick served with Pickett's troops on the island and remained after his discharge. After he eloped with Lucy Morris, a Haida from Sitka, Alaska, her family tried to kidnap her and take her home. They were unsuccessful. Lucy is seated in front, holding granddaughter Helen Beigin (Fleming).

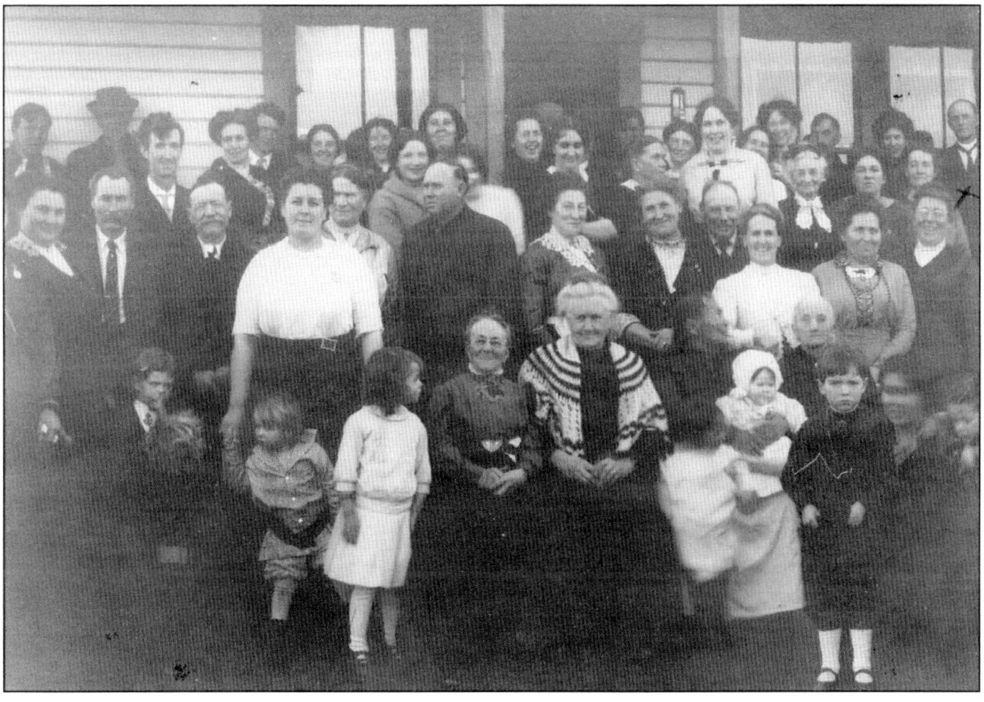

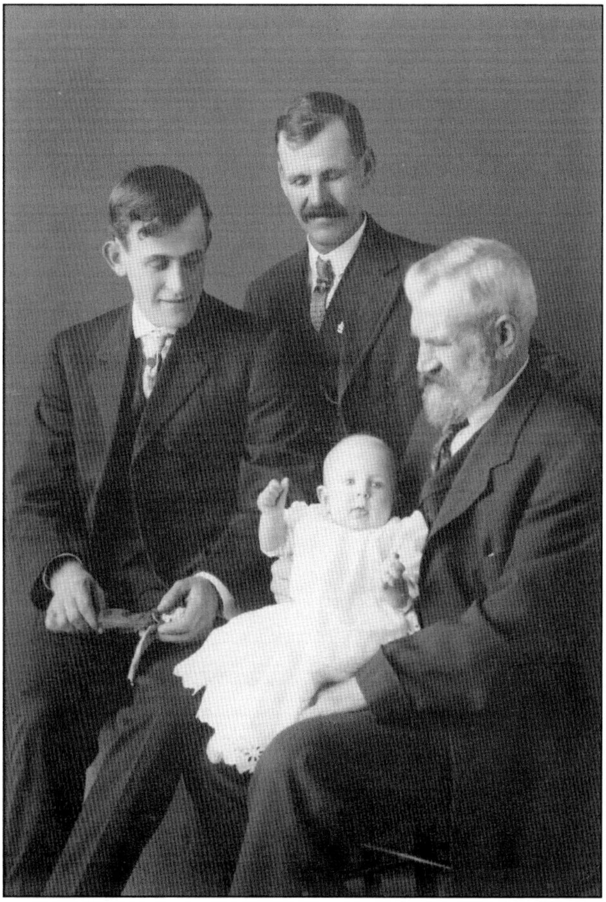

Baby Paul Guard is admired by father Roy (left), grandfather Frank, and great-grandfather Paul around 1914. Frank and Paul Sr. farmed on adjoining 80-acre pieces in Beaverton Valley, planting orchards and growing wheat, hay, and oats (one account reported 50 acres of "great, tall, well-filled oats"). Roy bought what is now the Sundstrom farm on San Juan Valley Road, and Paul Jr. became a veterinarian in Everett. (SH.)

Laura Tenney Wright escorts an elderly woman up the boardwalk on Spring Street around 1912, passing a hitching post in the road. It would not be unusual in these years to see a Model T parked next to a tied-up horse. The child hiding behind Laura's skirt may have been her grandson, Carleton Wright King, son of her daughter, Agnes, and Lyle King.

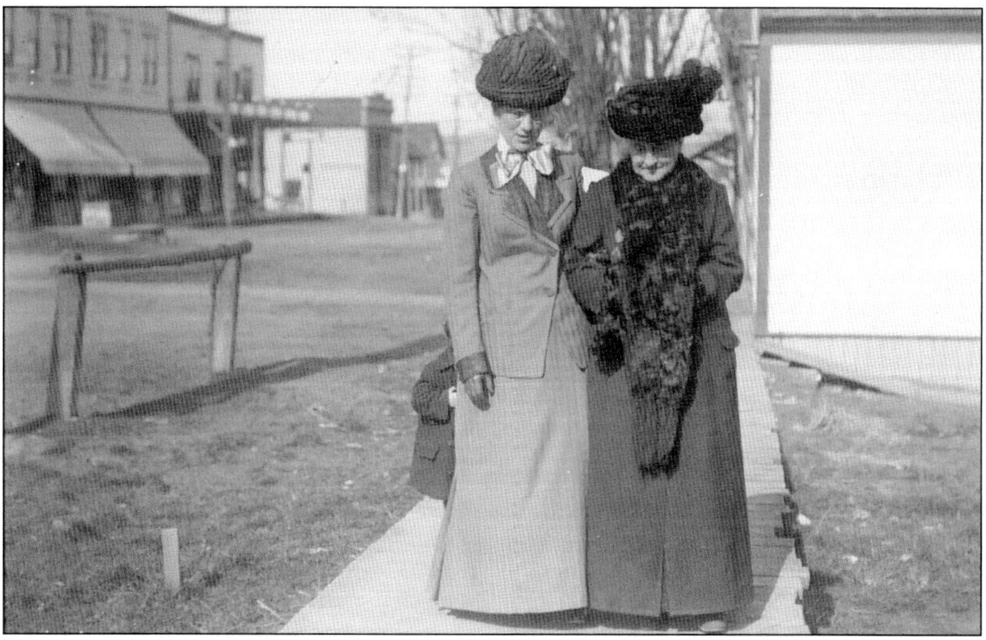

Six

The Schoolhouses

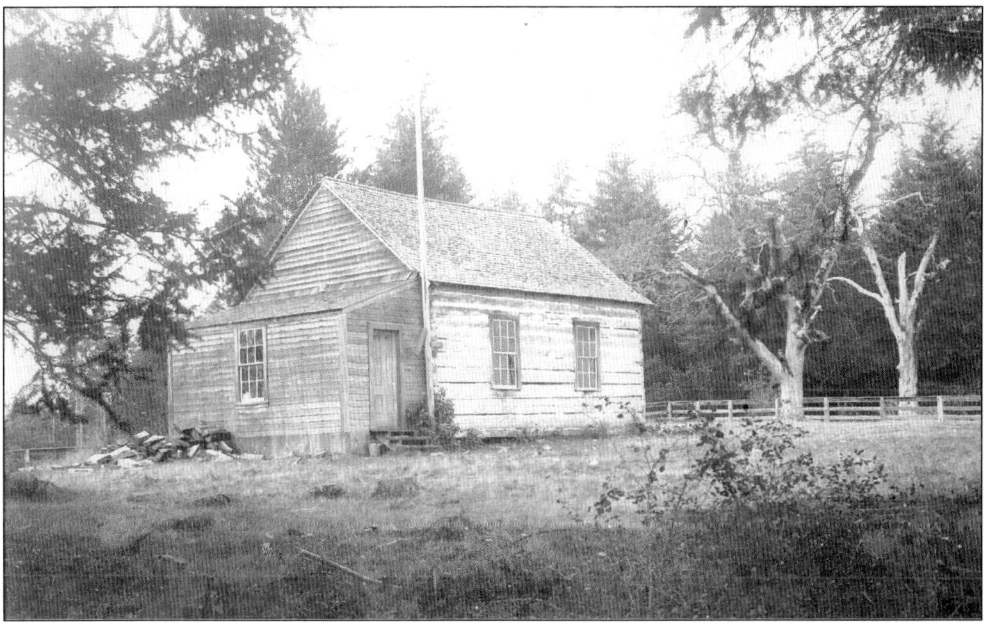

This is not the Number One Schoolhouse, as it has been depicted over the years This is the Number Two Schoolhouse, established in 1880 on No. 2 Schoolhouse Road (where else), about 100 yards from San Juan Valley Road. But it is fashioned of squared logs and has a shake roof, which also fits the description of the first community school organized through subscription in 1865 on Portland Fair Hill. Twenty-six dollars bought a two-room building, whitewashed inside and out, with long homemade tables and benches and a pot-bellied stove. Before then— and accounts vary widely—schools were organized in homes from Hannah Heights to Belle Vue Sheep Farm, the latter doubling as a church on Sunday. Most often mentioned was the home of William Bell, a future superintendent. One constant, however, is that some children walked three miles or more to school. This, combined with poor roads and harsh winters, limited classes to three summer months. However, as the population grew, five more schools were established and terms expanded to six months.

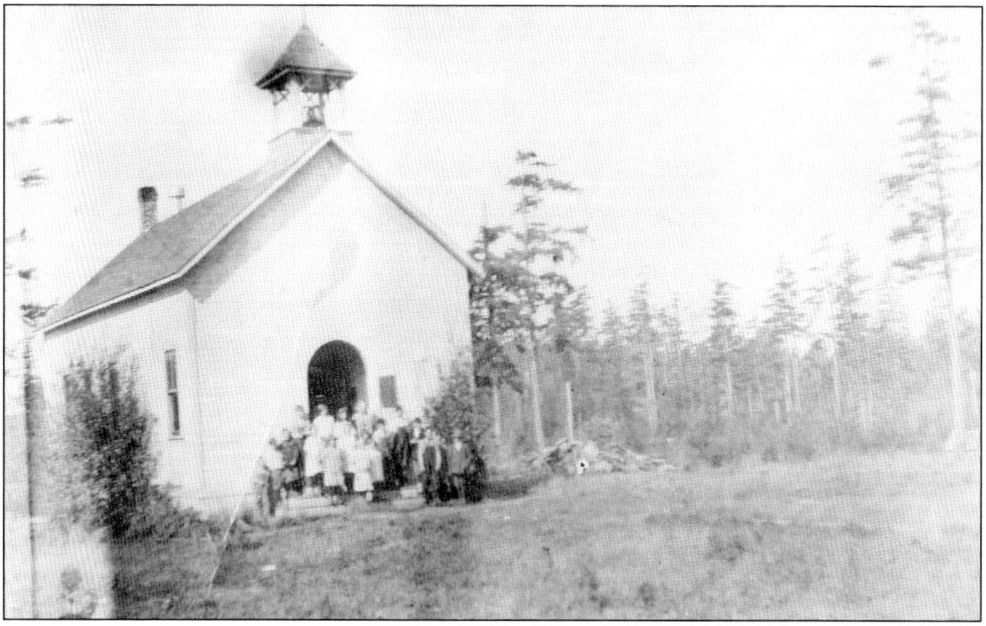

The student body gathers on the porch of the second Number One Schoolhouse, built in 1889. Parents provided books, slates, and pencils, and hired the teachers, one of whom was a former lime burner and surveyor, B. C. Gillette. Like most teachers of his day, Gillette was handy with a switch, but, recalled Henry Bailer, his tenure ended not long after sitting on a tack.

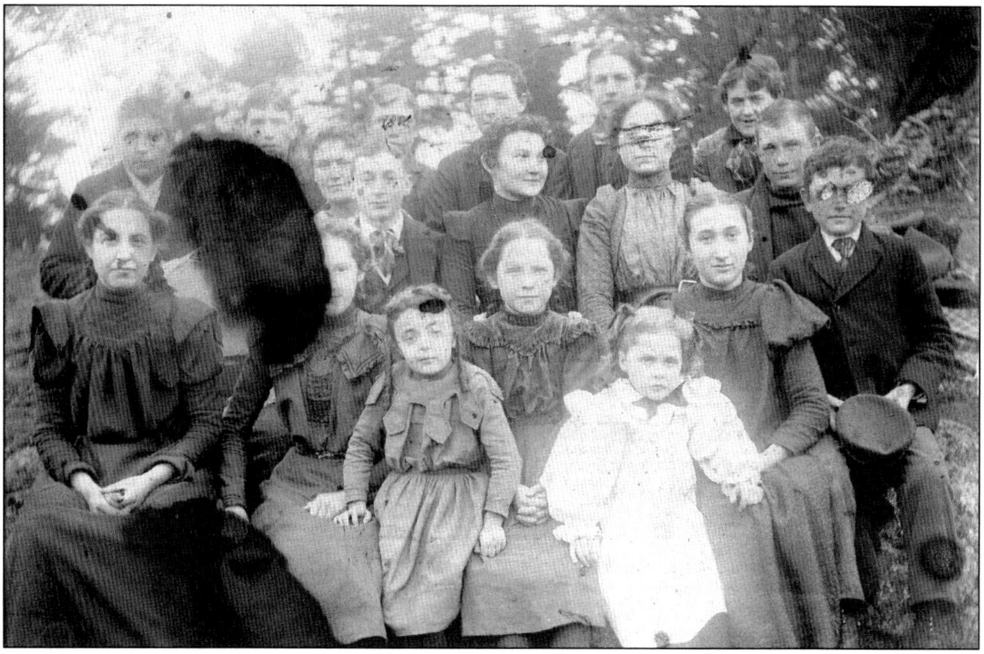

Number One Schoolhouse pupils gather for a class photograph, probably in the 1890s. By then, the terms usually ran eight months. The child at center is Sid Merrifield, daughter of Hattie Rosler and Stafford Merrifield. Four students have their eyes scratched out, including the boy and girl flanking another girl. Was this the fallout of a love triangle? Whatever, the sentiment is timeless.

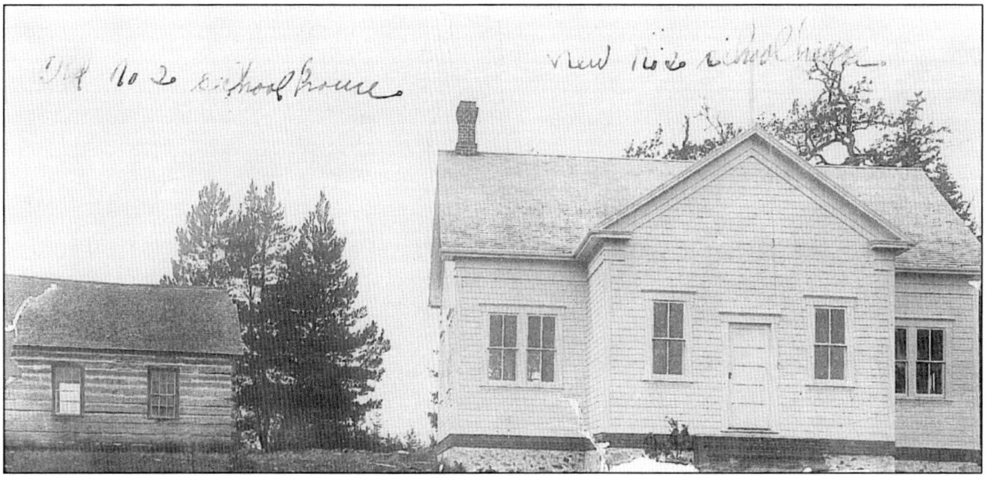

The classic lines of the 1889-vintage Number Two Schoolhouse are startling in contrast to the original log school at left and shown in full on page 93. This concrete and rock foundation was the first for any island schoolhouse, and the upper works were sound enough to provide lumber for additions to Clyde Sundstrom's house and barn. According to his son, Guard, he always regretted tearing it down.

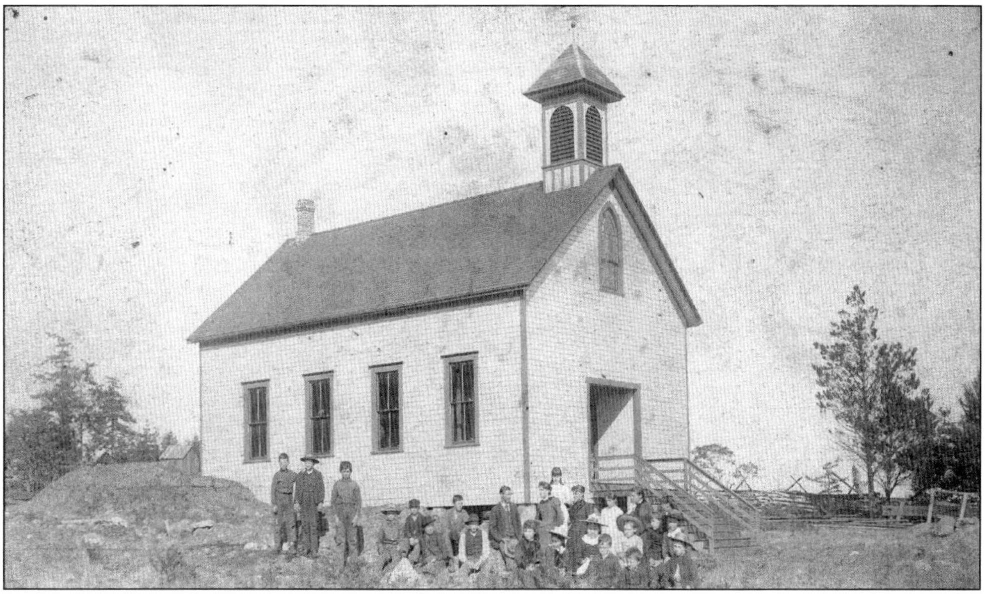

The Number 12 Schoolhouse made its debut in San Juan Valley at the base of Little Mountain in the 1880s, which was a relief to students who walked miles to Number One. As Lila Hannah Firth recalled, "From the north side . . . it was some climb for about a half mile . . . through valleys and up that terrible hill." It was one of the last schools to be consolidated.

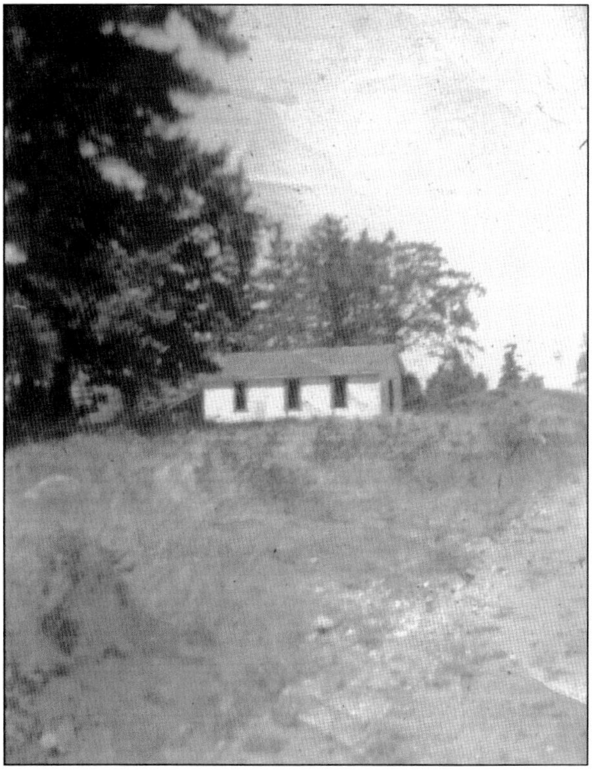

The Number Eight Schoolhouse also began as a communal effort in 1883 but was immediately too small for its 34 students. The one-room school, with Flora Guard as teacher (earning a district-wide $45 per month), was initially located on the slope of Young Hill, not far from the Royal Marine cemetery. Students attended mainly in summer. It was twice relocated, finally settling in the Mitchell Bay area in 1900.

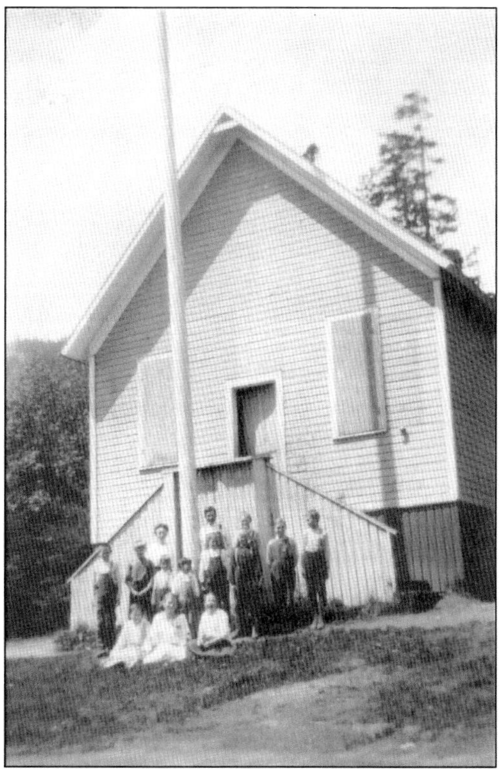

The Roche Harbor Schoolhouse was established in the 1890s for the children of lime works employees, plus spillover from the Number Eight Schoolhouse. It doubled as a church on Sundays, with services performed by a circuit rider minister. The building underwent extensive renovation from 1957 to 1960 and reopened as the Chapel of Our Lady of Good Voyage. Nondenominational services are performed to this day.

Seven

In the Spirit of Things

In February 2010, funeral services were held for Frances "Mickey" Cahail, whose casket was set beneath the altar in St. Francis Catholic Church on Price Street. More than 100 years before, Mickey was baptized near the same spot, in the same church. Then, it was on a hill overlooking San Juan Valley, at right. Across Madden Lane stands the Valley Church, once the home of the Emmanuel Presbyterian Church and the oldest house of worship on the island. It was here that the Lawson family sat in the box of a spring wagon in 1900 on their way to the cemetery, with pioneer Fanny Lawson in a casket set between them. The headstones of parishioners, from the earliest pioneers to present, surround these churches. Community spirit built them and others that followed. It moved young men to go to wars. It drew veterans to fire volleys in tribute to their sacrifices. It spurred celebrations on the Fourth of July. And, finally, it celebrated a war that never happened on San Juan Island.

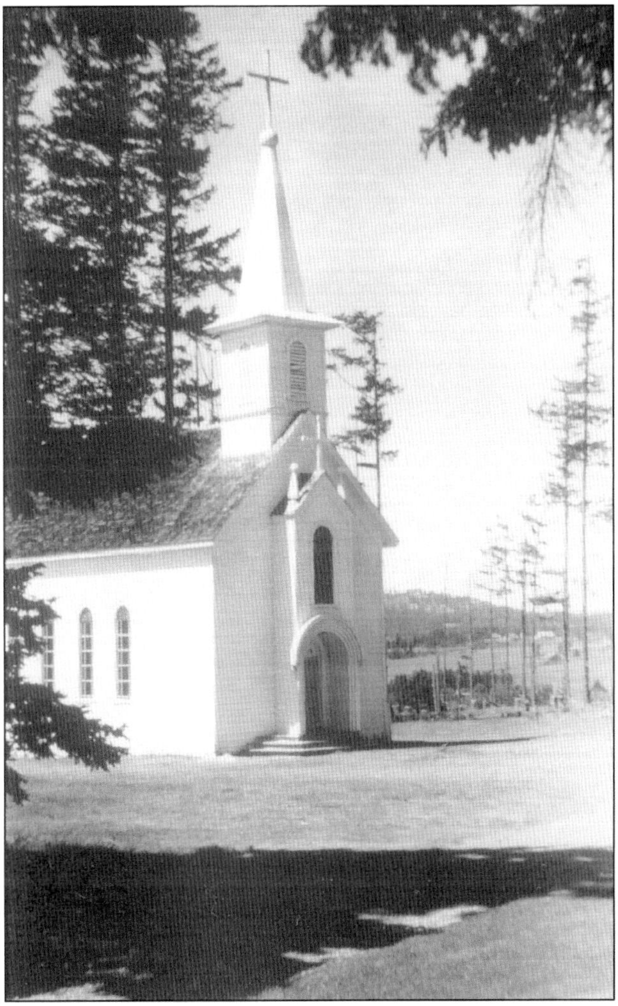

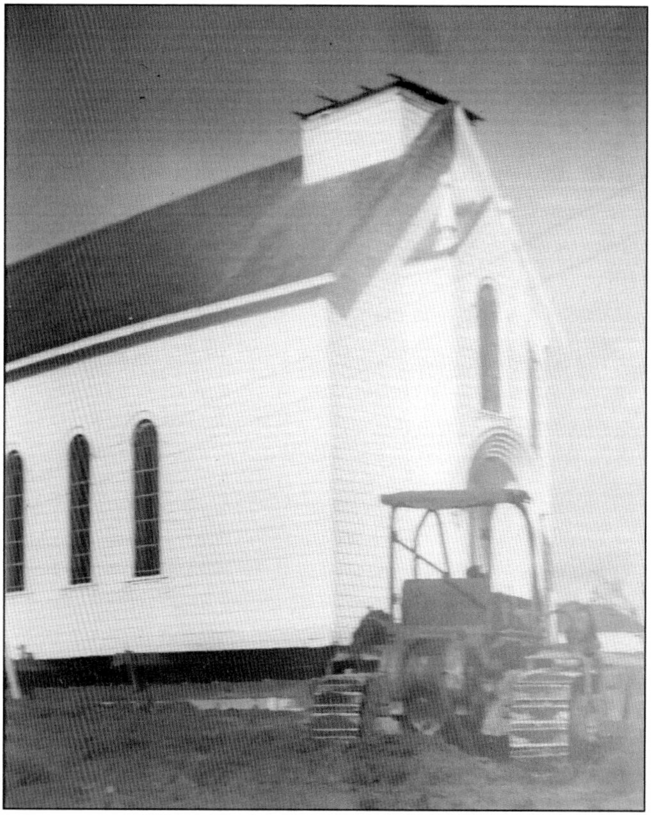

St. Francis Church began in 1860 as a Catholic mission in a log structure on Madden Lane. It was served by visiting priests, including one Canadian who went barefoot (except Sundays) to preserve his shoes. When it burned down in 1874, the present church was built with a $500 loan from the bishop and the sweat of parishioners. When moved in 1959, the steeple was shed to accommodate air traffic.

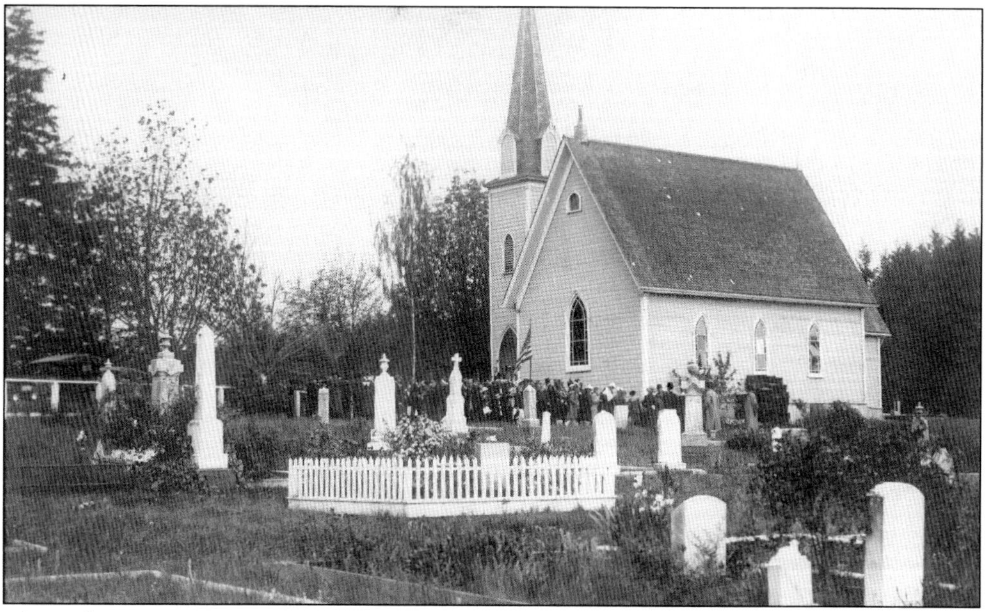

The Valley Church traces its beginnings to a cabin at Belle Vue Sheep Farm in 1860, then to the log schoolhouse at Portland Fair. Begun in 1878, the church required four years to build. The congregation moved in 1898 to a new church in Friday Harbor (still standing), which was eventually crowned by the belfry from the second Number One Schoolhouse.

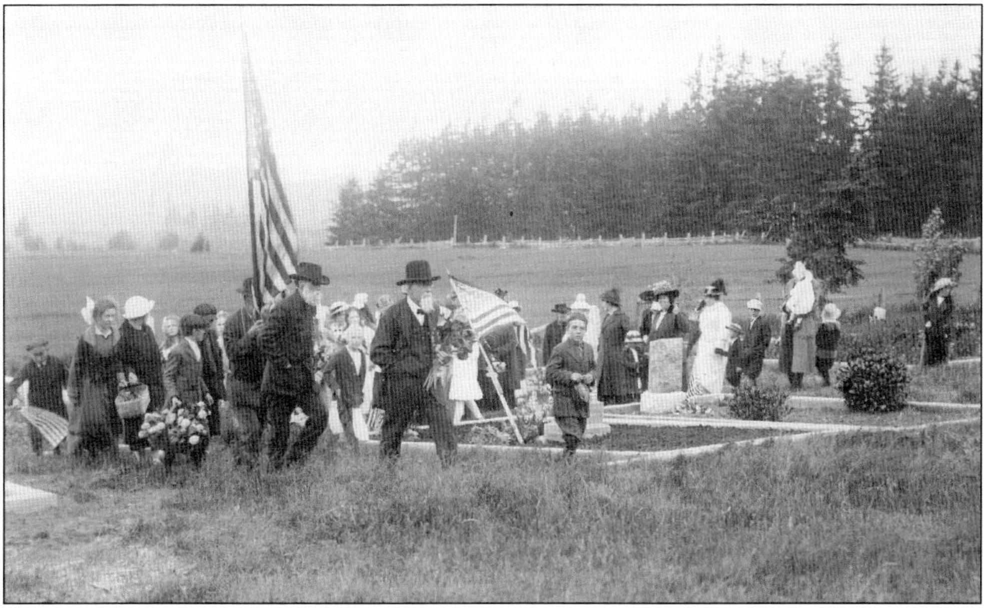

Grand Army of the Republic (GAR) members John Blair and John W. Smoots (two bearded men in foreground, Blair in the lead) head a *c.* 1914 Memorial Day commemoration at Valley Cemetery. Both fought in the Union Army during the Civil War. Memorial Day was first observed officially on May 30, 1868, but only in the Northern states.

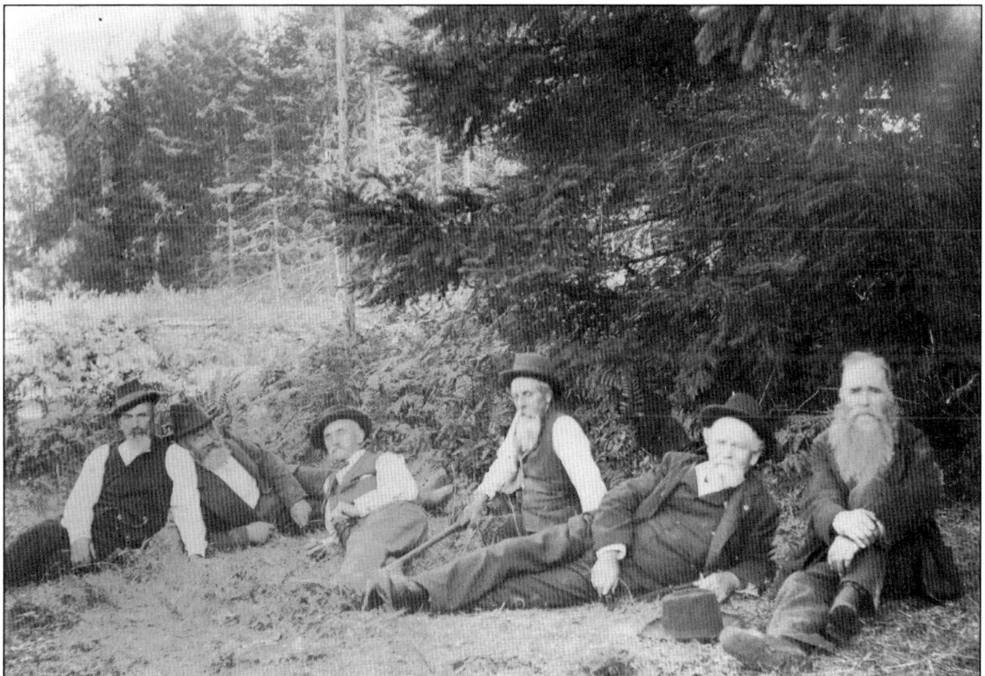

John Blair and George Dightman (second and third from right, respectively), and fellow (mostly bearded) Grand Army of the Republic (GAR) veterans take their ease on the edge of a woodland. The GAR began shortly after the war as a champion of racial equality, but when membership flagged, it redirected itself to veterans' rights and set the pattern for all succeeding veterans groups.

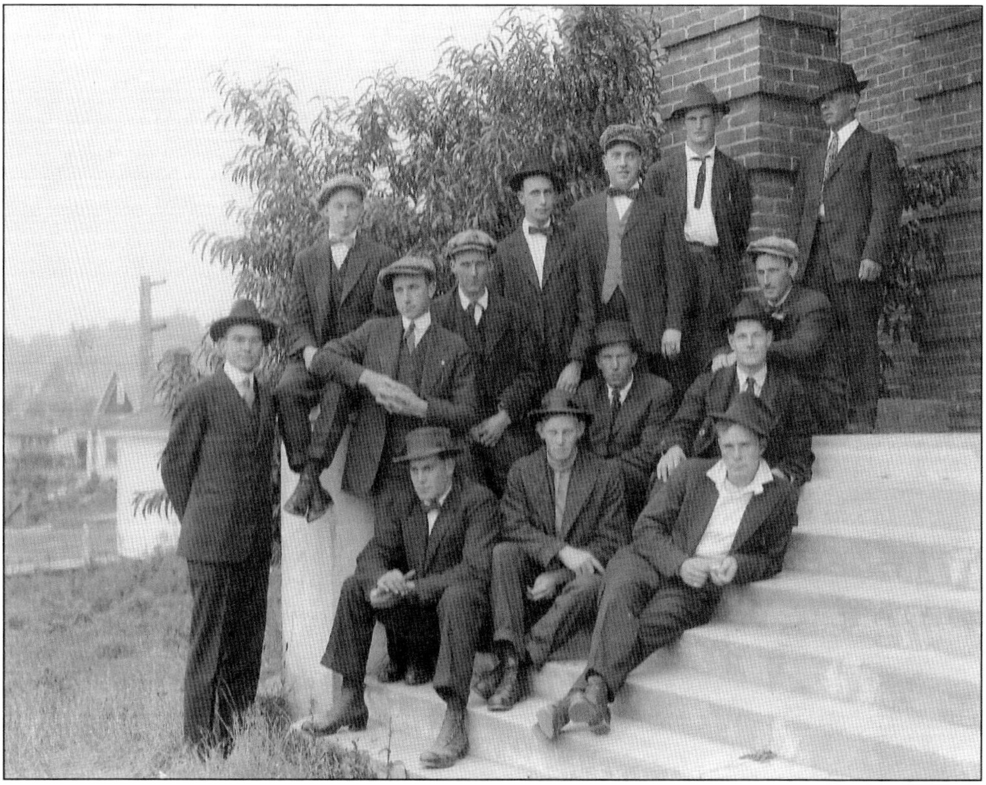

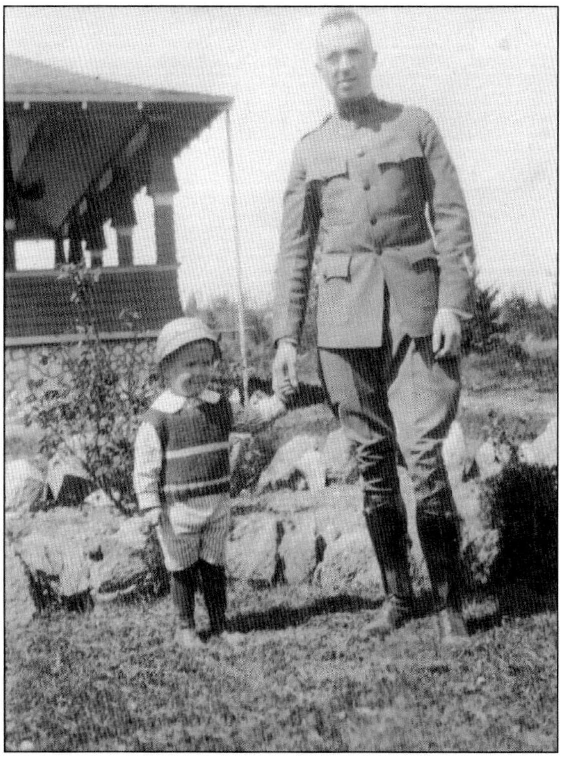

Though seated on the courthouse steps, these sober young men are not on jury duty but will soon be off to serve in the armed forces in World War I. One hundred and twenty four San Juan County men would serve. Among those pictured are Rodger Wills, seated on bottom step with hands folded, and above him, Walt Arend, whose arm rests on Calvin Lightheart's knee.

Fred Hackett, right, shown here with his cousin Frank Douglas, was one of nine San Juan County men killed in the war. Hackett was a private in the 1st Infantry Division when he fell near Montdidier, France, in May 1918. He was 19. American Legion Post 163 is named for Hackett as well as Bud Curtis Larson, who was killed on October 11, 1918, exactly one month before the Armistice.

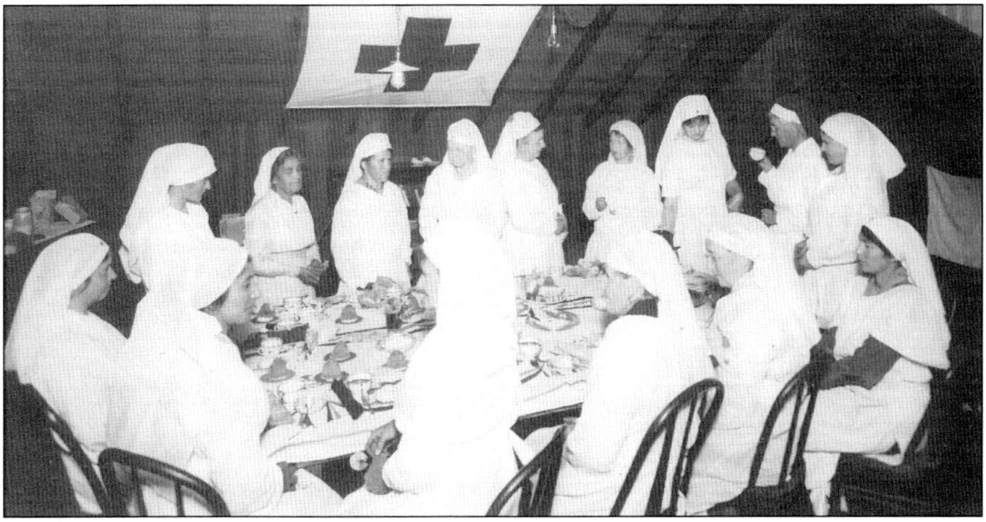

The San Juan Chapter of the American Red Cross meets for lunch in 1918 in the cannery complex. The "Home Front" effort on the island and throughout the county exceeded expectations throughout the war, purchasing nearly $300,000 in war bonds and raising $11,482 in relief funds. This Red Cross chapter earned national recognition for shipping more than 33,000 pieces of garments and battle dressings.

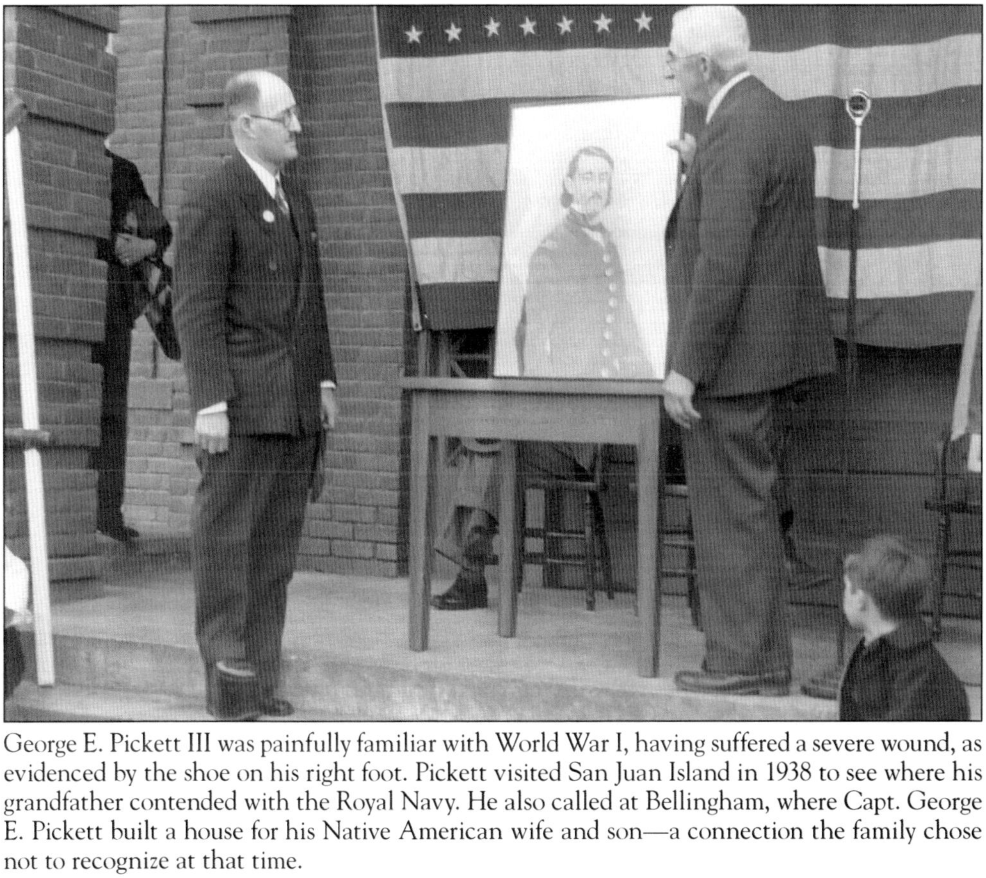

George E. Pickett III was painfully familiar with World War I, having suffered a severe wound, as evidenced by the shoe on his right foot. Pickett visited San Juan Island in 1938 to see where his grandfather contended with the Royal Navy. He also called at Bellingham, where Capt. George E. Pickett built a house for his Native American wife and son—a connection the family chose not to recognize at that time.

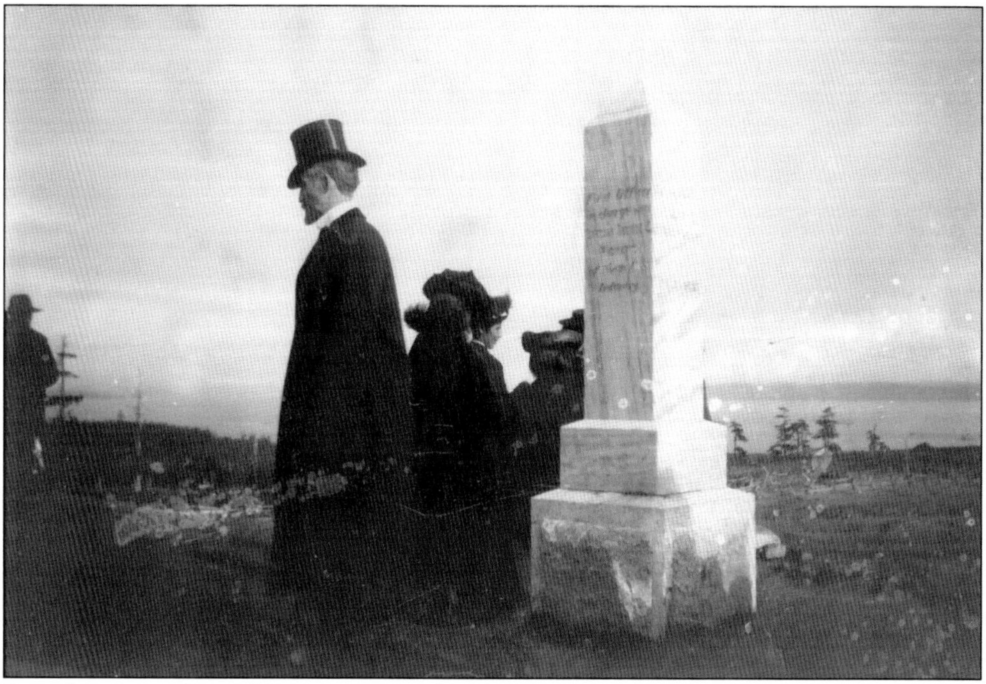

Forty-five years after 2nd Lt. Henry M. Robert built a redoubt at American Camp to intimidate the Royal Navy anchored in Griffin Bay, celebrants gather around a monument emplaced on its ramparts on October 21, 1904. This and an identical cenotaph at English Camp were placed by the Washington University State Historical Society to commemorate the shots that were never fired by the fortification.

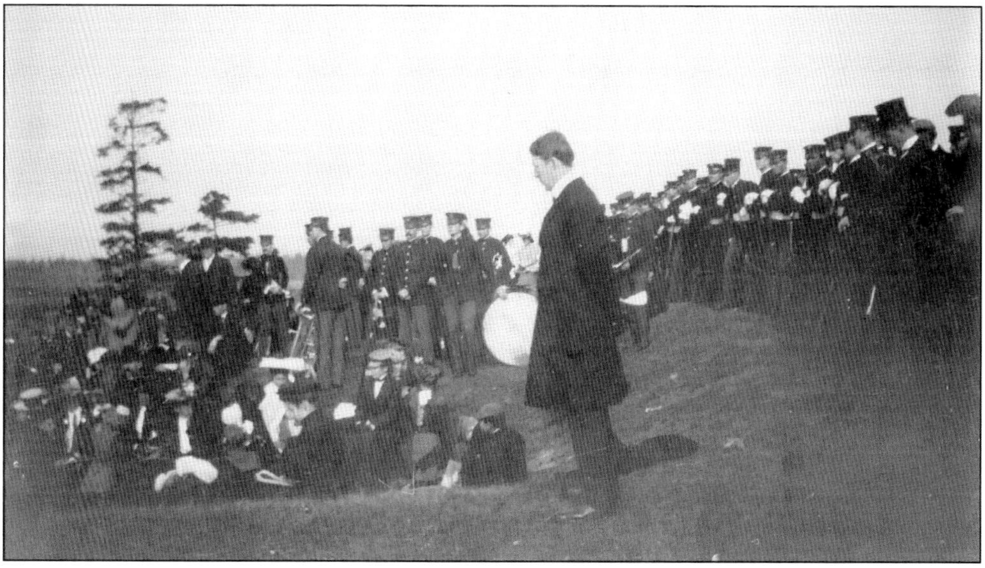

Rev. C. C. Pratt of Friday Harbor gathers his thoughts before speaking at the dedication of the Pig War monument at American Camp. The band and troops are from the Puget Sound Artillery, who accompanied the party from the site of the defunct San Juan Town. After speeches by U.S. and British officials and a keynote address by John McMillin of Roche Harbor, the monitor USS *Wyoming* fired a salute.

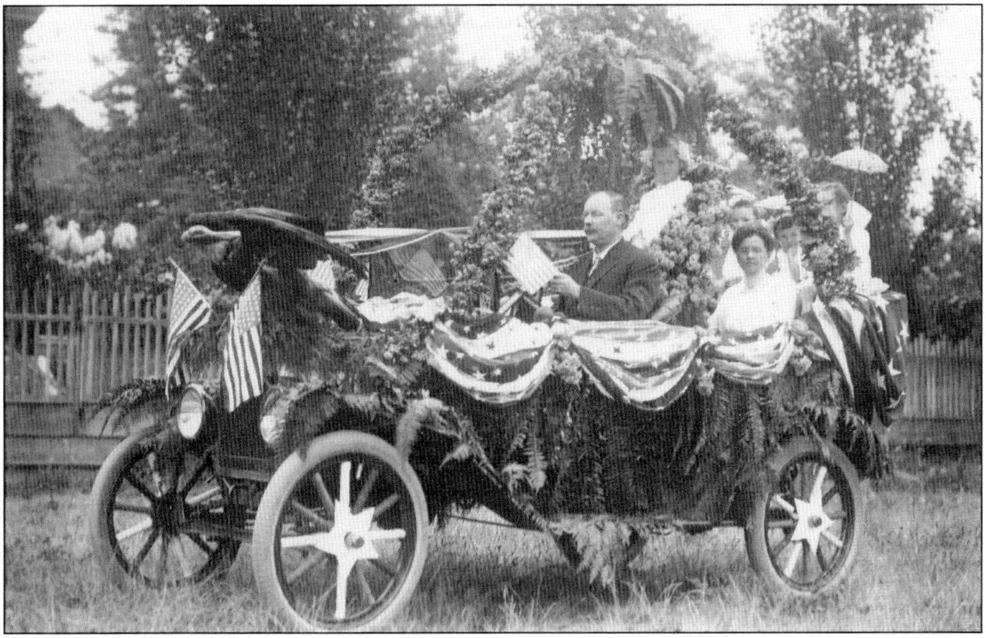

Clarence M. Tucker and family do not seem very excited about their winning entry in the 1918 Fourth of July parade in Friday Harbor. This car created almost as big a stir as the Grand Sweepstakes winner that had a cannon mounted on the radiator. Tucker founded the gristmill at Argyle in 1886 and went on to become vice president of San Juan County Bank.

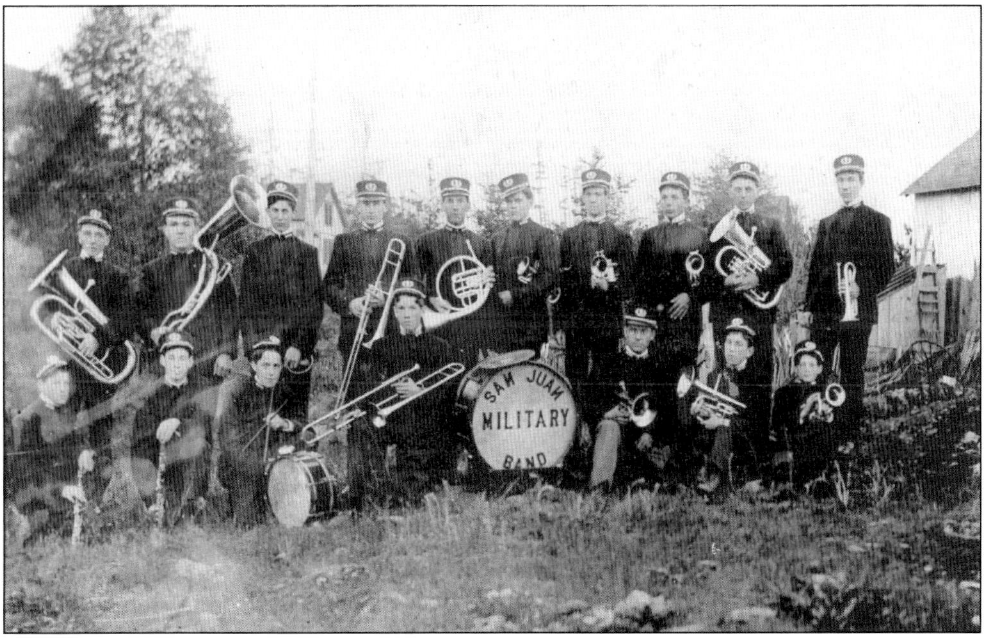

The San Juan Military band, around 1908, awaits the start of the Fourth of July parade in a vacant lot in Friday Harbor. The band's leader, Van Sargent, is standing at far right above diminutive trumpeter Stanley Madden. Cecil Carter kneels second from left next to snare drummer Homer Murray, who went on to form a popular dance combo with his wife, Marguerite, who played the piano.

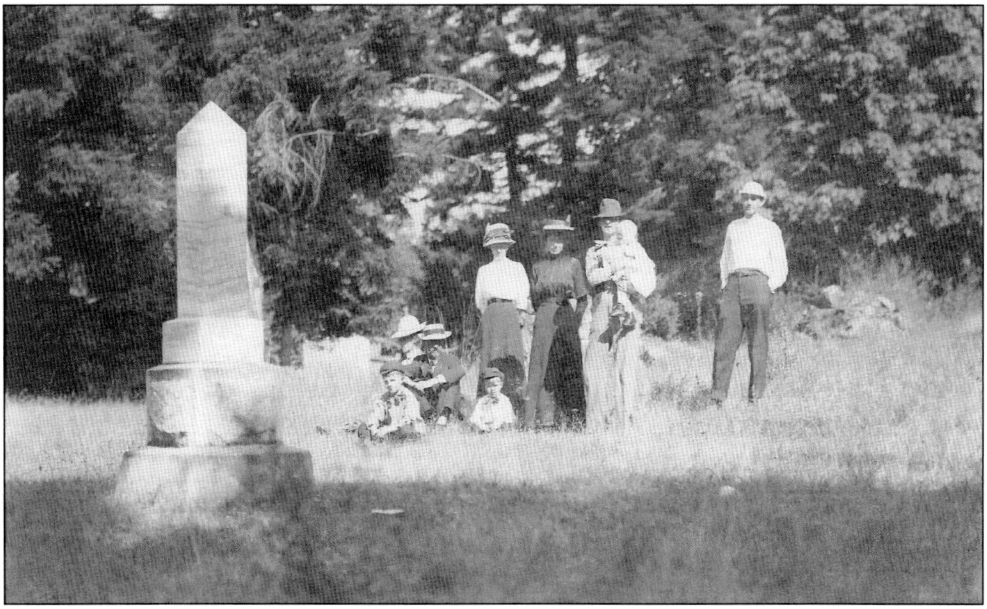

Cannery comptroller Claire Washburn and family visit the Pig War monument on the commanding officer's terrace at English Camp around 1913. Seated next to the children are Herbert and Mary Crook Davis. Nine years earlier on this spot, John McMillin said, "Forty-five years ago less than 45 people lived within the San Juan Islands . . . Today 3,500 people find happy homes."

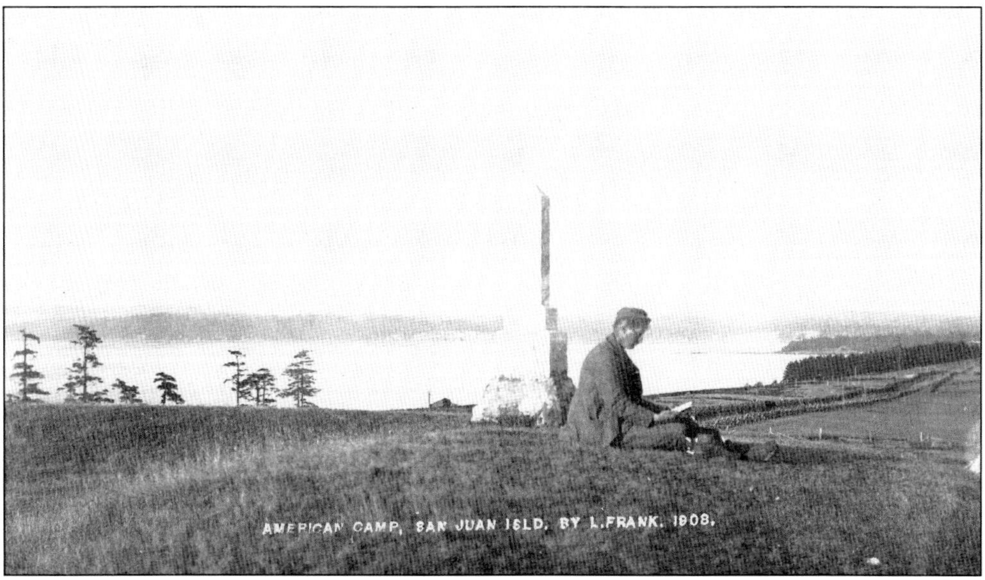

An unidentified young man reads while resting against the American Camp Pig War monument (erected in 1904) in this *c.* 1908 image. The county road, bordered by a split-rail fence, follows pretty much the same route as the Redoubt Road in San Juan Island National Historical Park, only then it terminated near today's Jakle's Lagoon trailhead.

Eight

Community Connections

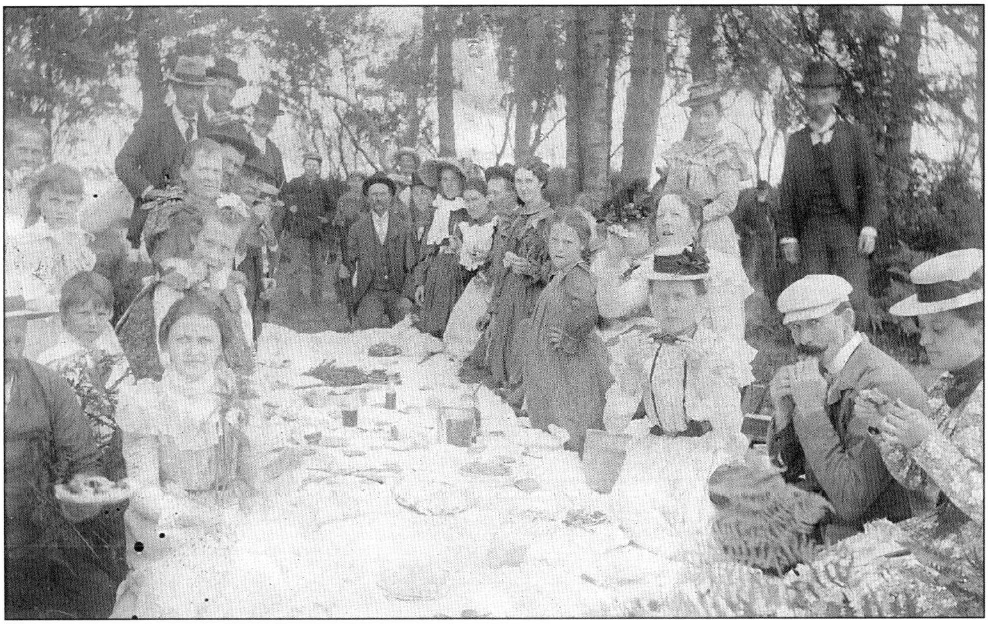

In the tough, early days of the frontier, San Juan Island's pioneers were closely connected, sharing in one another's lives and pitching in as help was needed. They raised barns together, shared farming equipment and chores, traded vegetables for fruit, fresh turkey for lamb. People not only worked together, they played together. Huge, extended families, friends, and neighbors gathered for supper, dancing, music making, hay wagon rides, and games. At night, they would gather around a potbellied stove to spin yarns, sing songs, play cards, and perhaps fetch some apples from the root cellar for a treat. Whole families went to quilting bees as yet another opportunity to exchange news about crops, horses, relationships, and their children. And islanders loved picnics. Here in 1894, the Guard family and friends gather under the firs. At 4:00 p.m., all the men would go home to do chores, then return for more. Note Frank Guard, with gray moustache and hat, peering from the end of the table at left.

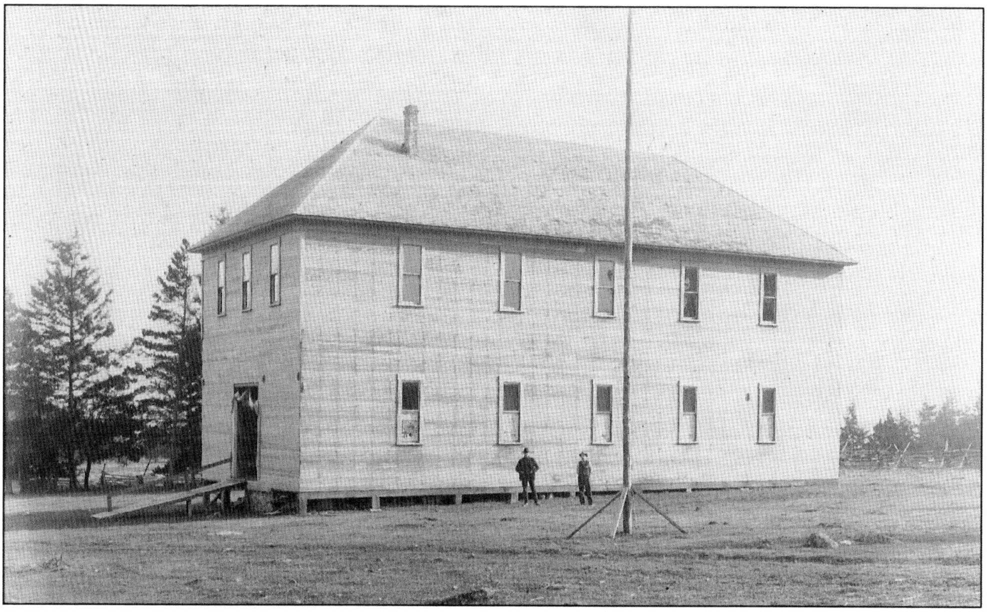

When Edna Dougherty married Julius Johnson on Christmas in 1928, her parents hosted a party in their home. When it became too crowded to dance, her father, Ed, chucked the Christmas tree out the door—decorations and all. This story sums up the islanders' love of dancing. Often they would gather at a large home, such as the Boyce or Bailer farm, where someone was always ready to play a fiddle or mouth organ. The Woodmen of the World Hall, above and below, hosted many dances on its French-milled timber dance floor that lasted from early evening until the next morning. This time, the men would leave at 4:00 a.m. to go home for chores and return for breakfast. "Oh, how these people can dance," wrote Bert Coffin in 1893. "Some ladies don't miss one dance until 5 or 6 the next morning."

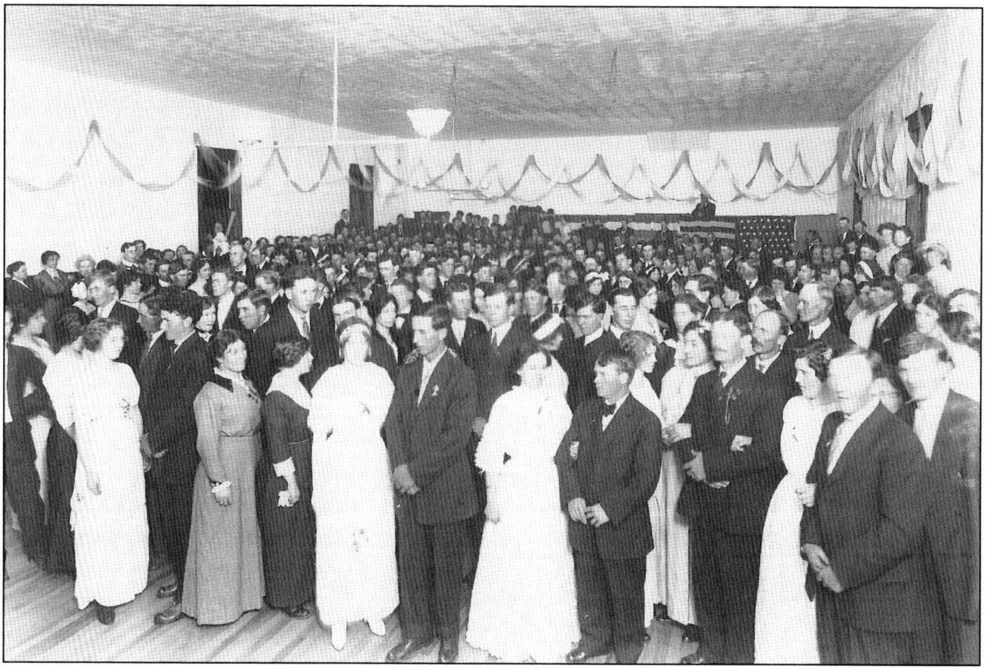

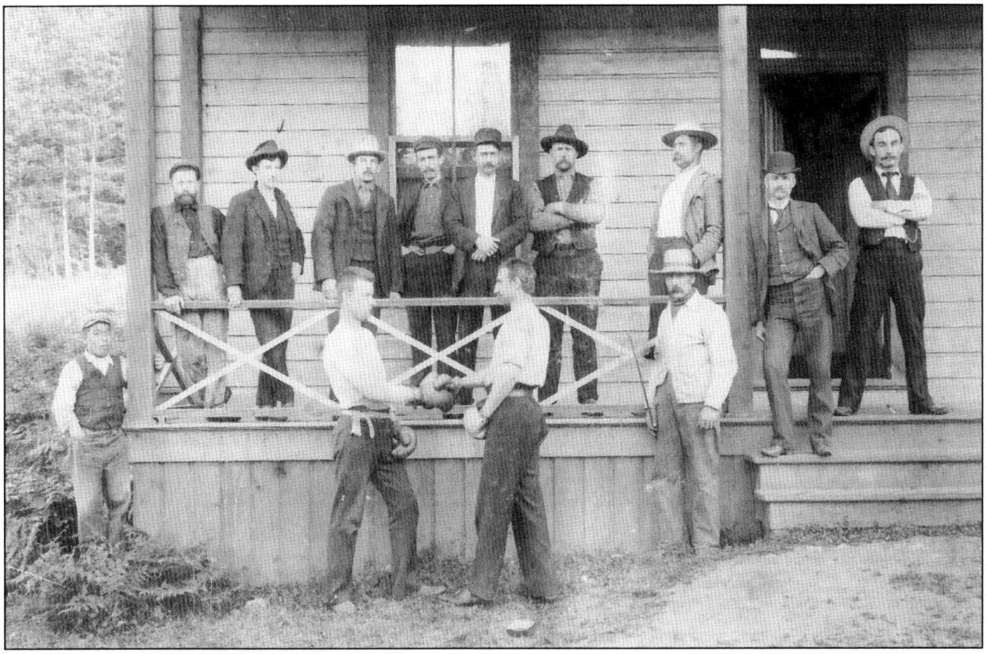

Amateur fisticuffs with money on the line, such as this set-to, were certain to draw interest from the young set as Bert Coffin attested in his diary. On Christmas 1894, after viewing a runaway team of horses and buying a turkey raffle ticket, Bert joined the sparring with several of the boys, "and for a wonder without getting a bloody nose."

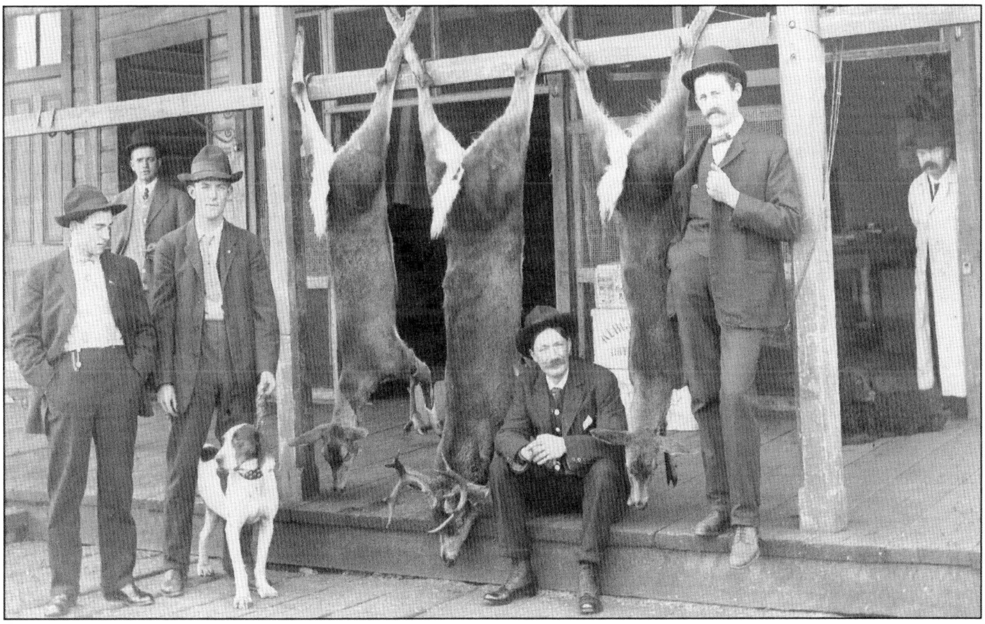

From left to right, hunters Gerry Terry (with dog), Jim Frazer, and Fred Terry proudly pose with their kill. The San Juans have always been abundant with Columbia blacktail deer that on rare occasions are spotted swimming between islands. Islanders have long been barricading their gardens from these indiscriminate nibblers. The fellow in the doorway wearing the duster undoubtedly did the slaughtering.

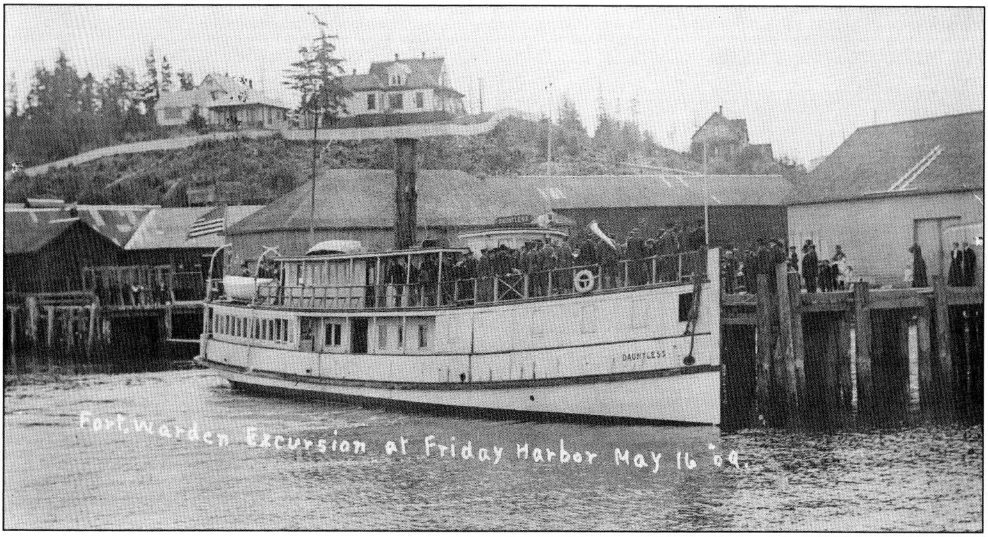

Soldier-baseball players and the Fort Worden Military Band, accompanied by "lusty rooters," prepare to disembark from the steamer *Dauntless* in anticipation of the big game with Friday Harbor on May 16, 1909. Cannery buildings are in the background, and the home of Friday Harbor's first mayor, Gene Gould, sets on the crown of Harrison Street hill.

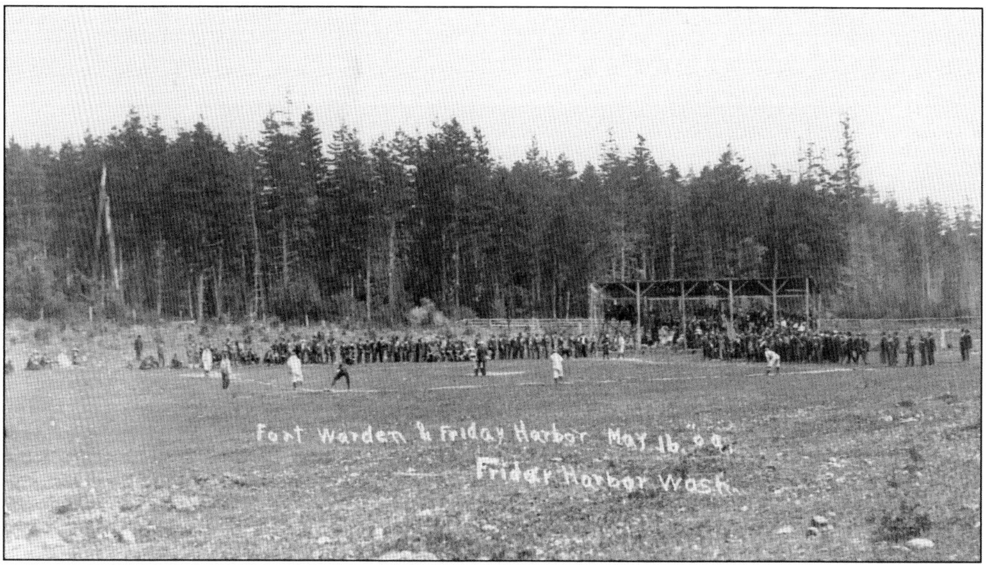

The *Friday Harbor Journal* reported more than 500 fans in the stands to watch star pitcher and former Northwest League professional "Cyclone Bill" Rosler frustrate the Fort Worden nine with "swift twirlers." Meanwhile, Friday Harbor batters "hit several skyward which floated gaily over the field, giving a home run or two, and occasionally much lung exercise." Rosler enjoyed later renown as a square dance caller.

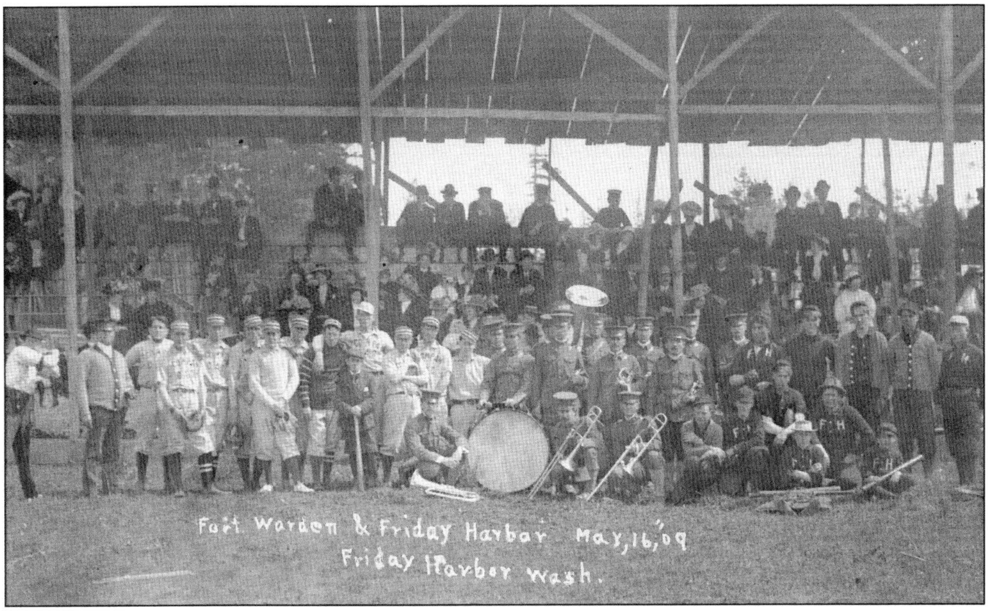

Friday Harbor won the ball game 11-8, thanks to some heavy hitting, as the score indicates that Rosler probably tired in late innings. Here the players and Fort Worden band conclude the afternoon with a commemorative photograph. The band won a gold medal at the Portland exposition and later played at the Alaska Yukon Pacific Exposition in Seattle.

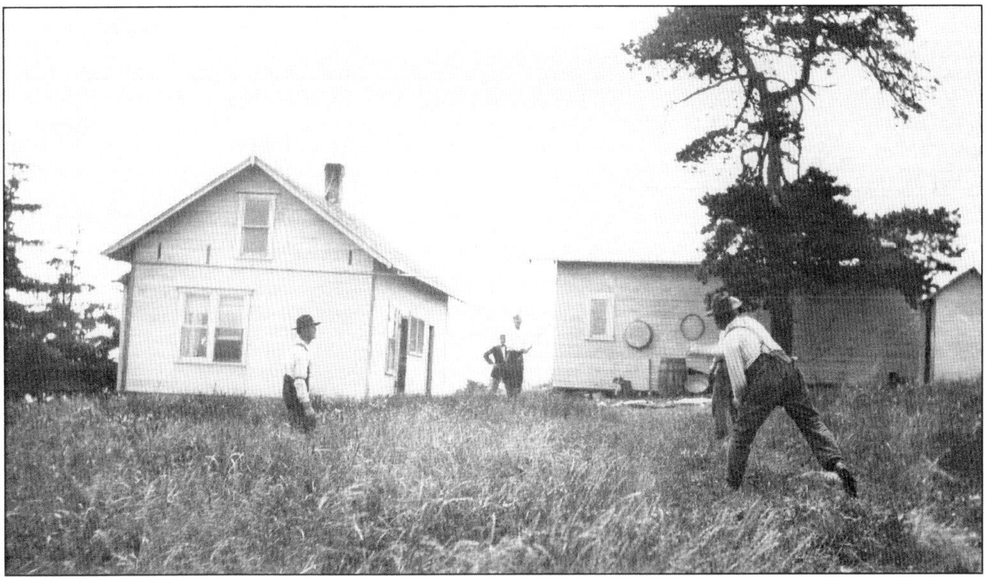

Baseball in the early 20th century was king, far surpassing football or any other team sport as the preferred activity for either viewing or playing, especially during Sunday afternoon picnics. Here the pitcher, probably Andy Johnson, lets fly with a "twirler" while hitter George Lawson prepares to take a cut in the backyard of Adeline and Anton Thrones.

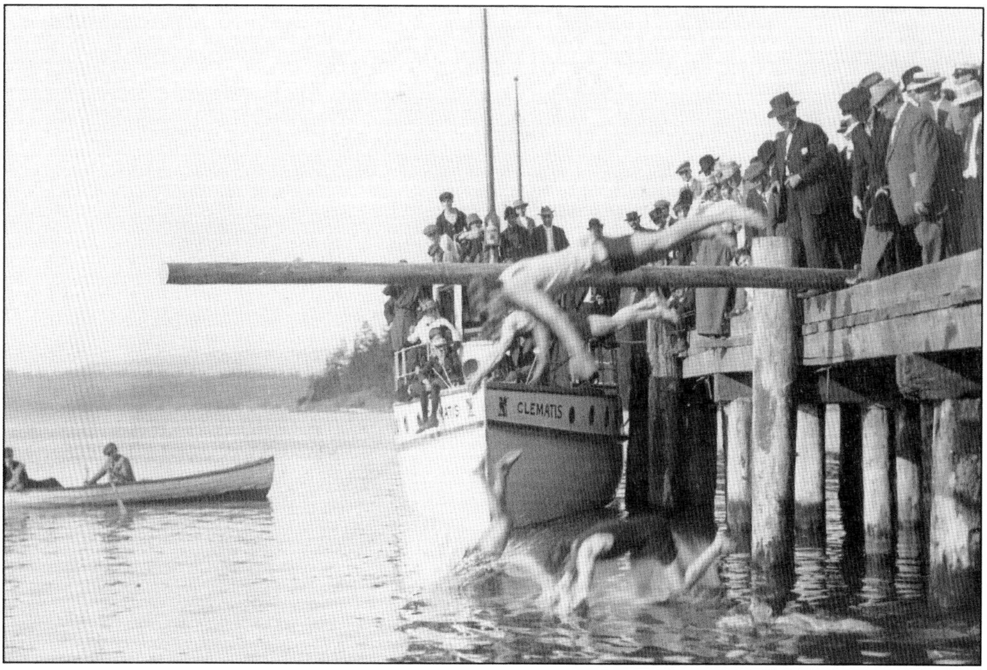

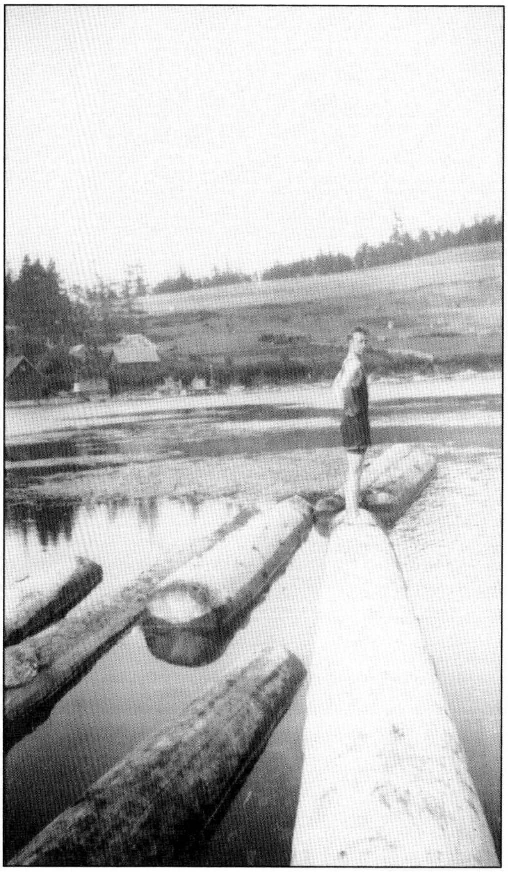

Some of the most popular events during Fourth of July celebrations were the swimming and grease pole contests. Kids jumped off the city float into the water, which was not as cold as one might imagine. For one thing, woolen bathing suits lessened the sting. But this is also where the sewer ran into the bay. The hardier kids used to swim clear across the harbor to Brown Island.

A swimmer poses before the dive at the lagoon, located on the landward side of Jackson Beach. This was a popular swimming hole because the creek winding down from Bald Hill warmed the water's surface. A raft was anchored in the middle, and occasionally a lifeguard was on duty. "We ran on logs and fished for bullheads until we all got wet and came home," said Jim Cahail.

Four generations of Boyces are, clockwise from right, Lucinda holding her great granddaughter (Josie's daughter, unidentified), granddaughter Josie Sweeney Turner, and daughter Alice Sweeney. Called the "First Lady of the San Juans," Lucinda was respected and beloved by Native Americans as well as Euro-Americans. Her grandchildren would sit for hours as she told stories, sang songs, and knitted, waiting for a trinket to pop out of her ball of yarn. (KR.)

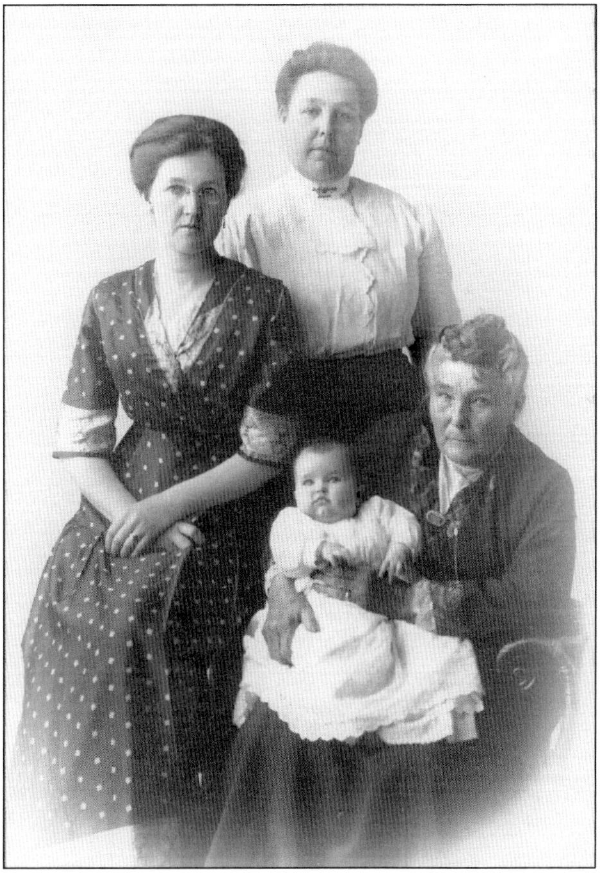

Paul Guard gives his son Robert (in sailor suit) and nephew Vic Reynolds a push on a swing set in Ray and Gladys Guard Madden's backyard on Pear Point Road. The occasion was his grandfather Frank Guard's 80th birthday party in June 1941. Molly Madden, daughter of Ray and Gladys, is at far left. The Guard family is linked with the Maddens, Wilsons, Douglases, Reynoldses, Prentisses, and Sundstroms. (SH.)

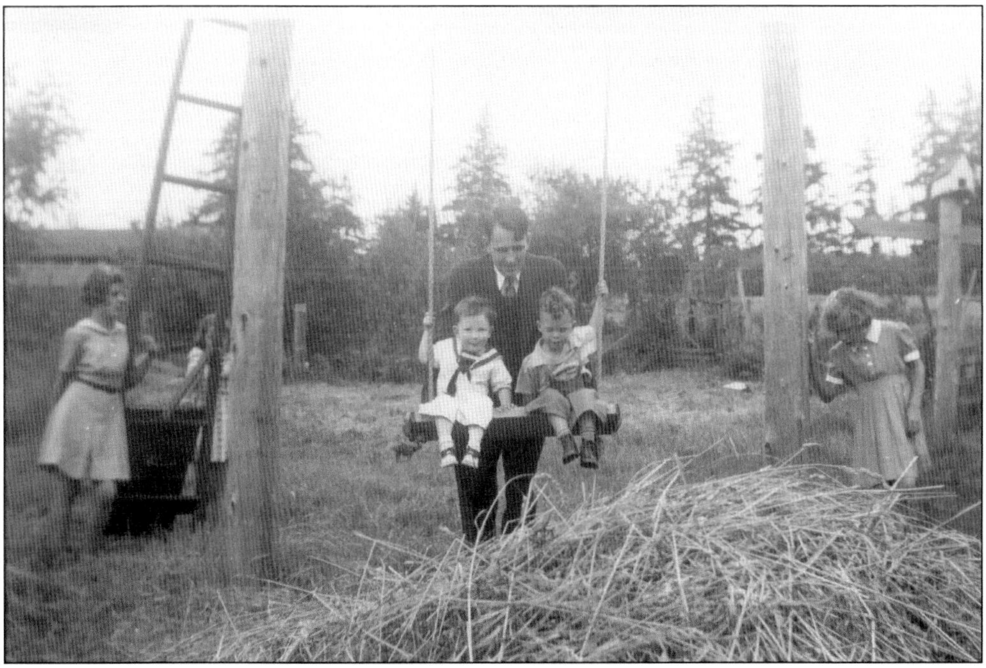

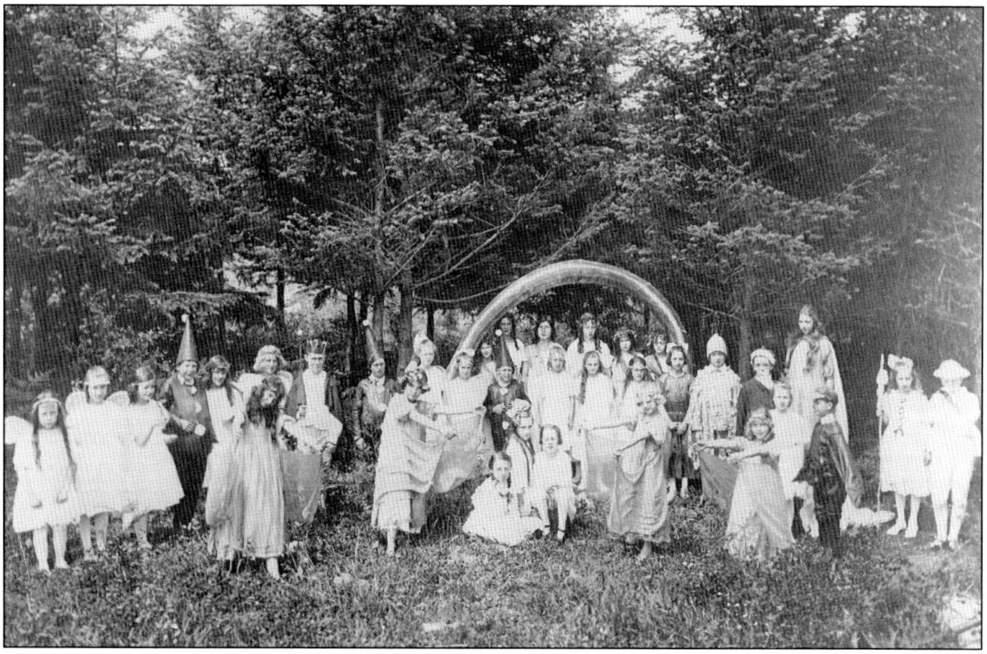

Even before Island Stage Left (the local Shakespeare company), San Juan Island residents entertained themselves with outdoor theatricals, including the occasional play by the bard. This Friday Harbor High School pageant presented a locally adapted version of *A Midsummer Night's Dream*. The photograph is entitled "Masque: What Fools These Mortals Be."

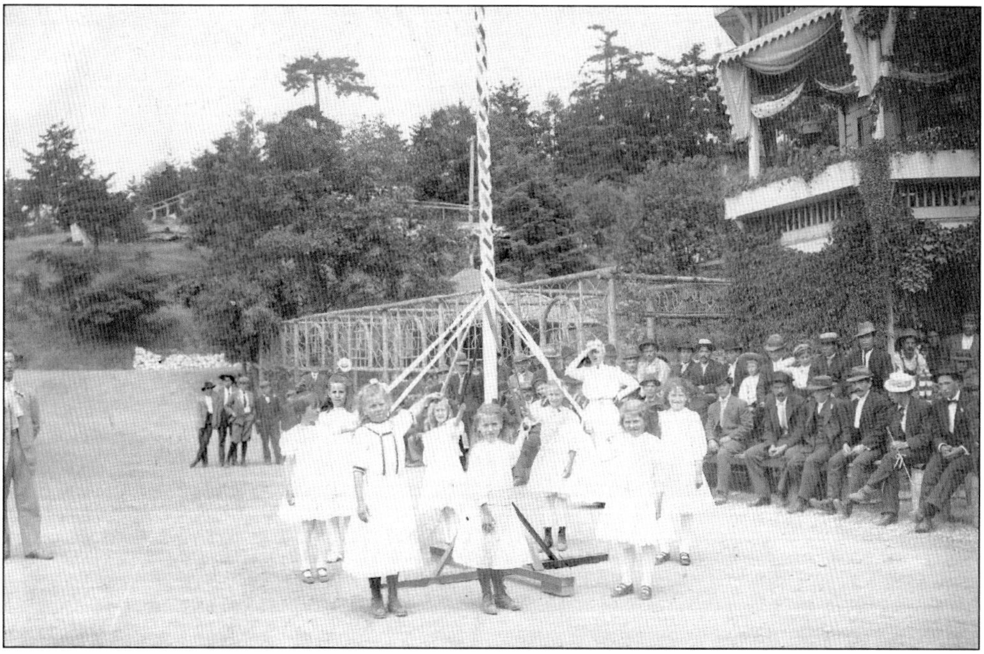

A rapt audience—all in hats—watches as schoolgirls in white dresses dance around the maypole in a rite of spring in Roche Harbor around 1910. Each holds a ribbon attached to the top of the pole, and as they go 'round, the ribbon decorates the pole in spring colors. To the right is Hotel de Haro, festooned with ivy, and an outdoor dining area enclosed in a handmade fence.

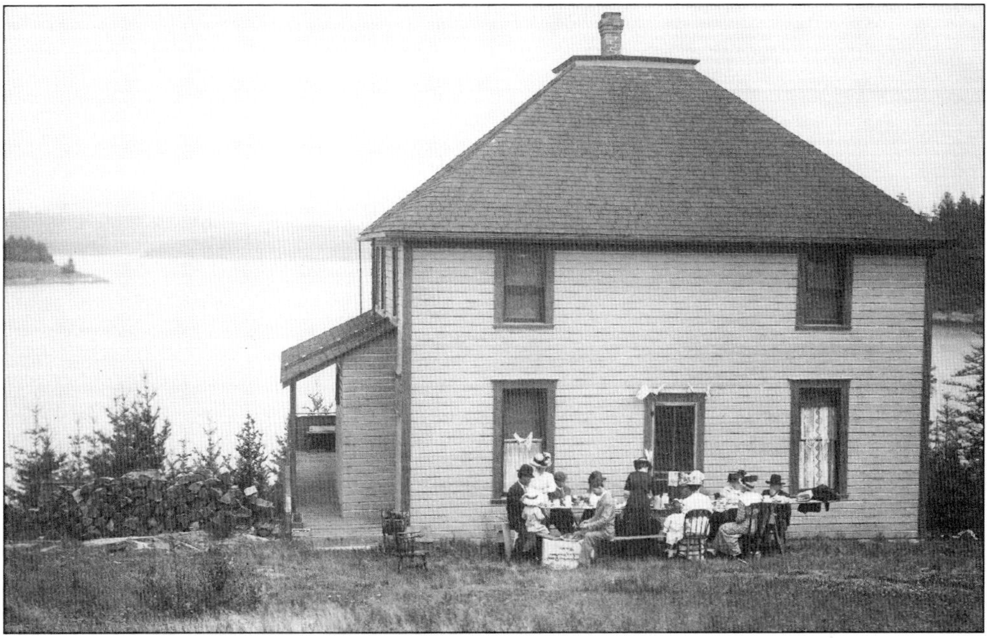

Fourth of July revelers picnic around 1914 at the home of school cook Orpha Sutton, who also boarded teachers. The house stood where the Cannery Restaurant is today. Note John Blair with hat and long white beard at right. Orpha's son Bing was a house painter whose nerve failed him only when it came to church steeples. "He'd get drunk and then go do it," according to Jim Cahail.

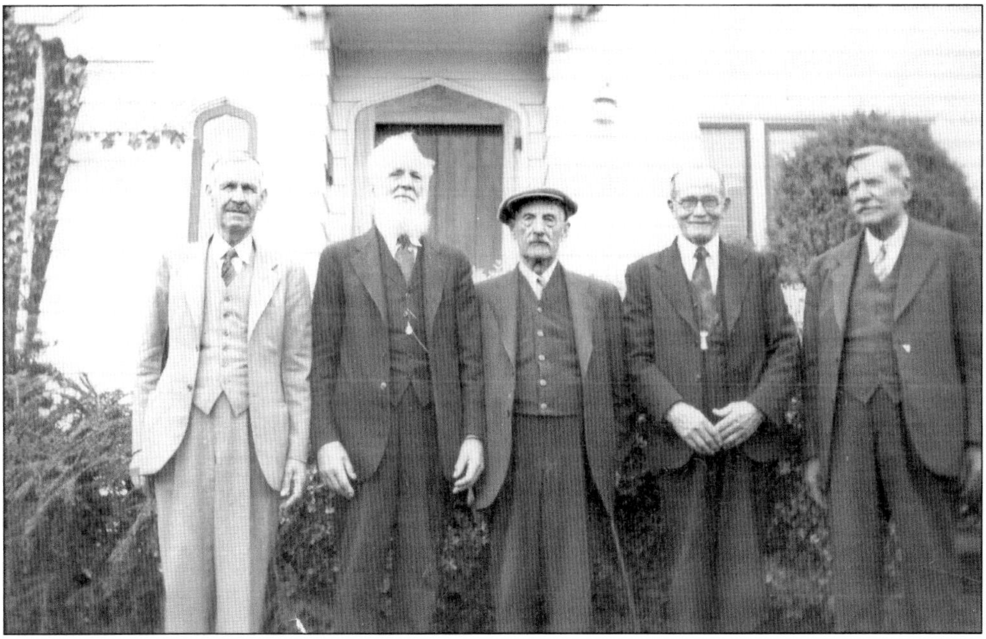

From left to right, Frank Guard, John Murray, L. B. Carter, Jack Douglas, and V. W. Talbot celebrate Frank Guard's 80th birthday. Talbot was the school superintendent and bought Browne Lumber from Herbert H. Davis. But he is mostly remembered for controlling the speed of his automobile by working the clutch and never letting off the gas. "You could hear him all over town," recalled one islander. "He kept the mechanics in business."

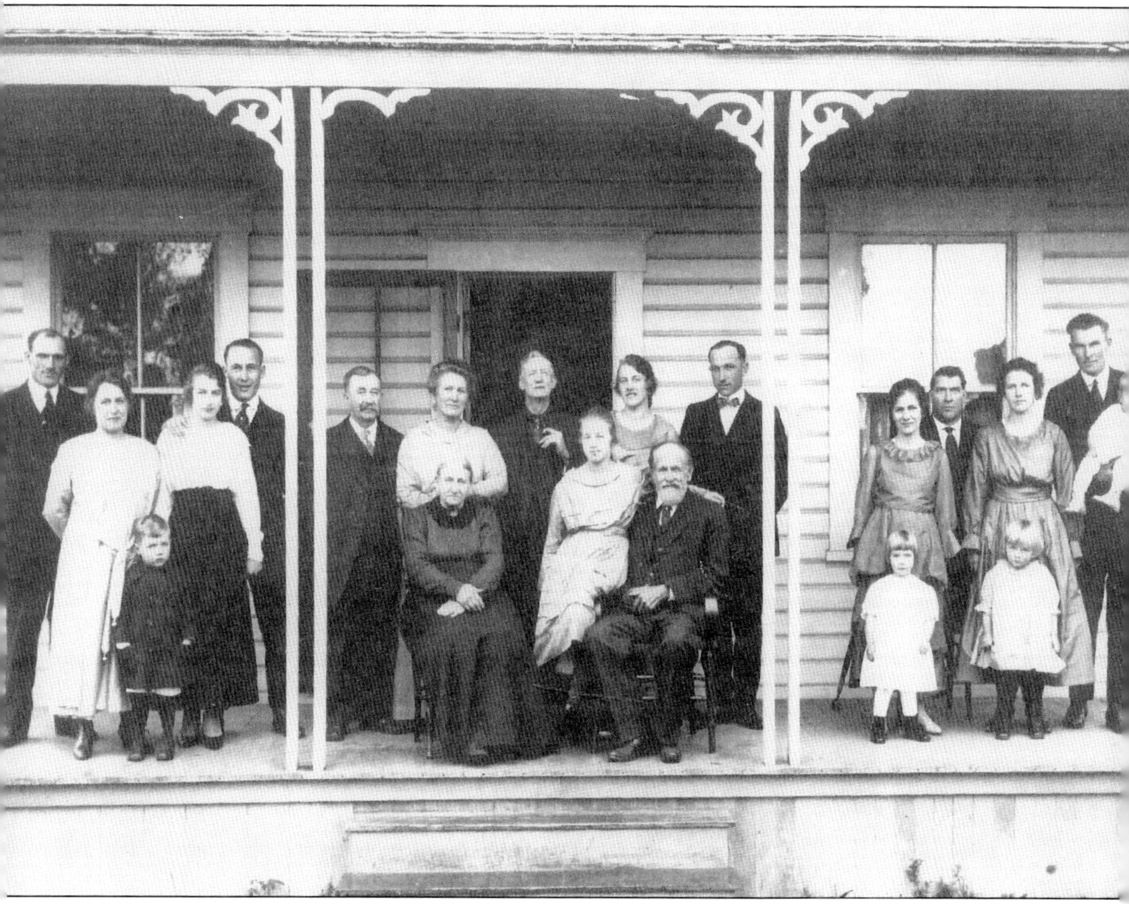

Ethel Perry Sandwith, at far left with her husband, Dr. Colin Sandwith (a veterinarian), son Perry, and family at the Perry home (now the Spring Street School annex), was one of the first female politicians on the island. In 1912, upon graduating with the first Friday Harbor High School class at age 21, she campaigned for county clerk and defeated C. L. Carter in the Republican primary by 100 votes. She quit politics when she married Sandwith in 1915 and, when he died in 1933, followed in her mother's footsteps as a nurse and midwife. Her parents, Park and Laura Baker Perry (sixth and seventh from left), arrived in Friday Harbor in 1903 and, in 1922, opened their home as a birthing and recuperating clinic. Like Lucinda Boyce before her (see page 17), Laura delivered many babies and was fondly known as "Mother Perry." All the bedrooms were painted in pastels, decorated with handcrafted pillows, quilts, and rugs, and filled with flowers from her garden. She also traveled by boat or over narrow, rutted roads to make house calls.

Claire P. Washburn, bookkeeper for the Friday Harbor Packing Company, has been given the chore of distributing flyers touting, that's right, another dance! This one is a Halloween Barn Dance sponsored by the local Elks Lodge around 1910. During those years, it was nothing to have dances three nights running—all year long.

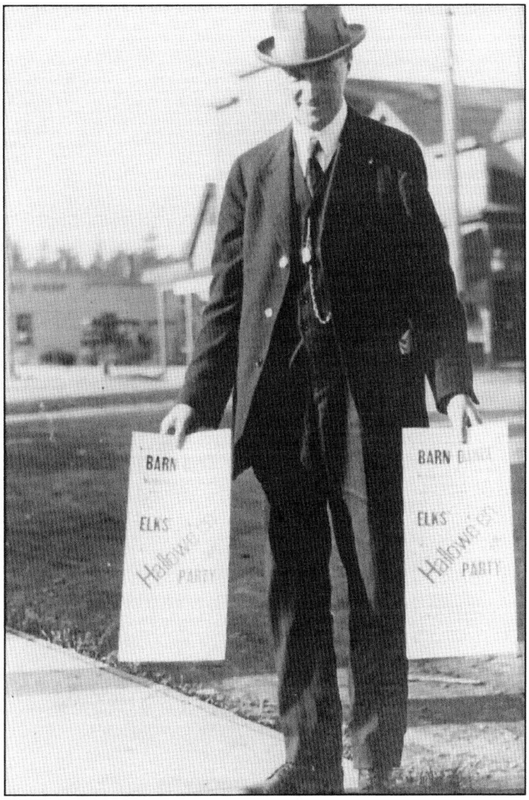

A few townspeople make their way down Argyle Avenue to the dock for a picnic, complete with guitar, picnic basket, and dog, around 1905. Town boys would crawl under the boardwalk and spook passersby. The home in the background, owned by Ralph Rich, now houses the offices of the San Juan County Land Bank.

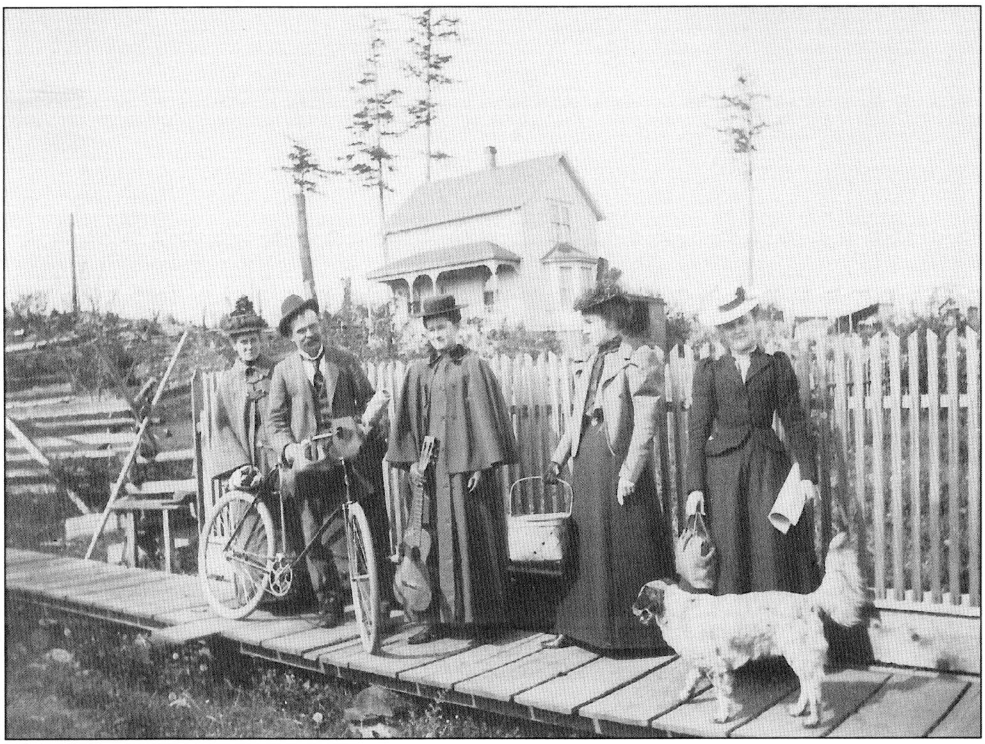

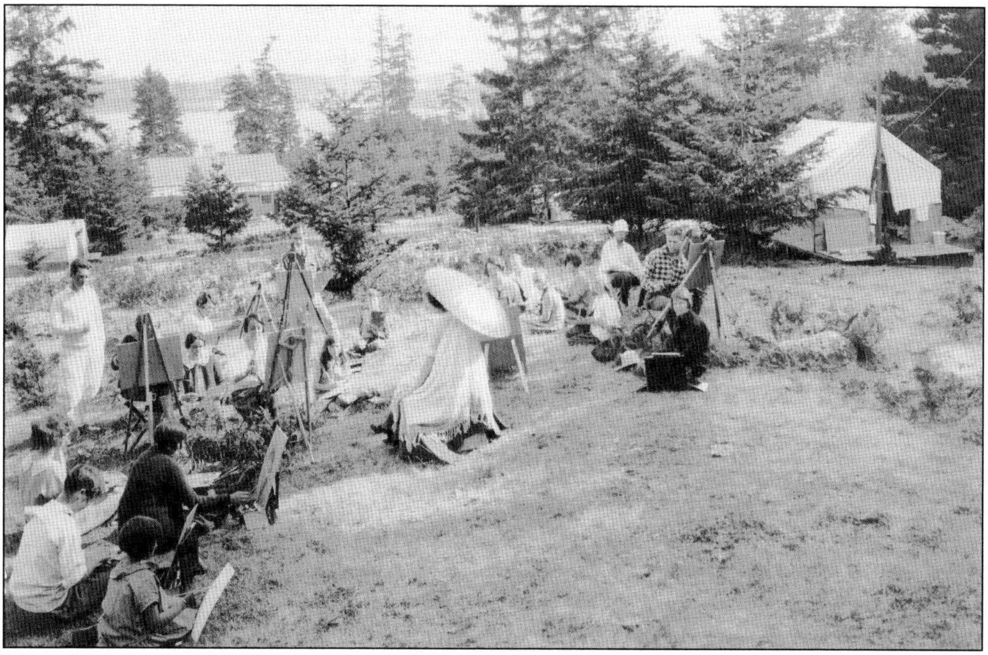

A model poses under an umbrella for artists attending a workshop at Camp McCormick in 1925. This was located on the grounds of the University of Washington Labs, which moved to Point Caution in 1921. Architect Carl F. Gould, notable for redesigning the University of Washington campus, designed the dining hall at left. The tent at right housed summer students.

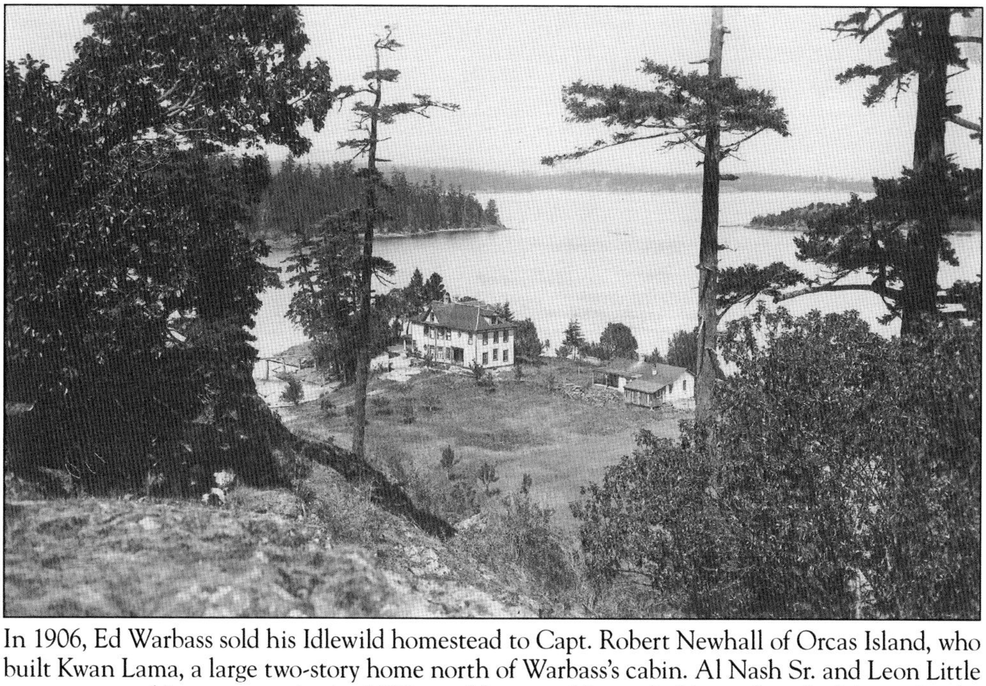

In 1906, Ed Warbass sold his Idlewild homestead to Capt. Robert Newhall of Orcas Island, who built Kwan Lama, a large two-story home north of Warbass's cabin. Al Nash Sr. and Leon Little next converted it to a resort in the 1920s, and Leon and his wife, library founder Minnie Little, ran it for several years. The viewpoint was called "Horse Heaven," for the red-eyed stallion rumored to haunt this spot.

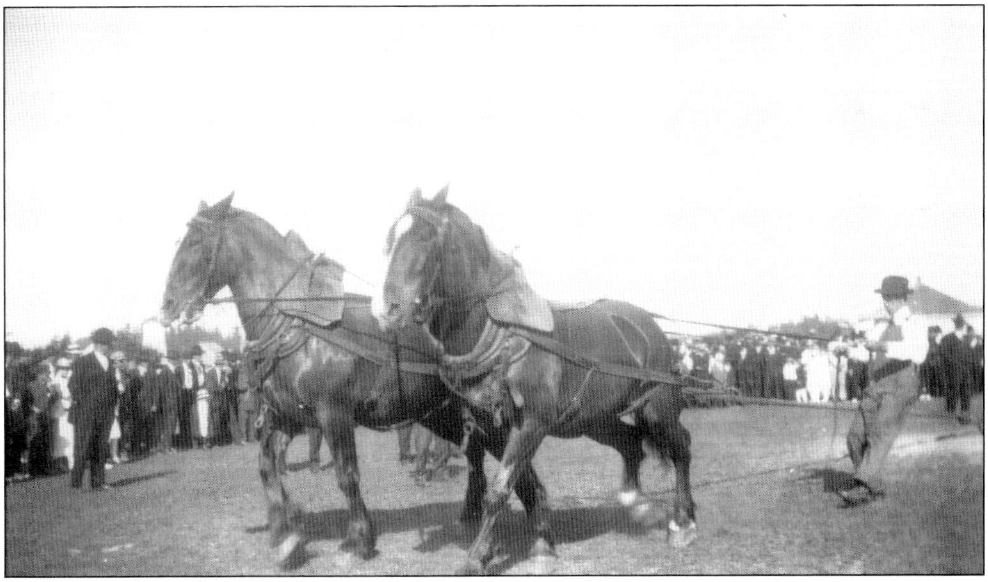

One important county fair event was the Horse Pull. Fairgoers, in lieu of horse racing, could wager (stealthily) on draught horse teams contending for honor of "strongest" in the archipelago. The horses pulled sleds, or "stone boats," of glacial stones—a common sight on the island—over a 27-foot course in a prescribed time. Each horse weighed nearly a ton.

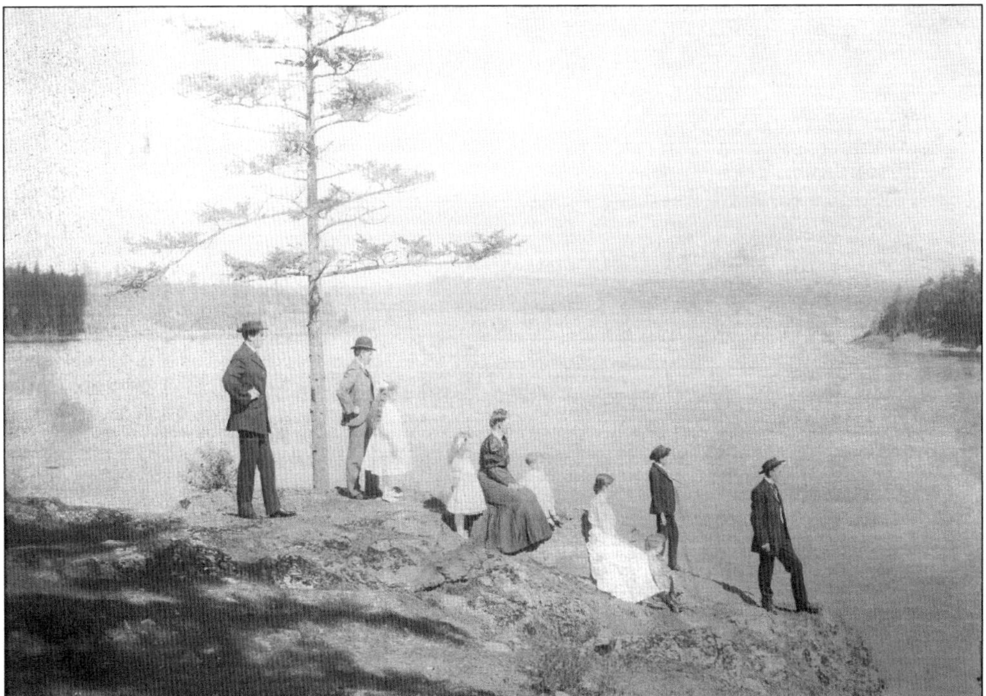

Saloon Best owner John Douglas (in the derby) with his family, around 1908, surveys the lot on which he would soon build a new family home. John Jr., far left, took over the saloon after the town went dry. He ran it as a pool hall, with cards, snacks, and cigars, until he sold it and left the island in 1938. The Friday Harbor House now stands on this site.

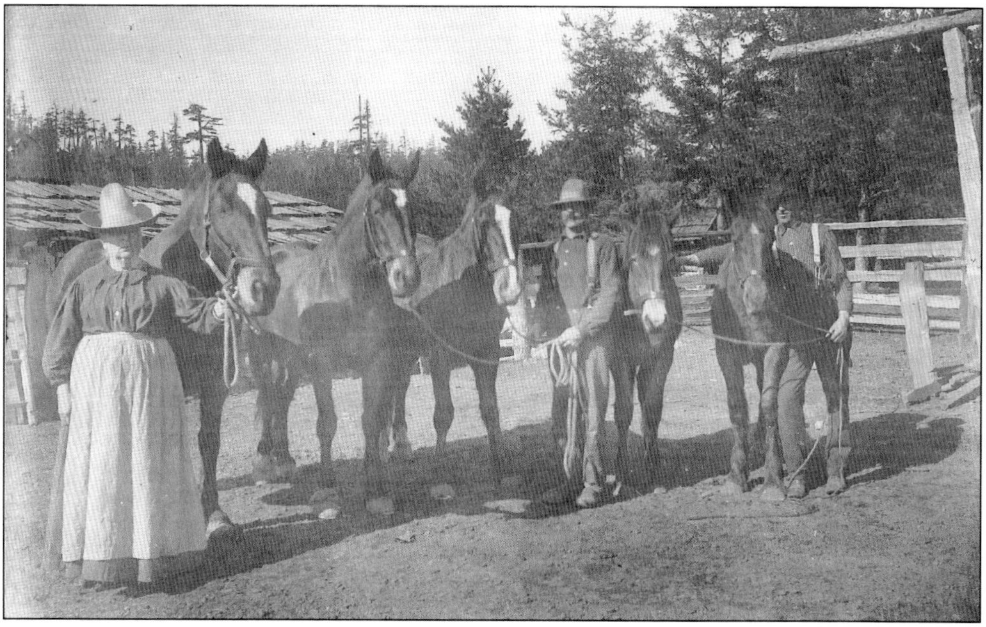

Minnie Sherwood tends her horses at her Sportsman's Lake farm, which was comprised of 40 acres and a few cattle. Island lore has it that the cabin, still standing across Roche Harbor Road from the lake, was moved from Belle Vue Sheep Farm at American Camp. Her husband, Charlie, one of the town barbers, was so talkative that his clients set aside at least an hour for a haircut.

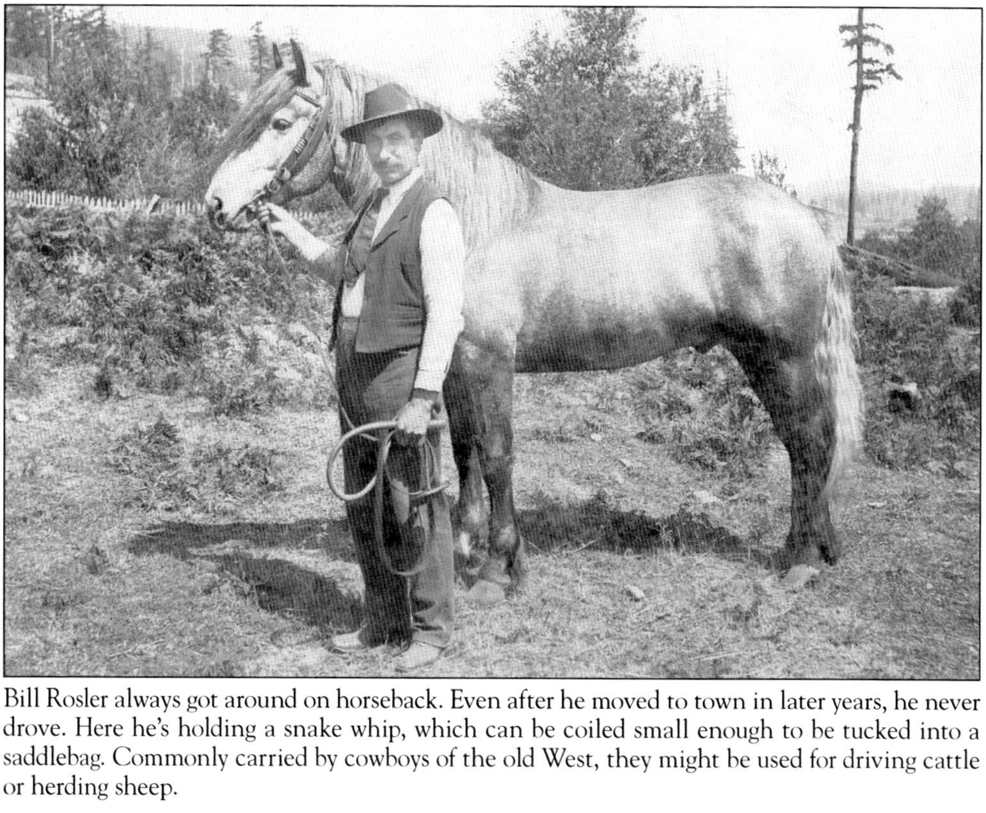

Bill Rosler always got around on horseback. Even after he moved to town in later years, he never drove. Here he's holding a snake whip, which can be coiled small enough to be tucked into a saddlebag. Commonly carried by cowboys of the old West, they might be used for driving cattle or herding sheep.

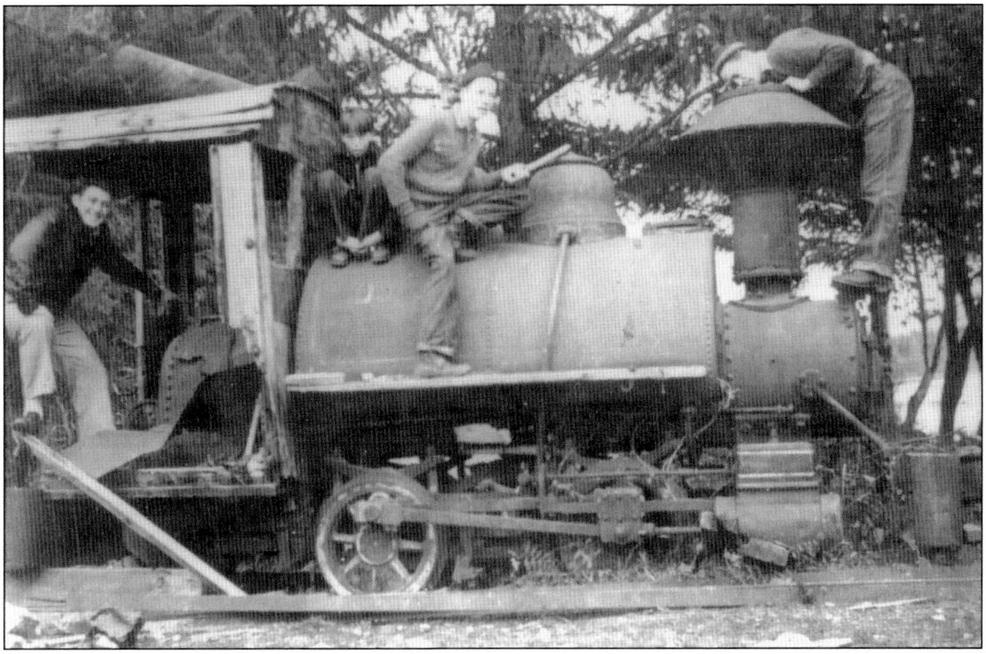

The always fun-loving Sundstrom brothers crawl about an old steam locomotive around 1938, by then lost among the weeds at Roche Harbor. By the 1920s, gasoline-powered trucks replaced the locomotive that once hauled limestone from the quarries to the kilns. The brothers are (from left on the boiler) Lindy, Wade, and Al (looking down the stack). The man in the cab is unidentified.

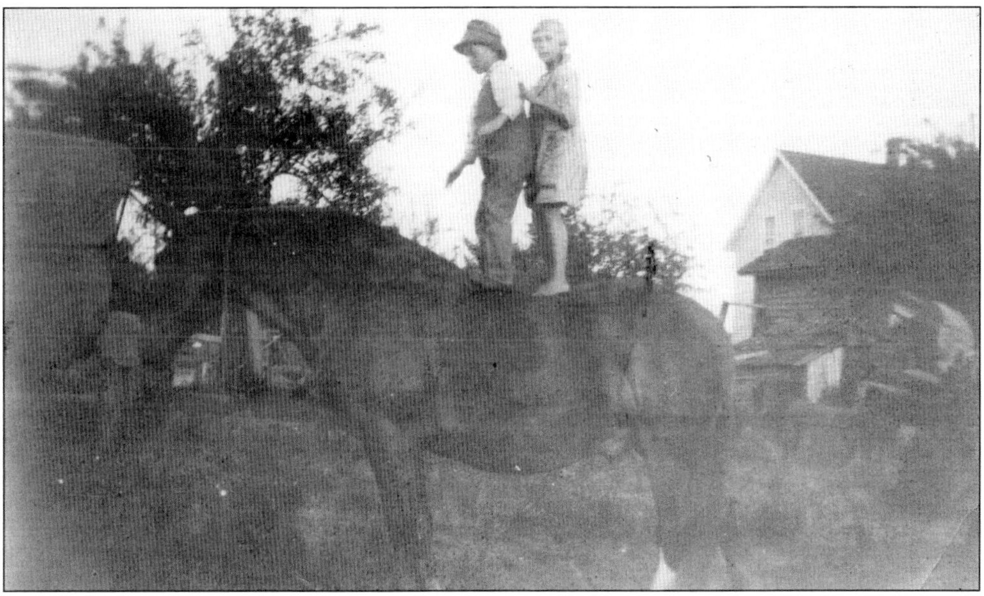

Siblings Juanita and Edward Egeland play circus acrobats on one of the farm workhorses around 1900. Edward died of polio at age seven. Their father, Harry, worked as a shingle weaver and later raised turkeys and chickens. Mother Etta was a green-thumbed gardener and grew tomatoes, peas, asparagus, cabbages, squashes, corn, pumpkins, rutabagas, parsnips . . . and her celebrated dahlias. Juanita lived in the same house in old Argyle for 55 years.

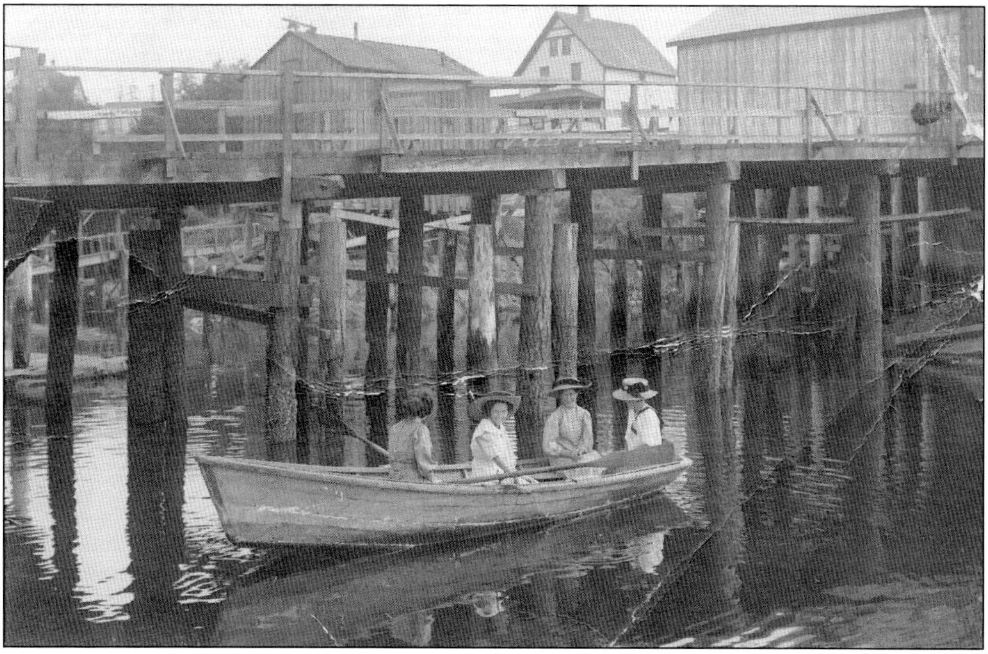

Personal water transportation at the turn of the century was by sail, rowboat, or canoe, unless you owned a steamship line. Here, in the early 1900s, women in hats and dresses embark on a journey from MacKenzie's dock on the harbor. The house in the background, now an espresso bar, was the cannery manager's home. Note that the bark has not been stripped from the log pilings.

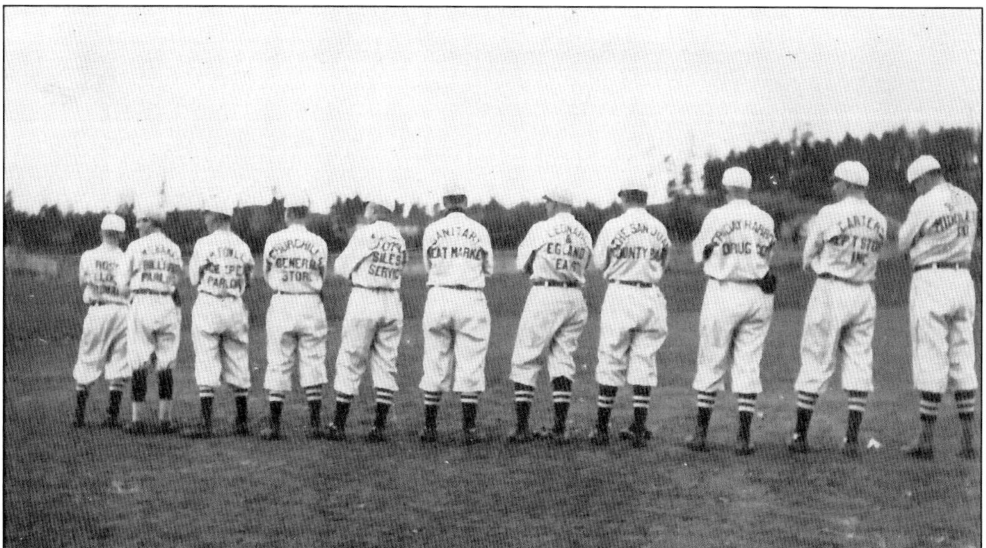

The Friday Harbor baseball club leaves no doubt as to who provided money for uniforms, bats, and balls in this 1921 team photograph. All the biggies are here, including the Sanitary Meat Market, Carter's Department Store, San Juan County Bank, Friday Harbor Drug, and so on. Note the odd juxtaposition of the billiard and ice cream parlors.

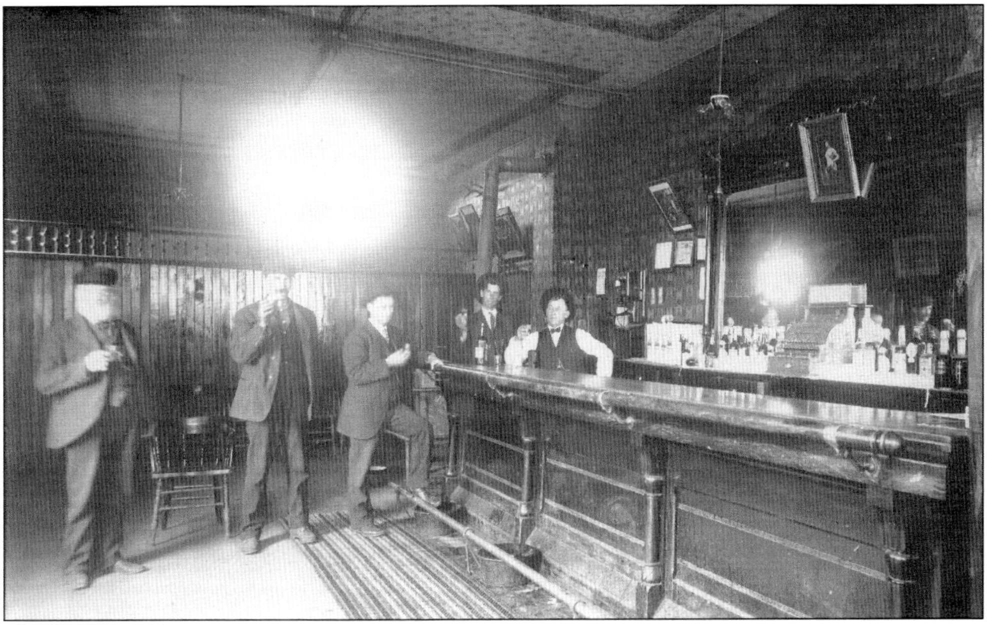

Alex and Fred Lightheart ran their saloon franchise in the Tourist Hotel until the town went dry in 1910. They next hauled cordwood. Alex also ran a livery stable on First and Spring streets, where he had a two-seat spring wagon for hire. He was said to be something of a horse whisperer, and his handsome team of horses minded him without use of a whip.

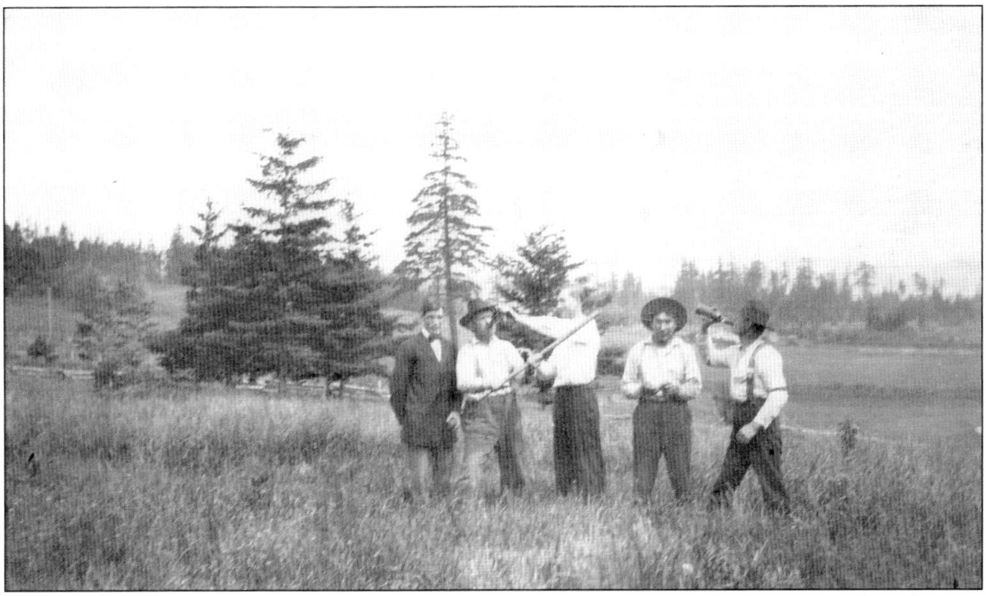

Players pause to refresh during a backyard ball game (page 109), with Andrew "Andy" Johnson, second from left, taking one of the first pulls. Swedish immigrant Johnson and Isabella Firth had nine children, plus two from her first marriage to Joseph Sandwith, who died in 1887. Good-natured Andy was proud of his horse team. He would clock his ride to town from his Olympic Lights farm, claiming the fastest horses around.

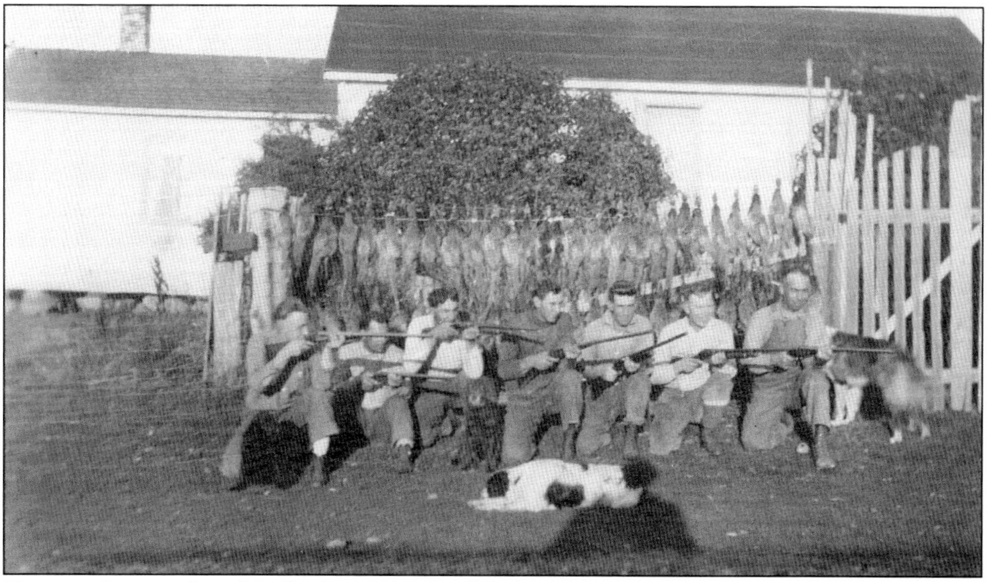

Pheasant hunters kneel with their prizes and shotguns around 1912 in front of Peter Lawson's home at Eagle Point. Hunting attracted Seattle businessmen and a few tourists even then. Only the dogs—Cole, resting in front, and Shep, at far right—are identified on the back of this image. However, guides Calvin Lightheart and Bill Rosler are believed to be at far left and third from left.

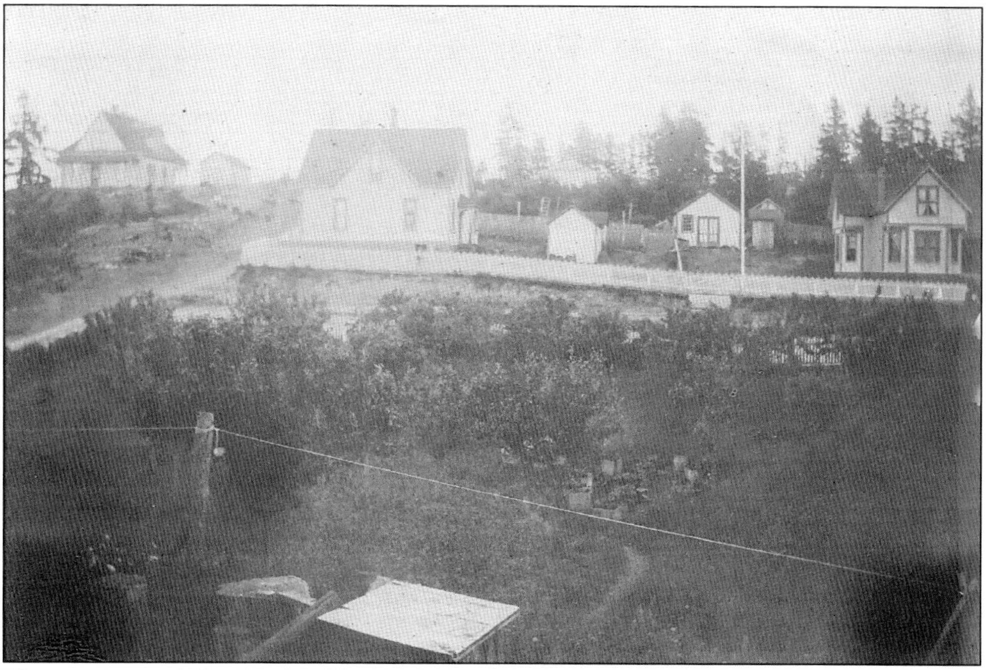

The town set aside lots bordered by Harrison, Nichols, and B Streets for a kind of "sunken" park within town limits shortly after incorporation, around 1910. At the time, they were considered worthless, as they occupied the gully that ran uphill from the harbor. Here it serves as a nursery for potted fruit trees. The house at left was torn down for condominiums, and the Tucker house, at right, remains.

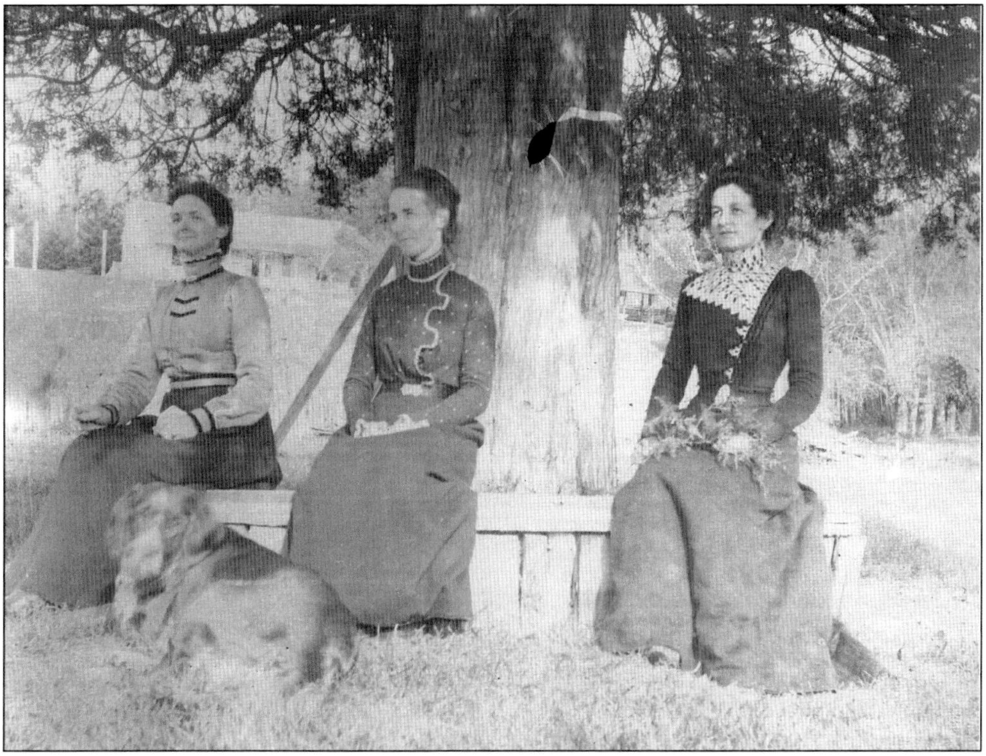

Mary Crook Davis (center) and friends sit in the shade of a giant cedar on the English Camp parade ground around the 1890s. One of the old Royal Marine noncommissioned officers' buildings is visible on the cleared terrace above. These were torn down to make way for the Crook farmhouse, which still stands overlooking the national park. Children said Mary always smelled like the bread she baked fresh daily.

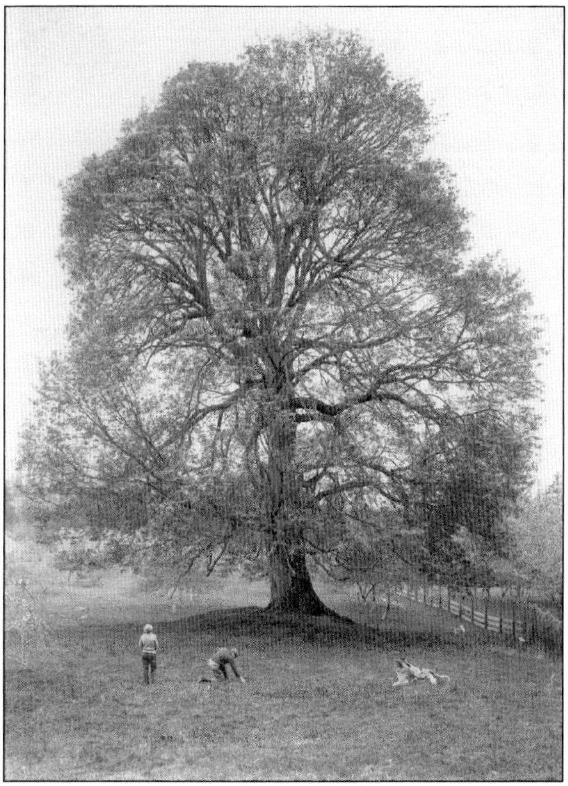

This Bigleaf maple in English Camp was already 227 years old in 1900 and was the largest of its class in the world until a lightning bolt destroyed a portion of its crown in the 1980s. Jim Crook planted apple, cherry, and pear trees in the orchard, at right, on the old parade ground. Deer still nibble on ripe, fallen pears.

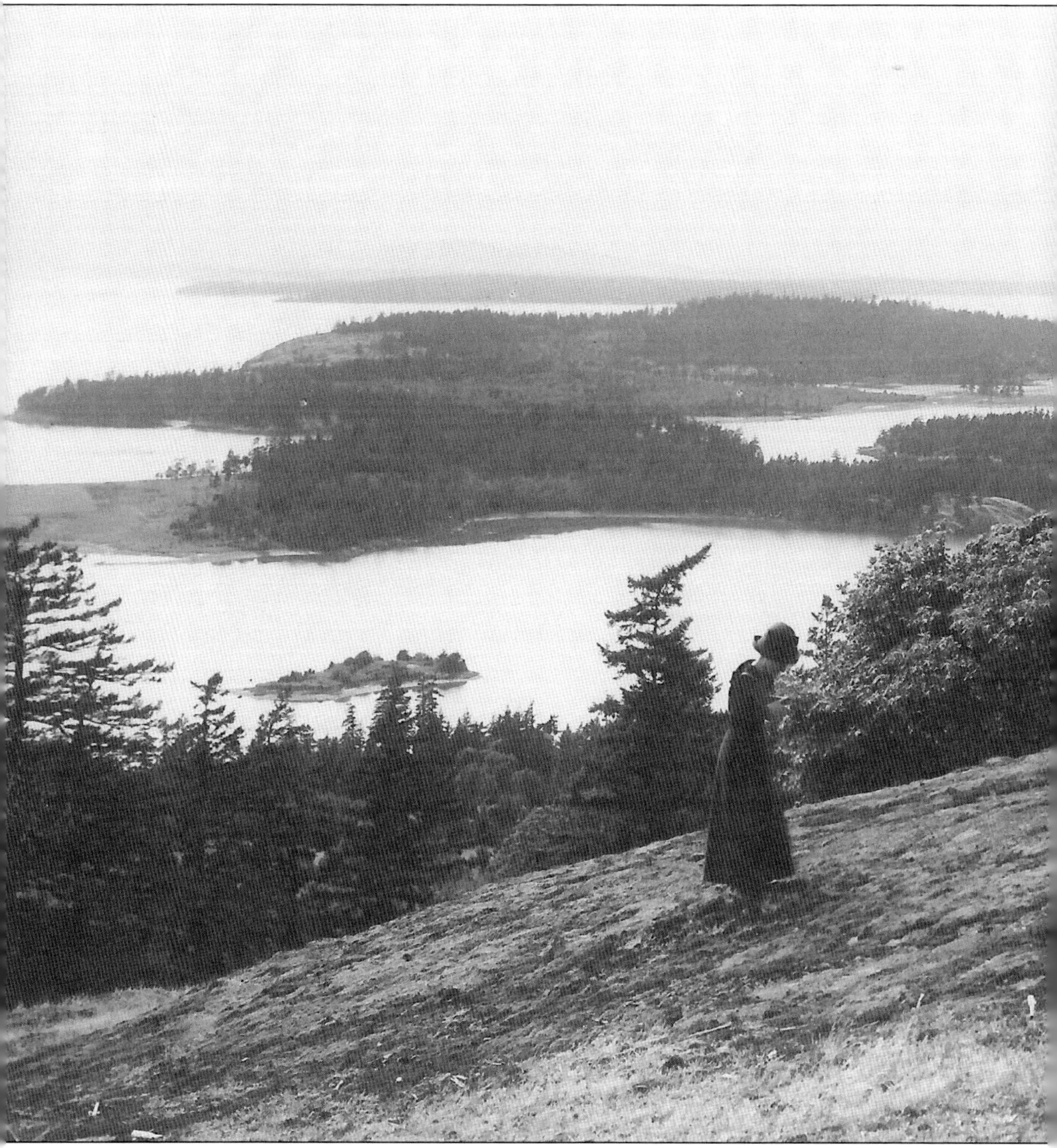

The summit of Young Hill has attracted islanders and visitors for millennia, from the Coast Salish and U.S. Boundary Survey teams to the Royal Marines who constructed a gazebo on the summit so officers and their wives could enjoy the sunset on summer evenings. The panorama takes in western views across Haro Strait and the Strait of Juan de Fuca to the Olympic Mountains

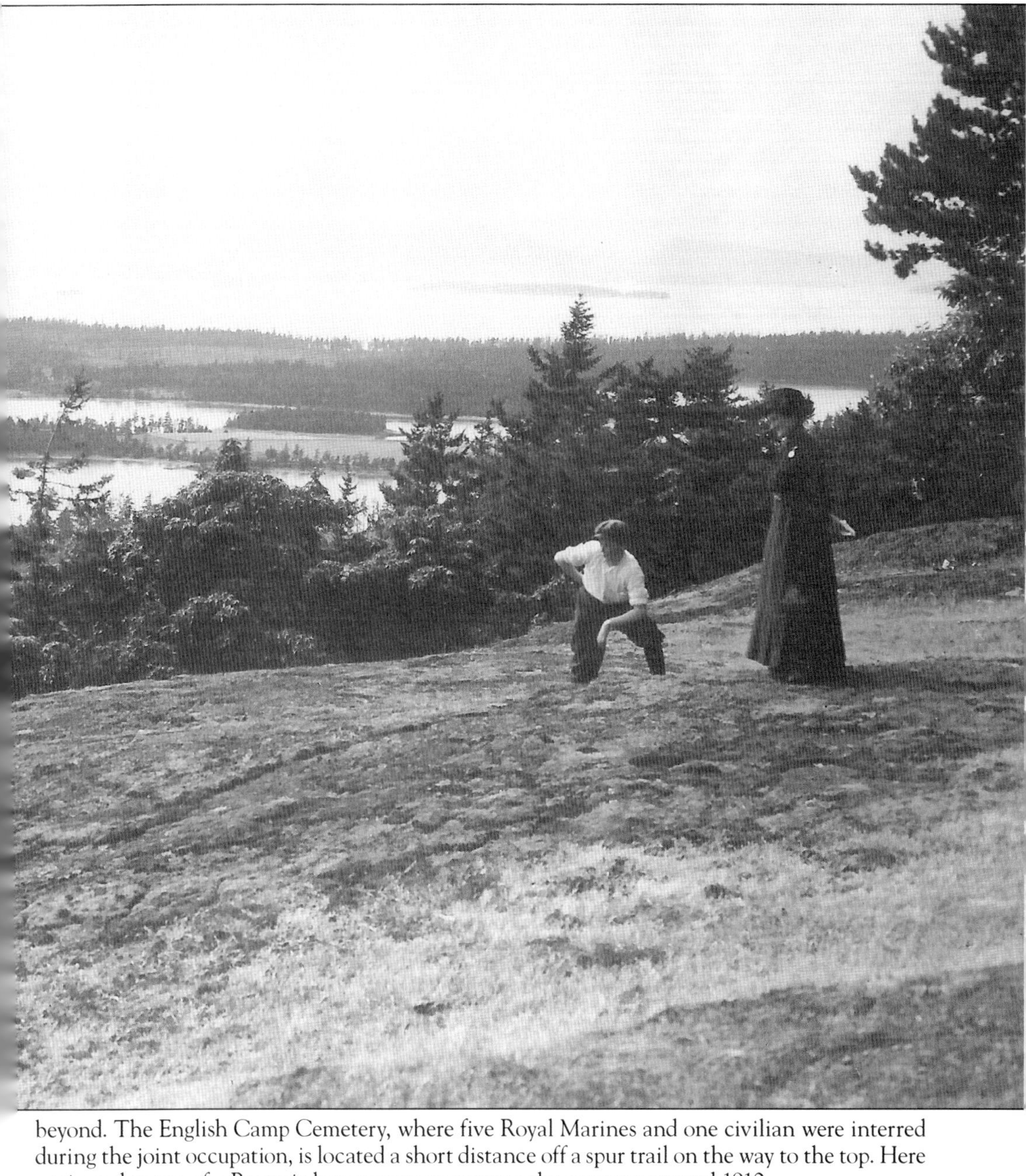

beyond. The English Camp Cemetery, where five Royal Marines and one civilian were interred during the joint occupation, is located a short distance off a spur trail on the way to the top. Here a trio makes use of a Brownie box camera to capture the moment around 1910.

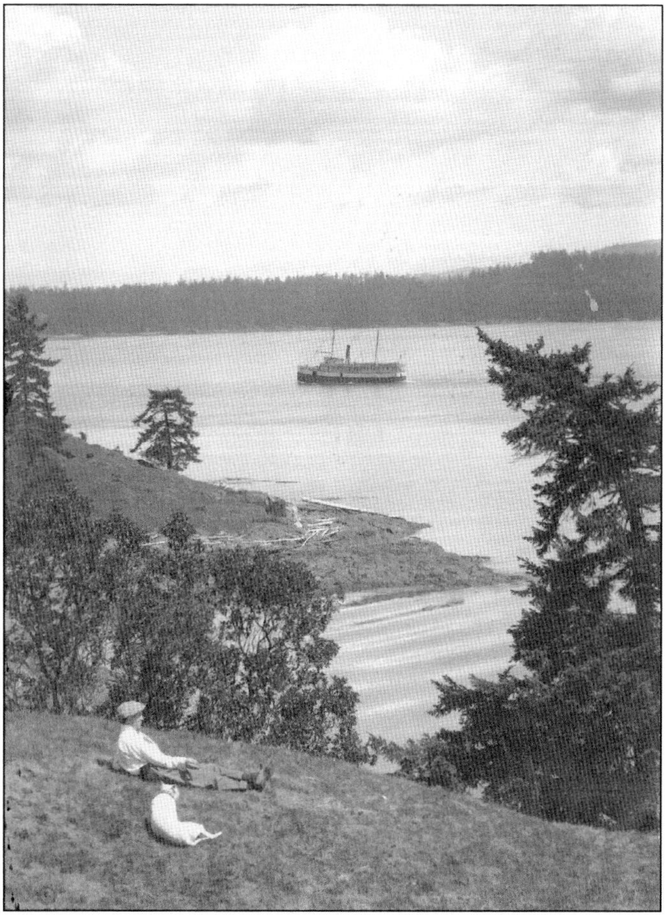

A man and his dog meditate on the view from a rock escarpment rising above stands of Pacific madrones and Douglas firs somewhere on the island's east side. A Mosquito Fleet steamer, probably the *Islander*, makes its way up San Juan Channel, possibly en route to Bellingham by way of Orcas Island. One can almost hear the dog panting.

In addition to being a source of bounty, San Juan Island's western coastline, which gives onto the Salmon Bank, has always been a splendid place to catch a rough sea or sunset on film. With the introduction of the Brownie camera in the late 1890s, capturing a landscape such as the rocky shore at Pile Point, below, was possible for anyone who could afford the modest price.

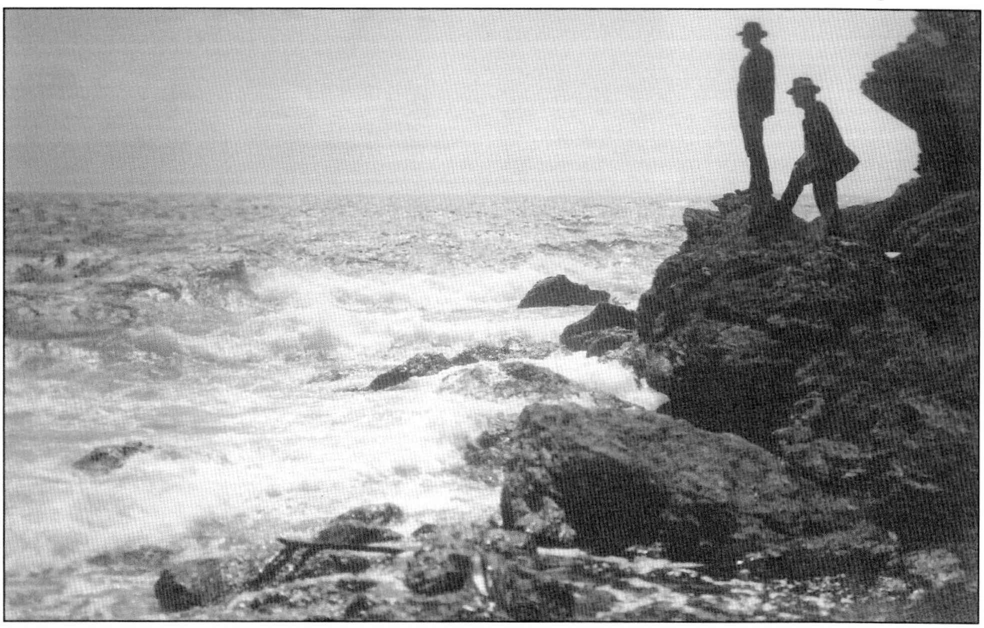

BIBLIOGRAPHY

Boxberger, Daniel L. *San Juan Island Cultural Affiliation Study.* Seattle: National Park Service, Pacific West Region, 1994.

Firth, Lila Hannah. *Early Life on San Juan Island.* Unpublished manuscript. San Juan Island National Historic Park archive.

Pratt, Boyd C. *The Disputed Islands Ordinary Life in Extraordinary Times: The San Juan Archipelago, 1850–1874.* MMS. Friday Harbor, WA, 2008.

Radke, August C., Radke, Barbara S., Ed. *Pacific American Fisheries, Inc.: History of a Washington State Salmon Packing Company, 1890–1966.* Jefferson, NC: McFarland and Company, Inc., 2002.

Richardson, David. *Pig War Islands.* Eastsound, WA: Orcas Publishing Company, 1971.

Suttles, Wayne P. *Coast Salish Essays.* Seattle: Talonbooks, University of Washington Press, 1987.

Vouri, Michael. *The Pig War: Standoff on Griffin Bay.* Friday Harbor, WA: Griffin Bay Bookstore, 1999.

———. *Outpost of Empire: The Royal Marines and the Joint Occupation of San Juan Island.* Seattle: Northwest Interpretive Association/University of Washington, 2004.

Vouri, Michael and Julia. *Images of America: Friday Harbor.* San Francisco: Arcadia Publishing, 2009.

Walker, Richard. *Images of America: Roche Harbor.* San Francisco: Arcadia Publishing, 2009.

Wray, Jacilee. *The Salmon Bank: An Ethnohistoric Compilation.* Port Angeles, WA: Olympic National Park/San Juan Island National Historical Park, 2003.

Discover Thousands of Local History Books Featuring Millions of Vintage Images

Arcadia Publishing, the leading local history publisher in the United States, is committed to making history accessible and meaningful through publishing books that celebrate and preserve the heritage of America's people and places.

Find more books like this at
www.arcadiapublishing.com

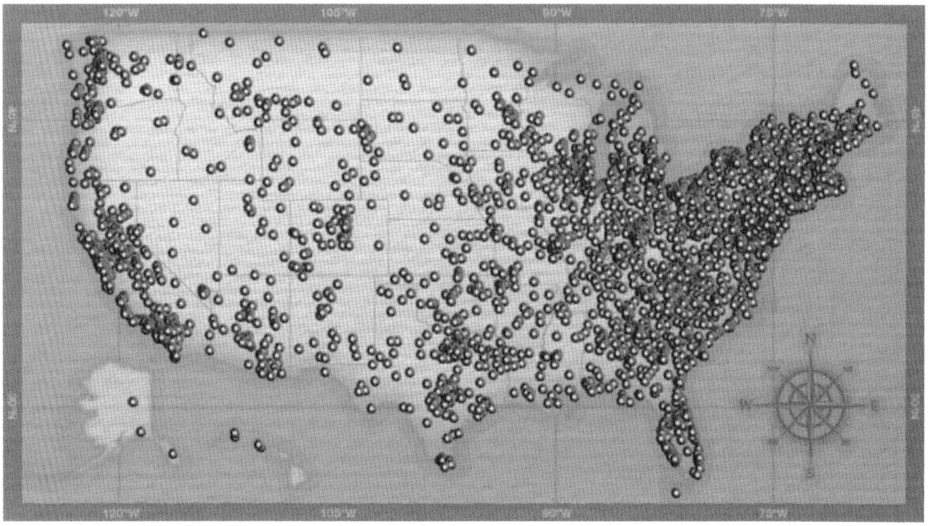

Search for your hometown history, your old stomping grounds, and even your favorite sports team.

Consistent with our mission to preserve history on a local level, this book was printed in South Carolina on American-made paper and manufactured entirely in the United States. Products carrying the accredited Forest Stewardship Council (FSC) label are printed on 100 percent FSC-certified paper.

MADE IN THE USA